❦ BARE-ARSED BANDITTI ❦

BARE-ARSED BANDITTI

THE MEN OF THE '45

MAGGIE CRAIG

MAINSTREAM
PUBLISHING

EDINBURGH AND LONDON

Copyright © Maggie Craig, 2009

First published in Great Britain in 2009 by
MAINSTREAM PUBLISHING COMPANY
(EDINBURGH) LTD
7 Albany Street
Edinburgh EH1 3UG

ISBN 9781845964108

A catalogue record for this book is available
from the British Library

Typeset in Bembo

Printed in Great Britain by
Clays Ltd, St Ives plc

This one's with much love for Alexander, who wanted
a book about the men, and whose keen intelligence,
sense of humour and unique way of looking at the world
brings so much laughter and nonsense into all our lives.

ACKNOWLEDGEMENTS

I should like to thank the following institutions and individuals who have helped me in my research for this book and the sourcing of illustrations to accompany the text: the National Archives of Scotland at Register House, Edinburgh, in particular the very knowledgeable and helpful Patrick Watt and his colleagues in the Historical Search Room; the National Library of Scotland, in particular Rare Books and Manuscripts; Inverness Library; Aberdeenshire Libraries and Information Service; author and classical scholar David Wishart, who most kindly translated two Latin poems for me; Her Majesty Queen Elizabeth II for permission to quote from letters in the Cumberland Papers regarding Major James Lockhart; Elspeth Morrison of the Incorporation of Goldsmiths of the City of Edinburgh; Colonel Dick Mason, Curator, Royal Scots Regimental Museum, Edinburgh Castle; Iain Milne of the Royal College of Physicians of Edinburgh; Mike Craig and Caroline Craig, Photographic Unit, Aberdeen University Library; Eileen Murison, photographer, McManus Galleries and Museum, Dundee; Sarah Jeffcot of the National Galleries of Scotland; Laura Yeoman, Archivist, Group Archives, The Royal Bank of Scotland Group; and Kate Holyoak, Picture Library Assistant, the Royal Collection, St James's Palace, London.

I should also like to thank all at Mainstream, in particular Editorial Coordinator Graeme Blaikie, and for their meticulous editing and fantastic cover design respectively, Karyn Millar and Kate McLelland.

My sincere thanks go to author, colleague and friend Maggie Kingsley and her family – James F. Gray, Nancy and Christina Gray – for giving me inside information on how the Panners felt and still feel about the Battle of Prestonpans.

I'd like to thank all my writing friends for their quick wits, generosity of spirit and lots of laughs along the way.

Finally, I want to express my love and thanks to the wonderful Tamise Totterdell, who's always there when I need her, and just for being herself, which is quite something; and to Will, as usual, for everything he quietly does – especially this time. Fools to the left of us, jokers to the right.

Contents

PREFACE

When I first published this book's companion volume, *Damn' Rebel Bitches: The Women of the '45*, I became used to men I met at talks and events taking a step back from me and asking nervously if what I had researched and written was 'a feminist book'. My answer to that question was the same then as it is now. It's a book about people. So is this one.

The Jacobite Rising of 1745 convulsed Scotland. While hostilities were raging many men and women simply wanted it all to be over. Many others, often with huge regret and after enormous soul-searching, saw armed conflict as the only way to achieve their political aims.

In *Damn' Rebel Bitches* – a book to which I gave a working title of *Not Flora MacDonald* – I wrote about the women who helped and supported the fighting men. With all due respect to Flora, I felt passionately that the contribution of so many other women had been ignored. They had been written out of history.

I went searching for them in libraries, archives and record offices the length and breadth of Britain and beyond. They were there all right, jumping out at me from original lists, letters, documents and contemporary newspaper reports. So were their men.

I did much research at the Public Record Office in London, then in its former home in Chancery Lane. It was charmingly Dickensian in style and atmosphere, with latter-day Bob Cratchits perched on high wooden stools peering over their specs at you to ensure you were treating the paper and parchment entrusted to you with due care.

It was in Chancery Lane that I read the transcript of the trial of Captain Andrew Wood of Glasgow, whose story is told in Chapter 30 of *Bare-Arsed Banditti: The Men of the '45*. He was interrogated beforehand, those questions and answers also recorded. Facing almost certain death on the gallows, he did nothing to try to save himself from that fate, obstinately refusing to cooperate with his captors. The one who questioned him noted several times that 'he refuses to answer further'.

Andrew Wood's comrade-in-arms, Captain Donald MacDonald, was asked during his interrogation to confirm his name. 'If you want to know my name,' the 25 year old replied, 'you may go ask my mother.' The heart-stopping defiance rang out at me across the centuries which separated us.

Yet men such as these have also been written out of history. If they are mentioned at all, they are depicted as gallant but misguided fools. In *Bare-Arsed Banditti* I have done my best to give them a voice, too. I hope they come across as real, living, breathing people who made choices and decisions which made sense to them in the context of their age and time.

The events and wider historical context of the '45 will be familiar to many readers. Those who are new to the subject might like to have some background.

Scotland and England waged war with one another for centuries. As an independent sovereign state, the ancient kingdom of Scotland always resisted England's attempts to conquer it. England found its northern neighbours troublesome both in their own right and because of Scotland's long-standing alliance with France, that country and England being equally long-standing rivals in an ongoing European power struggle.

More peaceful ways of resolving the conflict between Scotland and England were tried, for instance intermarriage between the royal houses of both countries. The resulting family relationships meant that when Elizabeth I of England died childless in 1603, the only possible successor was James VI of Scotland. He then also became James I of England, bringing the Scottish House of Stuart to the British throne and ushering in the Jacobean age. This term applies also to the style of the period in architecture, furniture, fashion and literature, and derives from *Jacobus,* Latin for James, the name of many of the Stuart kings.

James VI and I was succeeded by his son Charles I, whose arguments with Parliament led to civil war and his own execution. His son Charles II, restored to the throne in 1660 after the death of Oliver Cromwell, was a popular monarch. Father of several illegitimate children but no legal heirs, Charles II was succeeded by his brother, James.

King James VII and II was a devout Catholic, making him unpopular with many of his overwhelmingly Protestant subjects. Like his father, Charles I, he adhered to the doctrine of the divine right of kings, believing his position to be God-given. His reluctance to rule with Parliament as a constitutional monarch proved an even more insurmountable obstacle to his continuing to wear the British crown.

In 1688, in what became known to its supporters as the Glorious Revolution, James was deposed and forced to go into exile in Europe with his wife, Mary of Modena, and their young son, also James. The throne was offered to the deposed king's daughter Mary and her husband, the Protestant William of Orange. When they died without issue, Mary's sister, Anne, succeeded, ruling from 1702 to 1714. The last Stuart to wear the British crown married a Danish prince and endured 17 pregnancies. Many of these ended in miscarriage or stillbirth. None of her children survived her.

At this point Anne's younger half-brother – King James VIII and III to his supporters, and the Old Pretender to his opponents – might have been invited back. However, James could not bring himself to renounce his Catholic faith or his inherited belief in the divine right of kings. A German cousin, safely Protestant and willing to reign with Parliament, was offered the throne instead. The Elector of Hanover became George I and founder of what became today's House of Windsor.

There were several attempts made to win the throne back for the Stuarts, most significantly in 1715 and 1745. The Stuart Cause was given added impetus when, in 1707, during the reign of Queen Anne, the parliaments of England and Scotland united, putting an end to Scotland's status as an ancient and independent European country.

There was huge opposition to this move within Scotland, with rioting in the streets and impassioned speeches within the Scottish Parliament. However, Scotland's economy was in a bad way after the ill-fated Darien expedition, an attempt to found a Scottish colony in Central America, and some members of that Parliament saw the Union with England as the only way to secure Scotland's future prosperity.

Self-interest also played its part, with English bribes to other members of the Scottish Parliament ensuring they voted in favour of the Treaty of Union. On the day it came into force, the bells of St Giles', the High Kirk of Edinburgh, played a tune called 'Why am I so Sad on my Wedding Day?'

This mourning for the loss of nationhood was hugely significant in attracting men and women to what was now known as the Jacobite Cause. While some Scots did well out of Scotland becoming North Britain, as pro-Unionists were keen to call it, others felt themselves over-taxed, over-governed and under-represented. The Stuarts being the old Scottish royal house, there was also a deep-seated personal loyalty to them. This was especially so in the Highlands and, although by no means exclusively, among Episcopalians and Catholics.

The '15 ended inconclusively at the Battle of Sheriffmuir, leaving 'German Geordie' once more safe on his throne. However, discontent continued to simmer, boiling over most notably in Glasgow's Malt Tax riots and Edinburgh's Porteous Riot.

This discontent found a focus in the Jacobite Cause. In the 1740s, that Cause found a leader in Prince Charles Edward Stuart, the

Bonnie Prince Charlie of legend and song. My aim in writing this book has been to shine the spotlight on some of the lesser known but fascinating men who rallied to his Standard, playing their part in the dramatic events which unfolded in Scotland and England in 1745–6: the Year of the Prince.

Where they speak in their own words, I have, whenever possible, retained their eighteenth-century spelling, punctuation and frequent use of capital letters. This was correct at the time for nouns, as it still is today in the German language, but some people went a bit overboard, using capitals on other words, too, as the fancy took them. It can look wonderfully eccentric to modern eyes, and I think it gives a real flavour of the times. The only alteration I have made is to change the eighteenth-century *f* to a modern *s*. When it comes to names which can be spelled in more than one way, especially Highland names, I've done my best to be consistent. This is not always so easy when original documents, letters and even the owners of the names themselves sometimes moved between one version and the other.

I apologize to speakers of the 'language of the Garden of Eden' for not quoting the original Gaelic version of poems but only the English translations, albeit very fine ones.

In the hope of producing a flowing and readable narrative, I have chosen to use neither footnotes nor endnotes, a decision I also made when I wrote *Damn' Rebel Bitches*. My sources are cited within the text or are listed in my bibliography.

Throughout the book, I have alternated between 'Rebellion' and 'Rising', usually dependent on whether I am writing from the perspective of the Jacobites or their adversaries: and sometimes, as a proud daughter of Red Clydeside, I've used 'Rebellion' and 'Rebel' simply because I love the defiance inherent in the words.

The Rebellion of 1745 may have ended in failure. The spirit of the men who fought in it – and the women who stood beside them – lives on.

1

THE YEAR OF THE PRINCE:
HIGH SUMMER AT HIGH BRIDGE

TWELVE MEN AND A PIPER

John Sweetenham was an English Redcoat officer '& a piece of an Ingenier', a captain in Guise's Regiment. On 14 August 1745, he was travelling from Ruthven Barracks near Kingussie to Fort William, his mission to inspect and repair the fortifications there. This was the first Government response to the news that Prince Charles Edward Stuart had landed in Scotland. Charles's mission was to reclaim his birthright, place the crown of Great Britain on his father's head and put the Stuart dynasty back on the throne.

Those charged with the task of stopping him were putting their faith in what they called the Chain, the string of forts garrisoned by the British Army which lay along the Great Glen: Fort William, Fort Augustus and Fort George. At that time, Fort George was in Inverness itself. The one we know today, which lies on the coast between Inverness and Nairn, was built after the '45 and as a direct consequence of it.

The hope was that Charles could be confined to the north-west Highlands. That strategy was unlikely to succeed without remedial work being done on the long-neglected forts which made up the

Chain. Captain Sweetenham was not, however, destined to be the engineer carrying out and supervising that work. In a succinct but evocative description, he was 'surpriz'd at an inn' by a party commanded by Donald MacDonell of Tirnadris.

Tirnadris and his men took Sweetenham's sword and made him their prisoner – and, with this act of overt rebellion, the '45 began. Two days later, Tirnadris was at it again. Following in Sweetenham's footsteps, two companies of the Royal Scots were marching from Fort Augustus to reinforce the garrison at Fort William. From the Jacobite point of view, this they could not be allowed to do.

At High Bridge, a mile or two south-west of modern-day Spean Bridge, the Redcoats were ambushed. This first skirmish of the '45 has become a classic tale of a handful of wily Highlanders defeating a much larger military force. Tirnadris had only a dozen men and a piper at his disposal and there were 60 Royal Scots.

Outnumbered five to one though they were, Donald MacDonell and his men leapt about from rock to rock, raining sniper fire down on the hapless Redcoats from every possible direction. As they darted through the trees above the Spean, they held their belted plaids out wide, which also helped give the impression that their numbers were much greater than they were.

The Royal Scots didn't stand a chance. Most of them were raw recruits recently raised in Ireland, where the regiment had been stationed. They were not used to the terrain of the Highlands nor the fighting techniques of the Highlanders. They panicked, turned and fled, MacDonell and his men in hot pursuit.

In a cross between a rout and a running battle, they chased them for seven or eight miles, all the way up the hill on which the Commando Memorial now stands and back to Loch Lochy. Two were killed and several, including Captain John Scott of Scotstarvet in Fife, were wounded.

At Glenfintaig, he and his fellow captain, James Thomson, gamely tried to rally their men, forming the classic hollow square. When, however, reinforcements arrived for the Highlanders in the shape of a party of Camerons and another led by Tirnadris's chief, MacDonald of Keppoch, Captain Scott realized the game was up and surrendered.

It was here that the Jacobites – not yet officially an army but clearly feeling themselves to be under starter's orders – began as they were to go on, by showing mercy to their defeated foes. Captain Scott was carried to Cameron of Lochiel's home at Achnacarry and treated more as an honoured guest than an enemy, his wounds dressed by Lady Lochiel.

Meanwhile, Captain Sweetenham was being taken west. On 19 August 1745, three days after the engagement at High Bridge, he witnessed the Raising of the Standard at Glenfinnan. He later reported how the clansmen cheered and threw their bonnets up into the air, so many of them they looked like a cloud.

The novelist D. K. Broster took inspiration from the true stories of Captains Sweetenham and Scott in the creation of her fictional Captain Keith Wyndham. His unlikely friendship with the Highland Jacobite Ewen Cameron of Ardroy, an imagined kinsman of Lochiel's, is told in *The Flight of the Heron*, the romantic tale par excellence of the Jacobite Rising of 1745.

Despite the cheers and those blue bonnets tossed high into the air, Charles Edward Stuart was taking a huge gamble when he raised his Standard at Glenfinnan. He had landed in Scotland with 1,800 swords 'such as are fit for the highlanders' and several cases of pistols but only a few companions, the romantically named Seven Men of Moidart. (Actually, there were more than seven, but that number obviously had a ring to it.)

Despite the magic number, romance was not enough, even for committed Jacobites. They wanted to know where the previously promised well-armed French troops were, believing that without them the Rising had little chance of succeeding. In a famous exchange, one of the first Scottish Jacobites to meet the Prince, Alexander MacDonald of Boisdale, told him to 'Go home, sir.' Charles Edward Stuart's reply has gone down in history. 'I am come home,' he said.

He gave Cameron of Lochiel an equally telling response when, dismayed by the lack of those French troops, the chief of the Camerons expressed his reluctance to commit himself and his clan to the enterprise. If that was how Lochiel felt, then he would have to stay at home and read of the fate of his Prince in the newspapers. Like many others in the tumultuous year which was to follow, Donald Cameron found himself unable to resist that plea.

Others did say no. The chiefs of the MacLeods and MacDonalds of Skye were among the most significant of those, their refusal a crushing disappointment for the Prince. It was not simply the extra soldiers they would have brought to the Jacobite Army which mattered but also the influence the decisions of such powerful men would have on others who were trying to decide which way to jump. The consequences of failure were well understood by everyone.

Captain Sweetenham was well treated by the Jacobites, one of whom described him as 'the most polite among the few English officers who were at all sociable'. They released him two days after Glenfinnan on his parole of honour not to fight them or contribute in any way to the measures being taken against them, this restriction to apply for a year and a day. Not all the Redcoat officers who gave such an undertaking during the '45 kept their promise. Sweetenham did.

What the Jacobites kept was his sword, saddle and horse. Captain Scott's fine gelding had also been one of the first spoils of war. Although the Prince gave orders that Sweetenham was to be given two horses in exchange for his – it, too, must have been a handsome steed – this was forgotten about. Presumably the English officer decided not to contest the issue, preferring while the going was good to get the hell out of Dodge.

On his long walk back to Ruthven Barracks, he met several parties of well-armed Highlanders on their way to join the newly raised Jacobite Amy. He estimated he passed about 100 men in all. He spoke with several of them, so he must have had a safe conduct from his erstwhile captors to compensate for his now highly politically incorrect vivid scarlet coat.

Those erstwhile captors were not far behind him, although he was well away from Ruthven by the time they got there on 30 August 1745, 11 days after the Raising of the Standard. This outpost of the British Army, perched on a steep-sided man-made grassy motte on the opposite side of the modern-day A9 from Kingussie, was being held for King George by Sergeant Terry Molloy of Lee's 55th Foot.

The sergeant had all of sixteen men to help him hold back the newly formed Jacobite Army, and four of them were invalids. To say that the London Government, their representatives in Edinburgh and the British Army's commanders in Scotland were woefully unprepared for the Jacobite emergency would be putting it mildly.

It was a full month after the Prince's arrival in Scotland, the day after Glenfinnan, before General Sir John Cope left Stirling to march north with a Government army. Six days later, he reached Dalwhinnie, 'where the great Road divides into two; that on the Right, leading to *Inverness*, and that on the Left, passing over a remarkable Mountain, call'd the Corriarrick, goes to *Fort-Augustus*'.

Cope and Captain Sweetenham passed one another on the road, meeting at Dalnacardoch, halfway between Blair Atholl and the Drumochter Pass. Sweetenham gave Cope valuable first-hand information, confirming the reality of the Rebellion and the determination of the Rebels. He reported that they had plenty of 'Firelocks, Broad-Swords, Pistols and Cutlasses', and that they were planning to head Cope and his men off at the pass: the Corrieyairack, that is. Confirmation of this came from Duncan Forbes of Culloden, Lord President of the Court of Session in Edinburgh and a supremely loyal supporter of the London Government, who was then at his home near Inverness. Cope immediately feared an ambush.

Not only was the route through the pass 'of so very sharp an Ascent, that the Road traverses the whole Breadth of the Hill seventeen times before it arrives at the Top . . . the *Highlanders*, from their Knowledge of the Country, their natural Agility, and their Attachment to Ambushes and Skirmishes, would, in this Situation, have indulged their Genius, and would, doubtless, have proved most formidable Opponents'.

The general opted instead to lead his troops, depleted by desertions on the march north, to Inverness. In doing so, he left the road wide open for the Jacobites to march south to the Lowlands without having to fire a shot or draw a sword.

Delaying to make absolutely sure Cope was heading for Inverness, a 300-strong detachment of Jacobites on the hunt for arms and supplies called past Ruthven Barracks. In a conversation shouted over the parapet, they suggested to Sergeant Molloy that he surrender the little fortress to them.

Molloy was one of the many Irishmen in the British Army. He was, however, no raw recruit. The Jacobites informed him that if he put up no resistance they would allow him and his men to leave with their 'bag and baggage'. He told them he was 'too old a Soldier to surrender a Garrison of such strength, without bloody noses'.

The response to that was a threat to storm the barracks and hang him and every man in his garrison. Molloy told them to come on if they were hard enough – which they did. Unfortunately, there was not a ladder to be found anywhere nearby which would enable them to scale this complex of high-walled buildings set, as Colonel John O'Sullivan of the Prince's army put it, 'upon a sugre loaf'.

An attempt to burn their way in using an empty barrel 'prepared with combustible matters' also failed, Molloy employing the obvious method to put paid to that. On his parapet some way above, he simply poured water on it and extinguished the flames. This comic opera turned to tragedy when shots were exchanged and the Jacobites took their first casualties of the war. Three men were killed and four wounded.

Molloy lost one man. As he wrote to Sir John Cope the next day, this soldier was 'shot through the Head, by foolishly holding his Head too high over the Parapet, contrary to Orders'. So now we know why it's a bad idea to stick your head above the parapet – although some of us keep doing it, all the same.

Colonel O'Sullivan, one of the Seven Men of Moidart, ordered the withdrawal, regretting the attack on the barracks had ever been attempted. Nevertheless, it had, as blood had now been spilled on both sides. The deadly game had begun.

John William O'Sullivan was in his mid-forties in 1745. An Irishman who had sold his family's ancestral acres in Munster because the law would not allow him to keep them unless he renounced his Catholic faith, he was originally destined for the priesthood. Realizing he was more suited to soldiering, he saw action with the French Army in Corsica, Italy and Germany well before he became Adjutant General of the Jacobite Army.

A good organizer, O'Sullivan was dismayed in the days after Glenfinnan by how unwilling the Highlanders were to be corralled into companies along the military lines he thought necessary to form an efficient fighting force. In his later report to Prince Charles's father, James, he always refers to himself in the third person and shortens his name to Sullivan.

The spelling of the eighteenth century could be diabolically and hilariously bad. When it came to the mangling of the English language, O'Sullivan too was no slouch:

> The Prince staid at Glenfeenen to deliver armes & amunition to the men, to give time to Clenranold to raise all his men & to give some form to 'em, wch they wanted, for all was confused. Sullivan, who was the only officer there, or the only one yt acted, was charged with this; his propossition was to form into compagnies, to set fifty men, a Captn, Lt & four sergents, to each Compagny, but yt cou'd not be followed, they must go by tribes; such a chife of a tribe had sixty men, another thirty, another twenty, more or lesse: they wou'd not mix nor seperat, & wou'd have double officers, yt is two Captns, & two Lts, to each Compagny, strong or weak. That was useless . . .

Yet this army of tribal warriors, gathering its strength in one of the most remote parts of the British Isles, its ranks soon to be swelled by

Scotsmen and a few Englishmen from very different backgrounds, was to sweep south almost to London and come within a hair's breadth of tipping a king off his throne.

The stories of the men who played their part in this bold and dangerous adventure intertwine, as they must, with those of the men who were doing their damnedest to stop them. Some adversaries were more worthy than others.

2

THE PRINCE, THE PROVOST & THE GLASGOW SHOPKEEPERS' MILITIA: ANDREW COCHRANE

TWO THOUSAND BROADSWORDS, AT REASONABLE RATES

It was the high summer of 1745, and Provost Andrew Cochrane of Glasgow was a worried man. Rumours were flying that the young man known to his friends as Prince Charles Edward Stuart, and to his enemies as the Pretender's Son, had landed in the Highlands.

The Pretended Prince – as his opponents also contemptuously called him – was not going to march south on his own. Even without the thousands of French troops who featured so terrifyingly in the rumours, he would certainly be at the head of a body of ferocious Highlanders, all armed to the teeth and ready for action – and Glasgow was a sitting target.

A busy port full of warehouses, textile mills, workshops and wealthy merchants, the city had nailed its colours to the Hanoverian mast, its growing prosperity dependent on the political union with England. That union had given Glasgow access to England's colonies, opening up a mutually profitable trade with North America and the West Indies. By the 1770s, half of all the tobacco being exported from Virginia and North Carolina was being landed at quaysides on the Clyde.

Long before that, the tobacco ships were being sent back across the Atlantic laden with the goods the then colonists needed and which the city had geared itself up to manufacture. Sugar cane from the West Indies and the product from its subsequent refining also became hugely important to the economy of the west of Scotland.

Daniel Defoe, author of *Robinson Crusoe* and a Government spy, toured Scotland before, during and after the Union of 1707. Writing after the event, he said that 'the rabble of Glasgow made the most formidable attempt to prevent it, yet now they know better'. In other words, Glaswegians knew which side their bread was buttered. The Jacobite rallying cry of 'Prosperity to Scotland – and no Union!' cut very little ice here.

The Glasgow merchants, as Defoe also noted, traded with more than just the Americas. Their ships sailed to the Mediterranean, too, and far beyond it. The graceful vessel which rides the globe on top of the Merchants' House in the modern city's George Square is a model of the *Bonnie Nancy*. She belonged to Mr Glassford, one of the most famous of the Tobacco Lords and reluctant host to Bonnie Prince Charlie during the latter's unwelcome visit to Glasgow at the end of 1745. The real *Bonnie Nancy* went missing, presumed sunk, on a voyage to China.

When Provost Cochrane, Mr Glassford and their other friends prominent in the Virginia trade enjoyed their Glasgow punch – not, of course, to be confused with a Glasgow kiss – the toast before they drank their concoction of rum, water, sugar, lemons and limes was, 'The trade of Glasgow and the outward bound!'

When the '45 broke out, Glasgow's prosperity became a liability. Not only had the city's pro-Union stance made it, in Provost Cochrane's own words, 'obnoxious to the rebels', it was also filled with everything an advancing army needed: food, clothes, shoes and well-off citizens on whom taxes could be levied.

Glasgow was also completely undefended. Unlike Edinburgh,

it had no city wall. Nor, unlike both Edinburgh and Stirling, did it have a castle-fortress into which a garrison might withdraw and regroup. Nobody was more aware of these disadvantages than Andrew Cochrane.

He was in his early fifties in 1745, serving his third term in office. Born in Ayr in 1693, he had moved to Glasgow at the age of 30 and married Janet Murdoch. She was, in turn, a daughter, a sister and a wife to three successive Lord Provosts of Glasgow.

Cochrane had the opportunity to discuss his fears of a march on Glasgow by a Jacobite Army when the city's youthful Member of Parliament dined with him and other members of the Town Council at the end of July 1745, only a few days after Charles Edward Stuart had landed on the Scottish mainland.

Jack Campbell of Mamore was, after his father – Major General John Campbell of Mamore – heir to the Duke of Argyle. Travelling with his powerful relative to Inveraray, where the duke was building a fine new castle, Jack, just 22 years old at the time, wrote that the Glasgow magistrates 'were all extremely civil'. They were, he thought, also appreciative of how much the duke had done for them since Jack's election to serve as their MP the year before. His elevation to political office was not unconnected to his being the heir to one of the most powerful men in Scotland.

Andrew Cochrane's ability to remain civil to the lords and lairds who ran Scotland on behalf of the London Government was to be sorely tested over the months of turmoil which followed. So were his nerves.

Despite the city's lack of defences, Glasgow did have a military garrison. However, one of the first responses to the growing emergency – on 12 August 1745 – was to order those troops off to Stirling, a place of much greater strategic importance in military terms. A week later, a letter arrived from the Marquis of Tweeddale, then Secretary of State for Scotland. He was writing from London, where he spent much of his time, and he wanted to let Glasgow know:

that the Lords Justices had received intelligence that the
Pretender's son was already landed, or intending to land
in Scotland, and desiring them to exert there care and
vigilance on this occasion, and to use such precautions
as they judge necessary for preserving the publick peace
within there bounds.

At this point presumably Glasgow collectively rolled its eyes
heavenwards and asked to be told something it didn't know. Walking
a political tightrope as they were, Cochrane and the magistrates
sent a polite reply the same day telling the Secretary of State they
would do everything necessary 'for preserving the publick peace'
and assuring him that 'our inhabitants were all firmly attached to
his Majesty'.

It was to be the first of many such protestations of Glasgow's loyalty
to the House of Hanover. They pepper Cochrane's letters. Reading
them now, even allowing for the highly deferential tone the class
structure of the time obliged him to adopt, it can feel as though the
good provost was protesting a little too much.

As elsewhere in Lowland Scotland, there were those in Glasgow
who supported the Jacobites. Cochrane did his utmost to conceal this
and for entirely understandable reasons. If he was to protect Glasgow's
prosperity and its citizens' livelihoods, he had a difficult course to steer
through the rocks and reefs in which he found himself in 1745–6.

Given the source of Glasgow's wealth, he could not afford to sit
on the fence. Having then committed himself to what he had to
hope would be the winning side, he also had to assure its various
representatives that Glasgow's loyalty to the political status quo was
total. If the Rebellion ended in failure for the Jacobites, nobody was
in any doubt that there would be reprisals.

With the magistrates, Cochrane formed an emergency committee
of the 'principal inhabitants' of the city. The situation they faced was
daunting, the boulders in their path rolled there as often by their
friends as their enemies. The committee's first action was to take a

quick census, establishing there were around 500 able-bodied men who could form a citizens' militia.

Despite Glasgow's subsequent reputation for fighting men, the volunteers of the summer of 1745 were not used to wielding swords and guns. There weren't too many weapons available anyway, such as were to hand in a bad state of repair. A small detachment of dragoons under a Lieutenant Chisholm had remained in Glasgow. Now Chisholm told the provost he had orders to take himself and his men to Dumbarton Castle forthwith. On 4 September 1745, with the Jacobite Army having entered Perth the previous day, Cochrane wrote a frantic letter to General Guest, the Government military commander based at Edinburgh Castle, pleading for the dragoons to stay. He was particularly worried about John MacGregor of Glengyle, 'by whom we are threatened, or any stragling party'. Glengyle was the colonel of a regiment in the Jacobite Army which included two of the infamous Rob Roy's sons, and stragglers were always considered dangerous, ill-disciplined and on the hunt for booty.

The answer which came back was that no soldiers could be spared to help defend Glasgow. Nor could any arms and ammunition be supplied for distribution to the citizens' militia. Lord Justice Clerk Andrew Fletcher wrote to Cochrane from Edinburgh on 10 September 1745, while the Jacobite Army was still at Perth. He admitted things were in a sorry state 'owing to our not taking the alarm soon enough, and forming a proper and timeous scheme for putting the nation in a posture of defence'. He tried to reassure Cochrane that the 'Highland host' was not so numerous as previously thought and some of them were not even armed. The trouble was, lots of towns were asking for help. He would, however, try to put Glasgow to the top of the list for 'firelocks and ammunition'.

The next day, the Lord Advocate, Robert Craigie, wrote to Cochrane in reply to a letter from the provost. He too offered words of comfort:

and I assure you I sincerely sympathize with the city of Glasgow. That they should be under apprehensions that the fruits of their industry, as well as their persons and their families, may be exposed to the insults of a rabble of Highlanders, I am sorry to use the expression, assembled under the conduct of gentlemen of no fortunes, and, I think, of no principles, as they act under the direction of a Popish Pretender and his son, under the influence of France and Rome.

This was very much the party line but of little practical help to Cochrane. Adding insult to injury, the Lord Advocate went on to advise the provost that the 'friends of the government' should be on their guard:

> in this view, the inhabitants of this place are associating themselves under the direction of the Magistrates to defend the rebels, I hope you'll forgive me in suggesting that its the proper course for Glasgow to follow.

This must have infuriated Cochrane, whose fellow citizens had been getting themselves organized to do exactly that for the previous month. Still offering soothing words, Robert Craigie wrote that he thought many of the estimated 1,800 Highlanders at Perth were poorly armed and 'either very old or young'.

So that's all right, then. Although an army of nearly 2,000 occupying Perth still sounds pretty alarming, however decrepit at one end of the scale and not yet needing to shave at the other its soldiers might have been. Lord Justice Clerk Andrew Fletcher did at least seem embarrassed about the situation:

> I am sorry I have no power to be usefull to Glasgow. Those who differ from me, I am bound to believe they act according to the best of their judgment. I pray God may avert the evils we are threatened with. I would not

have you to permitt copies of my letter, or show it to
any but a few.

Despite being part of the Hanoverian establishment himself, clearly
Fletcher didn't want to be seen to be critical of it, either. At around
the very time he was assuring Andrew Cochrane that he was his most
obedient and humble servant, on the afternoon of 14 September 1745,
two officers of the Jacobite Army rode into Glasgow. They had a letter
to deliver and it was signed 'Charles P. R.'

> I need not inform you of my being come hither nor of
> my view in coming. That is already sufficiently known;
> All those who love their country and the true interest of
> Britain ought to wish for my success and do what they
> can to promote it. It would be a needless repetition to tell
> you that all the priviledges of your Town are included in
> my Declaration, And what I have promised I will never
> Depart from. I hope this is your way of thinking And
> therefore Expect your Compliance with my Demands.
> A Sum of money besides what is due to the
> Government not exceeding fifteen thousand pounds
> Sterling and whatever arms can be found in your City is
> at present what I require. The terms offered you are very
> reasonable and what I promise to make good I chuse to
> make these demands, but if not comply'd with I shall
> take other measures; and you must be answerable for the
> consequences.

The threat is scarcely veiled, and that 'at present what I require' cannot
have done much for Andrew Cochrane's stress levels. He himself wrote
of 'infinite disorder and confusion' in Glasgow – in other words,
blind panic. When his committee of magistrates and principal citizens
made the decision to negotiate with the Jacobites, the bulk of whom
were now at Falkirk, he knew this was going to be seen by many on
the Government side as both cowardice and treason. We don't talk

to terrorists. He also knew that not negotiating might lead to the plundering and sacking of Glasgow he so feared. The provost took the difficult decision to send a deputation to Falkirk in the hope of opening those negotiations with the Jacobite high command.

At the same time, Cochrane did his level best to explain the town's decision to 'truckle to a pretended prince and rebels', once again forced to bend over backwards to affirm loyalty to the Government and the House of Hanover. The letters to and from the Lord Advocate, the Duke of Argyle and the Secretary of State for Scotland flew backwards and forwards with a speed and frequency one might envy today, all the more amazing in a country in such uproar as central Scotland was by this stage.

Although the deputation of magistrates turned back at Kilsyth, persuaded the Jacobite Army was not now heading for Glasgow, Cochrane remained to be convinced. Other reports led him to believe that the city was 'expecting every moment a visit from the Highlanders; unable to resist, and absolutely at there mercy'. Naturally, Glasgow would remain loyal to the Government 'whatever our fate or misfortunes may be'.

Presumably Cochrane gave three small cheers when the Lord Advocate at last sent a warrant from the king to 'our trusty and wellbeloved the Provost, Magistrates and Town council of our City of Glasgow'. It graciously permitted its 'good subjects in that part of our kingdom of Great Britain called Scotland' to 'raise, assemble and arm such men as they shall judge necessary'.

As for supplying some of those arms – well, Robert Craigie did have a warrant for this, to go to General Guest at Edinburgh Castle, but this was impracticable now. The Lord Advocate also thought it inadvisable to send this second warrant with his letter, in case it should be intercepted by the Jacobites. If they thought Glasgow had a decent arsenal, they would be much more likely to pay the city that dreaded visit.

Again, this was all less than useless to Cochrane, especially when he received a further demand from Charles Edward Stuart. It was sent from the Palace of Holyroodhouse, four days after the Jacobite victory over Government forces under Sir John Cope at the Battle of Prestonpans on 21 September 1745.

> Seeing it has pleased God to grant us a compleat victory over all our enemys in Scotland, and as the present expedition we are now engaged in does not permitt us to visite the town of Glasgow, we have thought proper to intimate to you of the Town Council and University, that, whereas the exigency of the times do not permitt us to leave the publick money as should be done in time of peace, we are obliged to have recourse to you for a loan of fifteen thousand pounds sterling, which we hereby oblige ourselves to pay back so soon as the nation shall be in a state of tranquillity.

Charles promised his goodwill and protection for Glasgow and her university if his demands were 'chearfully and readily comply'd with by Munday first'. Helpfully, he also wrote: 'And furthermore, we are willing, in part of this sum, to accept of two thousand broadswords, at reasonable rates.'

This remarkable missive was delivered by John Hay of Restalrig, one of Charles Edward Stuart's private secretaries, who rode into Glasgow with an escort. Although he was an abrasive man, he did listen to representations from a meeting attended by what Provost Cochrane called 'our whole inhabitants', who managed to reduce the demand to £5,500, mostly in money but partly in goods.

The provost's justification for coming up with this ransom was the threat of violence from the Rebel army, whose members 'consisting of many thousands and daily increasing, were within a day and a half's march of us'. As if that weren't enough, MacGregor of Glengyle was 'in the town and suburbs' with some of his clansmen.

Cochrane sent this justification to the Duke of Argyle after the Government defeat at Prestonpans, reaffirming Glasgow's continuing loyalty to King George. He followed it up with another letter one week later. Lamenting the defeat and the Rebels' occupation of Edinburgh, he didn't neglect to mention that 'His Majesty's friends are without arms'.

> There is an absolute interruption of business; our manufactures at a stand, for want of sales and cash to pay there servants, and an intire stop to payments; the rebels harassing the burrows, distressing the collectors of the publick revenues, and endeavouring forcibly to get all the money they can, without regard to the merchant's drawbacks or laws of the revenue.

In that 'harassing the burrows', it must be regretfully assumed that Cochrane meant the villages and communities on Glasgow's outskirts, not that even Scotland's rabbit population was in danger from the wicked Jacobites. Although, given that an army marches on its stomach, it probably was.

Less than a month later, the beleaguered provost was fielding demands coming at him from the other side. These were first made by Major General John Campbell of Mamore, young Jack's father, writing from Somerset House in London on 25 October 1745 to say he was being sent north to take military command of the west of Scotland and the Highlands. An army also marches on its feet:

> as I flatter myselfe that my good friends in Glasgow will in every shape assist me in the publick service, I take this opportunity of beging you will be so good as to inquire if in your town there are any Highland shoo-makers who can make broges. I shall want about one thousand pairs, to be made immediatly; and as soon as any tolerable quantety are gott ready, you will order the contractor to send them by parcels to Dumbarton castle, where they will be secure till I shall have occasion for them. As I apprehend it to be one branch of your trade to the West Indies furnishing shoos, I need give

you no particular directions for contracting and fixing
a pattern, &c.

Andrew Cochrane must have been tempted to howl an exasperated
'Gie us a break, pal', and maybe he did. For public consumption, he
wrote to the Duke of Argyle to tell him how Glasgow had celebrated
King George's birthday on 30 October. This was despite another visit
from the Jacobites in the shape of a raiding party with drawn swords
who swept into town demanding horses and money, 'the Rebels
carrying matters with as high a hand as ever'.

Gallus Glasgow thumbed its nose at them, ringing its bells and lighting
its bonfires. The great and the good, including 'the Earl of Selkirk, several
persons of distinction, the principal inhabitants and gentlemen of the
colledge', proceeded to the town hall to drink numerous loyal toasts,
including one, of course, to the Duke of Argyle himself.

It's easy to imagine Cochrane, wig off and dressing gown on, asking
Janet over the breakfast table the next morning if she thought he had
laid it on thick enough. It would appear that he hadn't. In November
1745, he wrote to Patrick Crawford, a Member of Parliament in
London, bitterly expressing the view that Glasgow had suffered so
much because of its loyalty to the Government but was still getting
no thanks for it:

> our country robbed, plundered and harassed, by the rebel
> partys, and has got such a blow as it will not recover during
> my life. At same time we are represented as disaffected to
> his Majesty's government, when sure I am he has no such
> faithful subjects in his dominions as this place and adjacent
> countys. The rebels have been masters of Scotland for six
> weeks, yet not one man from this place has joined them,
> nor I believe six men from the neighbouring shires.

In denying that even one man from Glasgow had joined the Rebels,
the provost was being a little economical with the truth. He was still

having to be very careful about what he said. By this time, however, with Glasgow's trade and business at a standstill and 4,000 barrels of tobacco lying unloaded on the Clyde, he was finding it harder to conceal his anger and irritation, at least from someone he obviously trusted.

Patrick Crawford, not the MP for Glasgow but possibly a Glasgow man, seems to have been sounding out opinion about how the emergency had been dealt with. The provost was very clear in his own mind what the Government had done wrong, and it was almost everything.

The threat posed by the Jacobite Army hadn't been taken seriously enough, allowing them to quickly advance south. Sir John Cope had made the mistake of heading off too rapidly for the north instead of waiting at Stirling for more troops. The Rebellion could have been nipped in the bud if only the well-affected (those who were loyal to the Government as opposed to those who were disaffected to it) had been trusted with the arms and the authority to 'guard the passes' and defend their own towns and communities. He asked Crawford not to tell anyone his views:

> I desire not to be interested in any inquiry concerning
> my superiors' conduct. I have had great care and fatigue,
> and would not go through such another scene for a
> great deal of money: God grant it were all over.

The provost went on doggedly making requests for arms, asking if he should send carts to collect them. He finally got the weapons at the end of November, and the 500-strong Glasgow Militia and 150 men from Paisley were knocked into some kind of shape. They were promptly marched off to defend Stirling, leaving Glasgow in a worse situation than it had been before.

Demonstrating a fine grasp of dramatic timing, the Jacobite Army chose Christmas Day 1745 to march into Glasgow. For Andrew Cochrane, it was very far from being over. His nightmare was only just beginning.

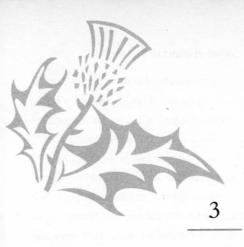

3

SOLDIER, POET & JACOBITE SPY: JOHN ROY STUART

WHEN YOUNG CHARLES COMES OVER, THERE WILL BE BLOOD AND BLOWS

The '45 did not explode out of nowhere. It had been brewing for years – but for the 'Protestant Wind', we might have known it as the '44. In February and March of that year, two violent storms blew up in the English Channel and wreaked havoc on a fleet of French warships gathered off Dunkirk. Poised to invade England in support of the restoration of the Stuarts to the throne of Great Britain, the fearsome weather rendered them useless. The invasion was called off – or at least postponed.

Previous attempts to restore the Stuarts had all failed and by the mid-1740s lay 30 years in the past. For many, the Jacobite Cause was yesterday's news, the House of Hanover and the Union between Scotland and England too well established to think of upsetting an arrangement which seemed to work well enough. On the other hand, dedicated Jacobites took strength in 1720 from the birth of Charles Edward Stuart.

As Charles and his younger brother Henry grew to manhood, the hopes of those people grew along with them. The reports were encouraging. Charles was fit and handsome, brave and bold, more than willing to fulfil his destiny. As the abortive attempt of 1744 showed, the French might be persuaded to help him achieve it.

There were Jacobites in many parts of Britain. They included powerful and influential men such as the Duke of Beaufort in England and Sir Watkin Williams Wynn in Wales. Many in the north of England had strong Jacobite sympathies, most especially in Northumberland. Oxford was considered a nest of Jacobites, and how many covert supporters of the Stuarts there were in London was anyone's guess.

Old loyalties to the House of Stuart remained strong, particularly, of course, in Scotland. A few highly placed Scottish Jacobites formed themselves into the Association or Concert of Gentlemen. They included the Duke of Perth, Lord Lovat and Donald Cameron of Lochiel. John Murray of Broughton, who was to become Charles Edward Stuart's secretary during the '45 and subsequently a notorious traitor to the Jacobite Cause, carried their coded letters backwards and forwards to the Jacobite court in exile in Rome.

In the years of plotting which culminated in the '45, there were many other messengers travelling secretly between Rome, France, England and Scotland. One of them was a man called John Roy Stuart.

John Roy is the quintessential romantic Jacobite: a warrior poet, dashing lover and cultured Highland gentleman. Iain Ruadh Stiùbhart in his native Gaelic, he was born in 1700 at Knock of Kincardine in Badenoch, not far from present-day Coylumbridge. The towering Cairngorms were the backdrop to his childhood.

His family traced its descent from Alexander Stewart, the much-famed and much-feared Wolf of Badenoch, and through him claimed kinship with the Royal Stewarts. Accounts of John Roy's life and adventures spell his surname in both variations, although he seems always to have used *Stuart*.

Perhaps he did so to emphasize his connection with the royal house. Or perhaps it was simpler for a man who spent a large part of his life in France. It is traditionally said to have been Mary, Queen of Scots, who invented the *Stuart* spelling. Spending most of her childhood and young womanhood at the French court, she adapted the name to be more easily pronounced by speakers of a language which did not include the letter *w*.

As was typical of many Highland gentlemen of his period, John Roy Stuart's impressive family tree did not go hand in hand with having any money. This may be why he sought employment in the British Army, serving as a quartermaster with the Scots Greys. The experience was to stand him in good stead in 1745.

When, however, he was refused a commission in the Black Watch, he resigned. Whether his rejection had anything to do with his Jacobite sympathies or whether it helped strengthen them is not clear. It does seem to be at this point, though, when he was in his early to mid-thirties, that he became a Jacobite secret agent.

While still in the British Army and serving in Scotland, he got into trouble for a certain lack of enthusiasm in pursuing a suspected Jacobite and ended up in Inverness Gaol. Lord Lovat, the Old Fox, a master of the esoteric art of fence-sitting, was Sheriff of Inverness at the time – and somehow John Roy managed to escape from prison. The two men spent the next six weeks together at Lovat's home, Castle Downie.

That they had a whale of a time there emerged at Lovat's trial for treason in 1746, when his luck and ability to serve two masters at last ran out. Proving his Jacobite sympathies, evidence was given that during those six weeks he and John Roy Stuart 'diverted themselves composing "burlesque" verse, that when young Charles comes over, there will be blood and blows'. Sadly, none of these Gaelic ditties have survived.

In addition to being a Jacobite spy, a poet, a cultured man, the master of several languages and having a fine head of red hair into the bargain, John Roy seems to have been something of a dandy. The Jacobites of 1745 were well aware of how important it was to dress to impress, and John Roy knew better than anybody that a man clad in shabby clothes did not inspire confidence.

Already on a monthly allowance from the Stuart court in exile, in 1744 he wrote to James Edgar, secretary to the king in exile, asking for a few more livres to enable him to buy 'cloaths & a little linen'. He was ashamed to go out in what he was wearing, believing that 'a tolerable Clean apportment & Cloaths are necessar to keep one from falling into contempt'.

He must have got the money from somewhere to smarten up his appearance. 'Cross-examined at the bar of the House of Commons' during Lord Lovat's trial, cattle-drover John Gray of Rogart in Sutherland was asked if he had ever seen John Roy Stuart with the Rebels and what he had been wearing. It was a standard question, tartan and any other form of Highland dress being taken as the badge of a Jacobite.

Gray's reply is guaranteed to raise a smile in the modern reader: 'He goes always very gay. Sometimes he had Highland cloaths, and other times long cloaths on.' Long clothes were, of course, full-skirted frockcoats and greatcoats, as opposed to the shorter jackets worn over the kilt.

Intriguingly, the officer serving under the Duke of Cumberland who confirms the colour of John Roy's hair gives us another detail of his appearance, referring to 'that officer with the red hair and the little hand'. Whether this was a deformity he was born with or the result of a wound, it did not prevent him from being a formidable fighter.

In May 1745, he fought for the French against the British at the Battle of Fontenoy in what is now Belgium. Astonishingly, he paid a visit to the British camp the night before the battle, spending an hour or so with a friend from Strathspey. If they came face to face the next day, did they give one another a wry smile, step sideways and fight someone else?

Like other men involved in the '45, John Roy could have faced an even worse dilemma but seems to have been spared it. He had an illegitimate son called Charles Stewart, who fought in Lord Loudoun's Regiment. Father and son may therefore have lined up on opposite sides to one another at the Battle of Prestonpans, but there is no record of any encounter between them there.

A month after Fontenoy, John Roy sailed from Holland to Scotland, leaving behind in Boulogne in France his wife, Sarah Hall, and their young daughter, asking that the exiled king should arrange for them to be looked after should anything happen to him. He landed quietly in East Lothian: a more discreet return home than disembarking at Leith, the busy and bustling port for Edinburgh.

He joined the Prince at Blair Atholl at the end of August. Charles was then on his way south after the Raising of the Standard at Glenfinnan. He knew John Roy well from his visit to Rome and trusted him implicitly. No time was wasted in sending him north with letters for Lord Lovat at Castle Downie.

What John Roy had been up to in the two months before then is not known. It's logical to assume that he visited family and friends, of whom he had many. Since he brought back from Europe letters from prominent people pledging aid to the Jacobite Cause, it's also logical to assume that he was doing his silver-tongued best to persuade them, and anyone else who would listen to him, that they should declare their support for the Prince. The man had a way with words.

Sometimes that got him into trouble. The English translation of his '*Oran a' Bhranndaih*', or 'Song to Brandy', paints a vivid picture:

> A thousand curses on the folly!
> Woe to him who would drink brandy!
> It fills us with wind and boastfulness
> And there will be much said of it.
> That's just what happened to me.
> In this glen I took to drinking.
> Temptation led me on
> And it struck me on the head.
>
> Woe to him who would go seeking
> Friendship, payment or pledge

Among some of the women of Kincardine!
I am ashamed to speak of them.
In particular, when I make love to them,
However sweet their words might be,
They would rather have a chance
To adjust my guts with a knife.

In 1746, after it all went wrong, John Roy Stuart was to pen some of the saddest verses imaginable. Mourning the deaths of his friends, the treachery and cruelty of his enemies, and the ravaging of the Highlands by an English army, they are melancholy laments for everything that has been lost.

In the summer of 1745, there was no thought of any of that. The time had come at last, and the endless waiting was over. The longed-for Stuart prince was here, and the pent-up frustrations of the past 30 years could explode into action.

Stepping out of the shadows of Jacobite espionage, John Roy Stuart was in the thick of it. With him were thousands of Scotsmen who were tired of rule from far-off London and the unfair taxes and restrictions which went with it – and they were all spoiling for a fight.

4

A Scholar & a Gentleman: Alexander Forbes, Lord Pitsligo

March, gentlemen

While Provost Cochrane in Glasgow was anxiously gathering scraps of information about the movements and intentions of Charles Edward Stuart and the Jacobite Army in the summer of 1745, a man of mature years at the other end of the country was doing much the same, albeit in a rather more eager frame of mind.

He was Alexander, 4th Lord Forbes of Pitsligo. His home at Pitsligo Castle, now an impressive ruin, stands on the hill above the old fishertown of Rosehearty in Buchan. It lies a few miles west of Fraserburgh on Scotland's north-east shoulder, where the Moray Firth gives way to the North Sea.

Alexander Forbes inherited his title and Pitsligo Castle – along with the estate's debts – at an early age, although, like many young Scotsmen, he completed his education in France, spending several years there. He became friends with François Fénelon, one of the greatest thinkers of his age. Fénelon advocated a mystical Christianity that appealed strongly to Alexander Forbes, the study and discussion of religion and philosophy to become a lifelong passion.

The French cleric also believed Christians should not shut themselves away from the world but had a duty to be involved in it. This philosophy took a liberal approach to education and politics, and believed in criticizing the state when it acted oppressively towards its citizens. It was a lesson Alexander Forbes learned well.

Returning home in 1700 at the age of 22, he immediately took his seat in the Scottish Parliament and was an active member of it. A boy of ten when the Stuarts were deposed from the British throne, he remained a committed Jacobite throughout his long life.

He was also a vehement opponent of Scotland's political union with England. In 1706, during the dying days of the old Scottish Parliament, he spoke out strongly against the proposal. When the majority of his fellow Members of Parliament chose – many persuaded by English bribes – to vote an independent Scotland out of existence, Alexander Forbes, not yet 30 years old, retired to Buchan.

He did not, however, retire from life. Burdened with debt though his estate was, the young Lord Pitsligo quickly won the affection of his tenants through his care and consideration for them. Although he was deeply spiritual, his Christianity was also of a very practical bent, and he hated unfairness and unkindness with a passion. Some described him as a saint. He would have laughed at that, being a convivial man who enjoyed good food, good wine and good conversation. He was an early supporter of education for girls and counted many women among his friends and numerous correspondents, both at home and across Europe.

His peaceful and sociable life at Pitsligo Castle with his first wife, Rebecca Norton, and their son, John, the Master of Pitsligo, was brutally shattered in 1715, when Charles Edward Stuart's father – James VIII to his friends, the Old Pretender to his enemies – landed at Peterhead, down the coast from Fraserburgh.

Following the Jacobite Standard raised by his cousin, the Earl of Mar, Lord Pitsligo, by now in his late thirties, picked up his sword, mounted his horse and went out for the Cause, fighting at the inconclusive

Battle of Sheriffmuir. When the Rising of 1715 guttered out, he was forced, like many other Jacobites, to spend several years in exile in Europe. By about 1720, when things had calmed down, he was able to slip quietly home.

The middle years of his life were spent studying literature and religion. In 1730, he published a book of essays on moral and philosophical questions. It's a wide-ranging work that includes a discussion on why we find it funny when someone falls over: 'What shall we make of that readiness to laugh, when one slips a foot and tumbles over? We are even afraid he is hurt, and yet cannot refrain from laughing.'

In 1745, when the call to arms came again, he was 67 years old and not in robust health, being a chronic asthmatic. Nobody would have blamed him if he'd stayed at home and let younger men rally to the Standard. Yet his loyalty to the Stuart Cause was unswerving. 'Did you ever know me absent at the second day of a wedding?' he asked well-meaning friends who remonstrated with him. He'd been out in the '15; it was his duty to go out this time, too.

Always ready to laugh at himself, he was amused when the young son of a friend brought a stool to help him mount his horse when leaving the house. Smiling down at the boy, he said, 'My little fellow, this is the severest reproof I have yet met with, for presuming to go on such an expedition.'

Yet go he did. The two hundred 'gentleman and their servants' of Pitsligo's Horse provided one of the Jacobite Army's seven cavalry regiments. Lord Pitsligo's son, John, the Master of Pitsligo, did not ride with them. This may have been because he did not share his father's politics. Or, like many Scottish families at the time, they may have been hedging their bets.

After the failure of the '45 Rising, Lord Pitsligo was one of the many Jacobite leaders declared an attainted Rebel, stripped of his title and property, his estate forfeit to the crown. His son took legal action to try to win some of this back, instructing his lawyer so soon after the event it might be thought he was poised to do so.

If father and son did agree that only one of them should go out for the Prince, it might seem odd that John Forbes was happy to allow his father to put his life on the line rather than the other way around. Then again, maybe he was not at all happy about it; his father might have insisted this was how it had to be.

This makes sense in the context of Lord Pitsligo's strength and nobility of character, and his devotion to the Stuarts. In the context of the '45, it is also noticeable how many of those Jacobites who were prepared to stand up and be counted were at opposite ends of the age spectrum.

The commitment of those in their twenties might be attributed to youthful passion and idealism. Their seniors, such as Lord Pitsligo, Gordon of Glenbucket and others, might have felt they had spent too many years compromising their principles. This was their last chance to go out and fight for them.

The value of Alexander Forbes to the Prince in terms of moral authority was incalculable. When he and his regiment joined the Jacobite Army at Duddingston near Edinburgh at the beginning of October 1745, a contemporary observer said it was as though religion, virtue and justice had just ridden into the camp, all embodied in the slight figure of Lord Pitsligo.

His decision to come out for the Prince persuaded many other Scots to do likewise, particularly his friends and neighbours in the north-east. Angus supplied Lord and Lady Ogilvy and the Forfarshire Regiment. Aberdeenshire and Banffshire provided not only Pitsligo's Horse but also regiments under Gordon of Glenbucket, Lord Lewis Gordon, James Moir of Stoneywood, Francis Farquharson of Monaltrie and James Farquharson of Balmoral. Despite the name, John Roy Stuart's Edinburgh Regiment also included many men from Aberdeenshire and Banffshire. After a lifetime spent researching through contemporary letters and lists, Jacobite historians Alistair and Henrietta Tayler estimated that around 20 per cent of the Jacobite Army's fighting men came from the north-east of Scotland.

Old loyalties and old religion had a lot to do with this. Although the persecuted Catholic Church clung on tenaciously in a few isolated pockets of Upper Banffshire, the beleaguered Episcopalian Church had a much larger membership in the area. All over Scotland, it was not the Roman Catholics but these Protestant believers who were most closely intertwined with the Jacobites and the Stuart Cause.

Before Pitsligo's Horse left its assembly point in Aberdeen, Alexander Forbes, 4th Lord Pitsligo, took off his hat and raised his face for a moment to the sky. 'Lord,' he said, 'Thou knowest that our cause is just. March, gentlemen.'

All over Scotland in the late summer and early autumn of 1745, thousands of men were doing exactly that.

5

JOHNNIE COPE & THE BARKING DOGS OF TRANENT

FOR SHAME, GENTLEMEN, BEHAVE LIKE BRITONS!
FOR SHAME, GENTLEMEN, DON'T LET US BE
BEAT BY A SET OF BANDITTI!

Condemned by a song: that's what happened to Johnnie Cope. The Battle of Prestonpans was barely over before the taunting, triumphant words were written:

> Cope sent a challenge frae Dunbar
> Saying, Charlie, meet ye an' ye daur:
> An' I'll learn ye the art o' war
> Gin ye'll meet me in the mornin'.

> When Charlie looked the letter upon
> He drew his sword the scabbard from:
> Come, follow me, my merry, merry men
> An' we'll meet Johnnie Cope in the mornin'.

> When Johnnie Cope he heard o' this
> He thocht tae himsel' that it wouldna be amiss,

For tae saddle his horse in readiness
Tae flee awa' in the mornin'.

When Johnnie Cope tae Dunbar came
They speired at him, 'Where's a' your men?'
'The de'il confound me gin I ken
For I left them a' in the mornin'.

Hey, Johnnie Cope, are ye waukin' yet?
Or are your drums a-beatin' yet?
If I were waukin', I wad wait
Tae gang tae the coals in the mornin'.

That's it, then: he was a bad commander, ill-prepared and taken by surprise. Worse still, he was a coward who saved his own skin, leaving his men in the lurch and to their fate. When a breathless Cope and his panting horse reached Dunbar, one smirking local remarked that he didna ken wha had won the battle but he kent fine wha had won the race.

Cope's bad press started early, so much so that after the emergency was over, a public enquiry was held into his conduct during it. He had already been found guilty at the court of public opinion, as the preface to the published report of the board of enquiry makes clear:

> From the Beginning of the Rebellion, and the first Motion of the King's Troops in *Scotland*, it was generally believed, that Sir *John Cope* had acted with less Vigilance than he ought to have done: and all the Advantages of the Rebels, previous to the Battle of *Preston-pans*, were, by the Publick, imputed to his Mismangement;

Examine the evidence, however, and it's not long before the word *scapegoat* springs to mind.

General Sir John Cope was a career soldier who found the time at certain periods in his life also to be a Member of Parliament. He actively sought high office in the British Army and achieved it. When the '45 broke out, he was commander-in-chief of King George II's forces in 'that part of Great Britain called Scotland'.

Duncan Forbes of Culloden was Lord President of the Court of Session in Edinburgh and the prime mover in Scotland of opposition to Charles Edward Stuart and the Jacobites. Forbes was the first to set the alarm bells ringing, firing off letters to everyone who needed to know about the rumours flying around the Highlands that the Prince had landed on the west coast. Many of the recipients of those letters dismissed the threat. Cope was one of the few who took it seriously.

The rumours were soon confirmed. On 13 August 1745, Cope received a letter from Alexander Campbell, the deputy governor of Fort William. Campbell was sorry to be able to assure the general that 'Part of the *French* Fleet, design'd for invading this Country, is arrived in *Moidart*' and that 'The Pretender's eldest Son is along with them, and has been a-shore a-shooting on the Hills.'

Cope was already making his preparations, having instructed the officers of the dragoons under his command to recall their regiments' horses from summer pasture and be ready for immediate action. He wrote to the commanders of the forts which made up the Chain, asking them to be vigilant and gather every piece of information they could on the Jacobite Army's movements.

It was Cope who realized the Rebellion might be nipped in the bud if Charles and his men could be kept on the wrong side of the Great Glen. Well aware of the importance of psychology in warfare, he believed, too, that the most effective way of stopping other clans and individuals that might be contemplating joining the Prince would be to present them with a resounding show of strength from the Government.

He knew this was not going to be easy. Many of the Government troops stationed in Scotland were untested in the field. There were not too many of them either, the experienced soldiers off fighting

Britain's wars on the Continent. Despite this, pinning his hopes on taking the war to the enemy, Cope marched into the Highlands – and came seriously unstuck.

He was leading his 1,500 dragoons and foot soldiers into bandit country, each and every step of man and horse taking them farther away from civilization. Even without a Jacobite Army heading towards them, this was hostile territory. So he took the sensible precaution of stationing his two companies of the Black Watch – then a young Highland regiment in the British Army – in the rear. That way they could keep an eye on the crests of the hills which rose on either side of the road and give warning of any imminent ambushes. It was not Cope's fault that most of these 200 men deserted before he reached Dalwhinnie.

A captain in Lord Loudoun's Regiment in the Government army, Ewan Macpherson of Cluny met Cope at Dalwhinnie and was ordered to return the next day with his company. As Lieutenant Colonel Whitefoord, with Cope on the journey north and one of his witnesses at the board of enquiry, rather plaintively put it: 'but he never came.' From the Redcoat point of view, Cluny had gone over to the Dark Side.

Feeding the expeditionary force once they had crossed the Highland line was a major problem. The general had done his best to prepare for this:

> I gave the utmost application to every one thing for bringing the troops from their respective quarters to Stirling, and for proving what was absolutely necessary for their march through the Highland: the ovens at Leith, Stirling and Perth, were kept at work day and night, Sunday not excepted, to provide Biscuit, which was no other way to be got. I contracted with proper persons for horses, to carry a small train of four field-pieces, and four cohorns, (the country horses being too small for that service) and with a butcher, to carry some cattle along with the army, to kill upon the march.

He needed bread as well as biscuit for his army. Knowing he would be lucky to find it once he left the towns of the Lowlands (and, intriguingly, finding it worthy of note that one of the bakers was Jewish), he set them to work on that too. 'Notwithstanding whereof, we were obliged to halt a whole day at Crieff, waiting for a hundred horse load of it, which was not quite ready when we marched from Stirling.'

Impatient though he was to get moving, Cope had to wait before leaving Edinburgh because he needed money with which 'to subsist the troops; I knew there was none to be got in the country we were to march into'. It was a fortnight before he received the necessary letters of credit from London which could be presented to the banks in Edinburgh. These came from the Marquis of Tweeddale, Secretary of State for Scotland, who helpfully also offered some advice:

> I have laid it before the Lords Justices, who entirely approve of your conduct . . . And their Lordships are of Opinion, that how soon you receive Information, that any Number of the Disaffected are gathered together, you should immediately attack them.
>
> A little Vigour shown in the Beginning, may prevent their coming to a Head . . . It is impossible at this Distance to give any particular Directions; your Judgment and Conduct will enable you, to make the best of the Circumstances that may occur.

Which all sounds remarkably like 'you're on your own, pal'. Cope must indeed have felt very much on his own when he met up with Captain Sweetenham on the road north and discovered that the delay in leaving Edinburgh had allowed the Jacobites to take control of the Corrieyairack Pass, barring his way to Fort Augustus.

Many of the Black Watch had by this time deserted and cantered off on mounts belonging to the British Army. Other horses had been rustled by the locals during the night, while their riders slept. There being 'no such thing as enclosures to keep them in', the sentries posted to guard them could do very little if a horse wandered off to graze and kept right on going.

With not enough horses to carry it, much of the precious bread had to be left by the road. Adding to Cope's woes, his hopes that the clans which supported the Government would join him on his march northwards had also been comprehensively dashed.

It's no wonder he and his senior officers decided at their council of war held at Dalwhinnie on 26 August that they should head north to the relative safety of Inverness. Turning around and going back the way they had come was not an option. They knew now, from Captain Sweetenham, that the Jacobites were armed, dangerous and on the march. The possibility of a party of them heading over the hills and ambushing Cope and his men before they reached Stirling could not be ruled out.

By the time Cope marched his men from Inverness to Aberdeen, the Jacobite Army had the upper hand. Well on its way south and thinking ahead, 'the Rebels had carried all the Boats on the Tay to the south side of that river.' So Cope shipped his men out of Aberdeen, although he had to endure yet another delay while they waited for a favourable wind.

On 17 September, the day the general arrived off Dunbar, a messenger came on-board his ship to tell him the Jacobites had taken Edinburgh earlier that morning. This they did by the simple expedient of walking in through the Netherbow Port when it was opened to allow a carriage to come out.

That Scotland's capital was now in the hands of the Rebels was a military disaster and a huge personal embarrassment for Cope. He'd been chasing them around Scotland for a month and had failed to even get in their way. Resolving to do so now, he chose the place where he would offer them battle with great care.

This was a flat plain between the Firth of Forth at Prestonpans and the rising ground to the south of it, on the ridge of which stood the mining village of Tranent, as it still does. In Cope's considered opinion, there was not 'in the whole of the ground between

Edinburgh and Dunbar, a better spot for both horse and foot to act upon'.

Although the Jacobites commanded the higher ground behind and to the west of Tranent, he considered that this advantage would be negated by the marsh which lay between them and his army. There was, he thought, no way they could approach him unseen and catch him unawares.

His choice of ground was giving the Prince's army a headache and not only because of the boggy ground. The area around Prestonpans and Tranent being one of the cradles of the Industrial Revolution, this was not a smooth and unblemished grassy field. There were open coal pits, the stone dykes which bounded farmland, and the Waggonway, one of the first railway tracks in the world. Long before the invention of the steam engine, horses pulled the trucks of coal along the iron rails. None of these obstacles was going to be easy to fight over.

On the other hand, this worked both ways, affording the Jacobites protection from Cope's cavalry. Land broken by these 'hollow roads, coal pits and enclosures' was no good for horses either. These difficulties led to much manoeuvring by both sides before they lined up to face one another in the early morning mist on Thursday, 21 September. At times it reads like an elaborate dance.

One of its passes and promenades involved the Jacobites occupying the kirkyard at Tranent and firing down on the Government army. Its gunners returned cannon fire, inflicting some casualties, and the Jacobites withdrew.

'About an hour before sunset', Cope spotted a large group of Jacobites marching down Falside Hill. Assuming an attack was imminent, he edged his men around so they weren't at right angles to their approaching enemies but facing them. Once again, a dancing image springs to mind. The Redcoats sound like a troupe of old-fashioned high-kicking chorus girls smoothly changing position – except, of course, that the soldiers' manoeuvre was carried out with deadly intent.

Now front-on to the enemy, they could let loose a full and

murderous volley of musket shot and cannon fire at the Jacobite Army. When they saw what the Government troops were up to, however, they once more withdrew.

The jockeying for position did not cease as night fell. Both armies sent out patrols which criss-crossed the area, each side trying to find out what the other was up to. Cope later recalled that 'two platoons were posted on our right, in the road that leads by Colonel Gardiner's house'.

This country road, which runs down from Birsley Brae, now crosses over the busy traffic lanes of the A1 and down into the new car park at Prestonpans railway station. Generations of Panners knew it as the 'Copie Stanes'. However, since modern-day Prestonpans decided the battle should be better commemorated – under the evocative slogan of 'Victory, Hope, Ambition' – it's now being referred to by its Sunday name of 'Johnnie Cope's Road'.

In none of the accounts of the Battle of Prestonpans, and the busy days before and after it, is much, if anything, recorded about what the locals were thinking, doing or feeling while all hell broke loose around them. In the case of the coal miners, the disturbances might have been going on above them, too. The popular view in Prestonpans and Tranent has always been that people kept their heads down and hoped and prayed it would soon be over.

Trying to let it all sweep over you cannot have been easy with all these patrols creeping through the September night. One group of Jacobites attracted the attention of some highly sensitive ears, as General Cope recalled at the board of enquiry:

> About nine of the Clock that Night, all the Dogs in the Village of *Tranent* began to bark with the utmost Fury, which, it was believed, was occasioned by the Motions of the Rebels. Upon which I visited some of the most advanced Guards and Centries, and found all very alert; but could see or hear nothing but the barking of the Dogs, which ceased about half an Hour past ten; in

which Time the Rebels had removed from the West to
the East Side of *Tranent*.

So the dogs of Tranent barked for a good 90 minutes – which cannot
have done much for anyone's nerves. Meanwhile, the Jacobite colonels
and captains were burning the midnight oil, wondering how they
might deal with the obstacle posed by the marshy ground lying
between them and the enemy. When a local man called Robert
Anderson offered to lead them safely through the bog by the paths
he knew because he often went wild-fowling there, they jumped at
the chance.

Setting off behind him at four o'clock on the morning of Thursday,
21 September, the Jacobite Army took about one hour to negotiate
the marsh. Colonel O'Sullivan was uneasy about that:

> for we cou'd not come to them but by two defiles
> between Morrasses and ponds, where two men cou'd
> hardly go together; if they had only fifty men at each of
> those passes, or let half of us passe, & fall upon us before
> we cou'd be formed, why all was over.

He needn't have worried. Despite the patrols, and although Cope and
his men 'lay upon our Arms all Night', the Government soldiers at
first thought the approaching Jacobites were nothing more than a
row of bushes, becoming visible as night slowly gave way to day. Then
those bushes raised their muskets and took aim.

It was the horses of the Government troops which suffered first,
shot in the head and neck. The dragoons who rode the horses – many
men and mounts alike new to the horror of battle – stared in terror
from the bleeding animals to the ferocity of what was now bearing
down on them out of the morning mist.

Tartan-clad warriors. Blood-curdling war-cries. Swinging, glinting
broadswords. And an even more vicious weapon.

Short of swords, Captain Malcolm MacGregor of the Jacobite Army

had looked around for what was available locally and come up with
scythes. Sharpened and lashed to poles seven or eight feet long, they
were wielded to bloody and horrific effect.

The horses were now deliberately targeted. James Johnstone, a well-
off young man from Edinburgh and one of the gentlemen volunteers
in the Prince's army, later described how the Highlanders rushed
towards the enemy:

> They had been frequently enjoined to aim at the noses
> of the horses with their swords, without minding the
> riders, as the natural movement of a horse, wounded in
> the face, is to wheel round, and a few horses wounded
> in that manner are sufficient to throw a whole squadron
> into such disorder that it is impossible afterwards to rally
> it. They followed this advice most implicitly, and the
> English cavalry were instantly thrown into confusion.
>
> Macgregor's company did great execution with their
> scythes. They cut the legs of the horses in two, and their
> riders through the middle of their bodies.

The Rebels kept on coming, causing ever more panic in the
Government ranks on the receiving end of this horror. All sense even
of self-preservation gone, many of the Redcoat foot soldiers came up
against stone dykes in a human log-jam, and were shot there. As James
Johnstone put it:

> The panic-terror of the English surpassed all imagination.
> They threw down their arms that they might run with
> more speed, thus depriving themselves by their fears
> of the only means of arresting the vengeance of the
> Highlanders. Of so many men in a condition, from
> their numbers, to preserve order in their retreat, not one
> thought of defending himself. Terror had taken entire
> possession of their minds. I saw a young Highlander,
> about fourteen years of age, scarcely formed, who was

presented to the Prince as a prodigy, having killed, it was said, fourteen of the enemy. The Prince asked him if this was true. 'I do not know,' replied he, 'if I killed them, but I brought fourteen soldiers to the ground with my sword.' Another Highlander brought ten soldiers to the Prince, whom he had made prisoners, driving them before him like a flock of sheep.

There is no sense of triumphalism in James Johnstone's description of what happened at Prestonpans, rather a shocked realization that this 'terrible carnage' was what war actually was, even if this was less like a battle than a massacre: 'The field of battle presented a spectacle of horror, being covered with heads, legs, arms and mutilated bodies: for the killed all fell by the sword.' And those gleaming, bloody scythes.

The man who had turned ploughshares into swords died in the battle. Yet even as Malcolm MacGregor lay bleeding on the ground, his body pierced 'through and through' by musket balls, he urged his men to fight on.

Horses whinnying in pain and fear, blood pouring down their long faces from the wounds they had sustained, men screaming in agony, the only thought in their heads to get away from flailing blades and flying bullets, it's hard to see how General Cope could have stemmed this tide of panic-stricken humanity. The evidence he gave to the board of enquiry is that he and his officers did their best:

> The Motion of the Rebels was so very rapid, that the whole Line was broken in a very few Minutes. The Pannick seiz'd the Foot also, and they ran away, notwithstanding all the Endeavours used by their Officers to prevent it. All possible Methods were taken to bring them back from the first Instant they began to run. I endeavour'd all I could to rally them, but to no Purpose. When they could not be brought to their Ground again, it was try'd to get them into a Body for

their own Safety; when that would not do, Endeavours were used to get them to load again in Hopes that they would then be brought to make a Stand; but that was likewise ineffectual. By this Time the Rebels were mixed with them. The Foot dispersed and shifted for themselves all over the Country.

A swift council of war came to the decision that the only thing for it was to retreat.

Johnnie Cope left his coach behind. It had been waiting for him close by the battlefield and contained some of his home comforts. Drinking chocolate being a rare treat in Scotland at this time, the Jacobites who triumphantly seized the general's coach tried to take the brown powder they found inside it as snuff.

What Cope also left behind on the battlefield was his reputation. Up until then, the threat posed by the Prince and his army had been seen as minor, a little local difficulty, easy to quash, not a problem, happening in distant North Britain, so who gave a damn? Not any more. The defeat of a British Army by a bunch of bare-arsed banditti sent out shock waves which ran all the way down to London.

As the preface to the published report of the enquiry put it: 'The Defeat at Preston-pans was attended by such a Train of Mischiefs . . .' Once the crisis was over, in that grand old British tradition, they looked around for someone to blame and thought they had found him in General Sir John Cope.

The board of enquiry was held at 'the Great Room at the Horse-Guards', their deliberations open to the public. This 'examination into the Conduct, Behaviour, and Proceedings' of Sir John Cope also called Colonel Peregrine Lascelles and Brigadier General Thomas Fowke, two of the commanders who served under Cope, to answer for their own conduct.

It began on Monday, 1 September 1746 and lasted for several days. There were five members and the board was chaired by Field Marshal George Wade. He was very well acquainted with the lie of the land that was being discussed. As General Wade, he had directed the great road-building programme which began in the 1720s with the aim of making it easier for Government forces to move quickly around the Highlands and thus more easily control them and their troublesome inhabitants.

'If you had seen these roads before they were made, you would lift up your hands and bless General Wade.' Among the first to bless him were the troublesome inhabitants. In a delicious and satisfying irony, the Jacobite Army found his roads extremely useful when it came to moving themselves and their equipment around.

The witnesses called included Captain Sweetenham, who told the board members what he had told General Cope about the strength of the Jacobites in terms of men and weapons. Lord President Duncan Forbes also gave evidence, confirming that he had warned Cope about the danger waiting for him should he try to lead his men through the Corrieyairack Pass.

David Bruce, who had been 'a voluntary Spectator in the Field of Battle, in which he arrived just at Day-Break, and kept in the Rear of the left of the King's troops till they were routed', gave evidence that he had seen 'no Misconduct or Misbehaviour in the General, or any of the Officers'. After the battle, in what may well be a masterpiece of understatement, David Bruce then simply 'went on to Edinburgh'.

Cope himself gave chapter and verse on the difficulties he had experienced which had led to his delay in heading north and consequent failure to intercept the Jacobite Army before it calmly walked down to the Lowlands. Other witnesses confirmed these difficulties, especially when it came to the problem of the bread to feed the troops.

Every aspect of what had happened on the march north, the return to Dunbar and at the Battle of Prestonpans was enquired into, Cope asked to justify every decision he had taken. This he comprehensively did. Deeply wounded by the allegations of incompetence, he left no stone unturned when it came to preparing his defence.

As well as the witnesses who spoke for him, he also brought with him reports of letters of support from officers who had served with him and under him. A dozen junior officers who had fought at Prestonpans – captains, lieutenants and cornets – spoke up in person for Cope, Lascelles and Fowke.

> They say, they saw Sir *John Cope* from their different Posts, ride along in the Front of the Line, just before the Attack began; giving Orders as he went along, speaking to the Men, and encouraging them: And after the Troops had broke, they saw him endeavouring to rally them again; and particularly Captain *Forester* says, He saw Sir *John* ride in among the Men when they were broke, and try to rally them: And Captain *Pointz* also says, that when the Foot began to break after the first Fire, Sir *John Cope* call'd out to them, *For Shame, Gentlemen, behave like Britons, give them another Fire, and you'll make them run*. And Lieutenant Greenwell also says, that after the Foot have given one Fire, they faced to the Right about, and Sir *John Cope* immediately rode up and called to them to halt, saying, *For Shame, Gentlemen, don't let us be beat by such a Set of Banditti!*

It's pretty convincing stuff. It certainly convinced the board of enquiry, whose members decided that Cope, Lascelles and Fowke had no case to answer, saying specifically of Cope that 'he used all possible Diligence and Expedition before, and in his March to Dalwhinny, considering the Difficulties and Disappointments he met with.' When it came to Prestonpans, the board's considered opinion was:

> That he did his Duty as an officer, both before, at, and after the Action. And that his Personal Behaviour was without Reproach.
>
> And that the Misfortune, on the Day of Action, was owing to the shameful Behaviour of the Private Men;

and not to any Misconduct or Misbehaviour of Sir *John Cope*, or any of the Officers under his Command.

So General Sir John Cope was completely exonerated, with not a stain or blemish on his character or professional integrity – but it's the Johnnie Cope of the song who's remembered.

6

SANDY THE STUDENT &
THE EDINBURGH VOLUNTEERS:
DR ALEXANDER CARLYLE

HE HAD ONLY FOUR BOTTLES OF BURGUNDY,
WHICH IF WE DID NOT ACCEPT OF, HE WOULD BE
OBLIGED TO GIVE TO THE HIGHLANDERS

Alexander Carlyle was a son of the manse. Following in his father's footsteps, he became minister of the same church, serving his parishioners at St Michael's kirk in Inveresk, right behind Musselburgh, for 55 years. He and his wife are buried to the left of the church's front door. A luminary of the Church of Scotland, he was so esteemed for his intellect and Old Testament-prophet good looks that he was nicknamed 'Jupiter' Carlyle.

In the summer of 1745, he was young Sandy Carlyle, 23 years old, impulsive, passionate and with a lively interest in the opposite sex. After studying at Edinburgh University, he spent a year at Glasgow. Like many a student before and since, he paid as much attention to his social life as to his studies, throwing himself into what he called 'college theatricals'.

He and his friends wanted to put on the tragedy of *Cato*, written by Joseph Addison earlier in the eighteenth century. The play was both popular and influential, and its central message of an individual standing up to the tyranny of the state in the cause of personal liberty found a huge resonance in what became the United States. The famous battle-cry which rang around St John's Church in Richmond, Virginia, in the run-up to the American War of Independence, of 'Give me liberty or give me death!' is said to have been inspired by Joseph Addison's play.

While Sandy Carlyle was at Glasgow University, he attended lectures by Professor Francis Hutcheson. The economist Adam Smith, who had been at Glasgow a few years before Carlyle, described this gifted professor, born in Ulster to a Scottish father, as 'the never to be forgotten Hutcheson'. He lectured not only to the students but to the people of Glasgow, throwing open the doors of his lecture theatre on Sunday evenings at six o'clock to anyone who cared to attend. Sandy Carlyle remembered that he used no notes, walking backwards and forwards as he spoke.

One of the fathers of the Scottish Enlightenment, Hutcheson believed in religious tolerance and political liberty, and that men and women were basically good, contradicting the prevalent religious view of humankind as miserable sinners. He also believed people should see themselves as citizens and not subjects of the state. If you lived under a tyrannical regime, you should not only be expected to rebel but consider it your duty to do so. These ideas, too, were to have a profound influence on the American revolutionaries.

Alexander Carlyle was a man of huge intellect. As young Sandy Carlyle, he and his friends were also interested in *Cato* for rather less elevated reasons than its noble message of freedom:

> McLean and I allotted the parts: I was to be Cato; he was Marcus; our friend Sellar, Juba; a Mr. Lesly was to do Lucius; an English student of the name of Seddon was to be Styphax; and Robin Bogle, Sempronius. Miss Campbell was our Marcia, and Miss Wood, Lucia; I have

forgot our Portius. We rehearsed it twice, but never acted it. Though we never acted our play, we attained one of our chief purposes, which was, to become more intimate with the ladies.

The plan being for him to go on to study at 'some foreign Protestant university', Sandy spent June and July of 1745 preaching as a probationer in Haddington, and in August went on holiday to Dumfriesshire. He was to stay with some friends from Glasgow at Moffat, a fashionable resort where those and such as those went to drink the whey from goat's milk, believing this to be good for their health. When he got there, he found the place in uproar at the news that Charles Edward Stuart had landed in the north, gathered together an army of Highlanders and was even now descending on the Lowlands. The enemy would soon be at the gates of Edinburgh.

Hurrying back home, Sandy enlisted with friends from Edinburgh University in a volunteer corps which was christened the College Company. On the very day he joined it, 14 September 1745, he had 'arms put into my hands'. How Provost Cochrane would have envied the student soldiers. Whether they knew what to do with their guns was another matter, although they did receive some rudimentary training.

Sandy Carlyle was not the only person to make the observation that two-thirds of the male population of Edinburgh was anti-Jacobite, while two-thirds of the female variety were for the Prince and his Cause. He also observed that some people, particularly Edinburgh's Provost Stewart and his friends, showed a distinct lack of enthusiasm for defending the city. The suspicion was rife that they were hoping the Jacobites would find a way in but without their overt help.

The raw recruits of the College Company, on the other hand, declared themselves happy to 'expose our lives in defence of the capital of Scotland, and the security of our country's laws and liberties'. On the morning of Sunday, 15 September, they were marched up to the Lawnmarket.

While some women wept at the sight of these fresh-faced young intellectuals ready and willing to do their bit, the Edinburgh mob expressed its derision in various ways. A group of ladies at a row of windows overlooking the street laughed and made fun of the volunteers. They drew back and hurriedly closed the windows when the students threatened to fire warning shots into the rooms – on a mere two or three hours' training, no wonder.

While the students were eating the bread, cheese, ale and brandy supplied by the friendlier local publicans, Sandy Carlyle was found by his 15-year-old brother William, who had been anxiously searching for him. He took William aside and 'endeavoured to abate his fears'. The Volunteers weren't going to be in any great danger, he told the boy, their march out of the city designed only to make the Highlanders delay their approach.

Unfortunately, Sandy then asked William to look after his money for him. William burst into tears, saying his brother really must be going into danger if he was willing to part with his cash. Sandy redoubled his efforts to comfort the boy, and the two brothers arranged a meeting place for nine o'clock that night.

Other people were worried about the College Company, too, a group of ministers addressing them with a plea that they should not march out to meet the Rebels. They were 'the flower of the youth of Edinburgh, and the hope of the next generation'. Their loss would be irreparable, and didn't they think they should stay inside the city which would otherwise be defenceless? That suggestion allowed youthful ardour an honourable method of withdrawal, and, after another hour or so milling about the Grassmarket, the Volunteers were marched back to the College.

That evening a few of them – 'twelve or thirteen of the most intimate friends' – had a late supper at Mrs Turnbull's, whose tavern stood next to the Tron church in the High Street. Spirits were high and fiery, proposals for marching off and offering their services to Sir John Cope as soon as he landed being put forward. Sandy Carlyle later wrote that it was difficult to put any counter-arguments without being damned as cowardly or a secret Jacobite, but he gathered courage from noticing that one or two other students weren't too enthusiastic about this mad proposal either.

The dozen or so young men then took their turn on nightwatch, guarding the Trinity Hospital in Leith Wynd, 'one of the weakest parts of the city'. This forerunner of Leith Walk began just outside the Netherbow Port, its Edinburgh end now lost under modern-day Jeffrey Street.

The students had a boring night. They had nothing to do but respond 'all's well' every half an hour, using a variation on MacDonell of Tirnadris's ploy at High Bridge in the hope that any approaching Jacobites would think Edinburgh was a lot better defended than it was.

At one o'clock, the little brigade was visited by Provost Stewart and his guard. To a man, the students were now convinced he actively wanted the city to fall into Jacobite hands, and they were thoroughly ashamed of him. 'Did you not see how pale the traitor looked, when he found us so vigilant?' asked one of Sandy Carlyle's friends after Stewart had left them to it. To which Sandy offered the practical reply that he thought it was just the light from the lantern that had made the provost look so pale.

The friend who made the comment was John Home. Born in Leith in 1722, the son of the town clerk, he too was to become a minister but is better known as a playwright, his most famous work being *Douglas*. This is the play which was so well received at its first performance that it famously prompted an enraptured member of the audience to shout out from the stalls, 'Whaur's your Willie Shakespeare noo?'

When the student volunteers came off duty the following morning, Sandy Carlyle returned to his lodgings and tried to get some sleep. It was too noisy outside, and he himself was too agitated, so he went out again at midday. It was Monday, 16 September, and it was to be a chaotic day for Edinburgh. The place was in uproar, arguments raging as to how to best defend the city, whether it should even be defended. If, as seemed likely, the Jacobites were going to take it anyway, why risk bloodshed in a futile attempt to save it?

The professional soldiers – two companies of dragoons – were little help. At about four o'clock that afternoon, they were seen hurrying away from Coltbridge, just on the city side of Corstorphine, towards Leith. On horseback, they clattered along what was then known as the Long Dykes and is now George Street in the New Town. This ignominious retreat swiftly became known as the Canter of Coltbridge.

With the professional soldiers having run away, the four companies of Volunteers once more rendezvoused in the Grassmarket. A free and frank exchange of views between two young men over what should be done grew heated. Hands went to weapons, each on the point of attacking the other, 'one with his musket and bayonet, and the other with his small sword', until their friends separated them. Tempers were running high.

Just then, a man on horseback rode past the Volunteers, calling out to them that the Highlanders were at the gates of the city and were 16,000 strong. The man 'did not stop to be examined, but rode off at the gallop'. At the same time, the provost was convening a public meeting whose mood was very much in favour of surrendering the city to Prince Charles and his army. The Volunteers were stood down. They took their weapons up to General Guest's garrison in the castle to prevent them from falling into the hands of the Jacobites.

Sandy and William Carlyle met up as they had previously arranged at a house near the Netherbow Port, but the gate was locked. It was eight o'clock at night before the brothers were able to squeeze through the large crowd assembled around it, some wanting in and some wanting out of the city. Then Sandy and William walked through Holyrood Park, where they met hardly anyone. There they chose to head for home along the coast, 'rather than the road through the whins', which was too 'dark and solitary' on a moonless night.

Walking slowly because they were both so tired, they eventually reached Lucky Vint's Courtyard – a tavern at the western end of Prestonpans – where they met a group of Government officers. After the Canter of Coltbridge, unconvinced that Leith was safe, these officers had moved further out.

Although Sandy assured them that Edinburgh was not yet in the hands of the Highlanders, the dragoons remained very panicky. As the Carlyle brothers headed through town towards their home at Inveresk, the soldiers began to move untidily and in a state of some confusion 'on the road that leads by the back of the gardens to Port Seaton, Aberlady and North Berwick, all the way by the shore'.

Scornful of their unreasoning fear, Sandy Carlyle told them the Highlanders had 'neither wings nor horses'. Nor were they invisible, able to suddenly appear out of nowhere in front of the dragoons. His robust common sense did not help one iota. When one of the dragoons guided his horse off to the side of the road so that it might find some grass to graze on, both man and animal fell into a coal shaft.

They fell with an enormous clatter, the noise robbing the dragoon's comrades of what little courage they had left. They bolted, in their haste dropping many of their weapons onto the road. The next morning, Sandy and a friend organized the gathering up and safe-keeping of these until they could be delivered to General Cope's army. He does not tell us whether the unfortunate dragoon and his horse made it back up out of the coal shaft; probably not, as the man's broadsword was later shown off by someone else as their booty from the battlefield.

At noon the next day, Tuesday, 17 September, Sandy Carlyle learned that Edinburgh had fallen to the Jacobites and that Cope was due to land at Dunbar later that afternoon or evening. He and a couple of friends resolved to head there to offer their services, delaying only for some dinner at the Carlyle home, the manse at Inveresk. They washed down their meal with a bowl of whisky punch: as you do.

While they were finishing it, a neighbour arrived. He invited the young men to join him for a 'small collation' at his house with his sister and himself. The would-be volunteers to Cope's army demurred. The afternoon was wearing on, and they had already eaten. The neighbour insisted. He had four bottles of burgundy. If they didn't help him drink the wine, he would have to give it to the Highlanders.

Since they obviously could not let that happen, Sandy and his friends repaired to the neighbour's house, where they ate apples, pears and biscuits, drank a bottle of claret to 'wash away the taste of the whisky punch' and then fell upon the 'excellent' burgundy. A mere one hour later, they considered themselves fit to take to the road. By this time it was five o'clock in the afternoon.

With a brief stop at Maggie Johnstone's pub, a mile or two to the north of Haddington, 'for some beer or porter to refresh us after our walk', they pressed on. At ten o'clock that evening, two of the party decided it might be a good idea to look for a bed for the night. Sandy and one of his friends went on to Dunbar, where Cope was setting up his camp. They were refused admittance.

It took them until two in the morning to find somewhere to sleep, waking up the occupants of the manse at Linton. Thinking they might be 'marauders from the camp', the minister kept them standing at his door for an hour before he could be persuaded to let them in. After only a couple of hours' sleep, they in their turn were abruptly roused from their slumbers by their friends who'd taken to their beds at ten o'clock the previous night. It sounds as though they were revoltingly bright-eyed and bushy-tailed.

At two o'clock that afternoon, Wednesday, 18 September, Sandy took his dinner with Government commander and family friend Colonel James Gardiner at his home, Bankton House at Prestonpans. The colonel's spirits were low, but the conversational shortfall was supplied by a young relative of his, Cornet Kerr, who teased Carlyle about his hunt for a bed the night before. He advised the civilian that an experienced soldier always took up the first half-decent quarters he found. Kerr thought the battle that they all knew could not be far away would be an assured victory – 'if God were on our side'.

Between then and that 'approaching event', Sandy met up with several of his comrades from the Edinburgh Volunteers, their ardour for offering their services to Cope undimmed. He had the chance to talk with a Redcoat officer and was astonished by the man's ignorance of 'the state of the country and of the character of the Highlanders'.

He also observed, with the pomposity of youth, that it seemed to him 'very imprudent to allow all the common people to converse with the soldiers on their march as they pleased, by which means their panic was kept up, and perhaps their principles corrupted'. As he put it, most of the common people in East Lothian and perhaps two-thirds of the gentry had 'no aversion to the family of Stuart'. If their religion could have been secured, they would have been very glad to see them on the throne again.

Later that day, around 25 of the student volunteers gathered together at an inn in Haddington. Their determination to throw themselves at the enemy was to be thwarted yet again when they received a message via a Captain Drummond that General Cope thought they would be more use to him if they reconnoitred the roads round about, going out in pairs. This they did, at eight in the evening and again at midnight. It was so quiet that Sandy Carlyle and his companion ended up having supper at Sandy's parents' house, with nothing to report.

By the time they got back to Haddington, all the beds were taken, and they had to sleep on benches and chairs in the kitchen. To their disgust, they later discovered that 'several Volunteers had single beds to themselves, a part of which we might have occupied'. It was quite usual at the time for men travelling together to share a bed at an inn.

Two of their fellow volunteers had rather more to worry about. Having been out on patrol all night, they were captured after daylight had broken by a party of Jacobite cavalry, who spotted them through an open window sitting in Crystal's Inn in Musselburgh enjoying a breakfast of white wine and oysters. It's hard not to see the College Company as a bunch of well-educated, well-bred, well-fed and well-lubricated young gentlemen having an awfully big adventure.

John Roy Stuart, the senior officer among the Jacobites who took the oyster-eaters prisoner, threatened to have them hanged. Hardened and experienced soldier though he was, this seems a tad out of character. Perhaps he too thought they were were well-off boys playing at soldiers and wanted to put the fear of God into them, sending them scurrying back home to the safety of their parents' houses.

Cope lined his men up later that day in a field whose crop of corn had been harvested only the night before and which was bare except for one solitary thorn tree. Sandy Carlyle spent most of that same day at the top of his father's church steeple in Inveresk, observing the movements of the Jacobite Army. He came down only to mount his horse and ride off to inform Colonel Gardiner and Cope's aide-de-camp of what he had seen.

When the fight which had been brewing for several nerve-jangling days finally erupted very early the following morning, Sandy Carlyle was asleep. Woken by the first cannon shot, he threw on his clothes, spoke hurriedly with his parents and headed for the field. By the time he got there, it was all over.

He estimated it could only have lasted ten to fifteen minutes. Lord Elcho, fighting on the Jacobite side, concurred. When he and Sandy stumbled upon one another, Elcho demanded to know where he could find a public house. This was probably because he was scouting out somewhere for the wounded to be taken rather than because he was desperate for a drink. The young student 'answered him meekly, not doubting but that, if I had displeased him with my tone, his reply would have been with a pistol bullet'.

Sandy then saw some Government soldiers running as fast as they could away from the field. 'Many had their coats turned as prisoners but were still trying to reach the town in hopes of escaping.' Many of these Redcoats voluntarily became turncoats, joining the Jacobite Army. Tradition has it that Alan Breck Stewart, immortalized by Robert Louis Stevenson in *Kidnapped*, was one of them.

By this stage, in the immediate aftermath of the battle, young Mr Carlyle seems to have been acting as tour guide, directing the Duke of Perth to the house which someone else in the Jacobite Army had designated the field hospital for wounded Government officers.

He was impressed by the duke's tone of 'victorious clemency' but highly critical of the tears and howling of the women camp followers. Crying over their wounded and dying men, their distress apparently 'suppressed manhood and created despondency'. Presumably they should have pulled themselves together, come to terms with their loss, drawn a line under their grief and stopped making such a terrible fuss.

Horrified by the bloodshed, Mr Carlyle senior was growing ever more worried about his elder son's safety. If the Rebels came to the manse and realized Sandy had been one of the pro-Government Edinburgh Volunteers, they might decide to take their revenge. With a farewell to Mrs Carlyle and the younger children, father and son rode out on horseback along the sands. At Port Seton, forced to come back up onto the road, they witnessed a Highlander shooting another man. Deeply shaken, they returned home.

To his credit, Sandy Carlyle then offered to help the surgeons treating the wounded Government officers, which soon had him out and about among the Jacobites, searching for a lost medicine chest. In the meantime, the Duke of Perth had ordered a guard to be assigned to the Carlyles. Whether this was to keep an eye on them or protect them is not entirely clear.

On the Sunday evening after the battle, a Jacobite officer by the name of Brydone, very young and very polite, managed to resist Mrs Carlyle's 'faint invitation to supper' but was persuaded to return for breakfast the following morning at nine o'clock. Mr Carlyle senior said prayers before they ate.

> We knelt down, when Brydone turning awkwardly, his broadsword swept off the table a china plate with a roll of butter on it. Prayer being ended, the good lady did not forget her plate, but, taking it up whole, she said, smiling, and with a curtsey, 'Captain Brydone, this is a good omen, and I trust our cause will be as safe in the end from your army as my plate has been from the sweep of your sword.' The young man bowed, and sat down to breakfast and ate heartily; but I afterwards thought that the bad success of his sword and my mother's application had made him thoughtful, as Highlanders are very superstitious.

Over the next couple of days, Sandy Carlyle tried to convince Brydone that the Rebellion had to end in failure. It may have worked. Brydone left the Jacobite Army shortly before the Battle of Falkirk the following January, and his name does not appear in any lists of prisoners.

Sandy Carlyle stayed at home for the next week and then, proceeding with his plans to complete his divinity studies in Holland, went to Edinburgh to buy some things he needed for his journey. The Prince had issued a proclamation to say he would pardon every member of the Edinburgh Volunteers who went to Holyroodhouse to 'pay their court to him'.

Sandy described Charles Edward Stuart as 'a good-looking man, of about five feet ten inches; his hair was dark red, and his eyes black. His features were regular, his visage long, much sunburnt and freckled, and his countenance thoughtful and melancholy.'

Sandy himself sailed from Newcastle to Rotterdam on Monday, 14 October. The following spring he returned home via Harwich, spending a few weeks in London on the way. He was still there in April when the news arrived of the defeat of the Jacobites at Culloden. With a new friend, writer Tobias Smollett, they were sitting in the British Coffee House in Charing Cross, a well-known meeting place for Scots in London, when the news came through. They walked home with their swords in their hands. The mob was out in force and 'London all over was in a perfect uproar of joy'.

Smollett warned Sandy Carlyle not to open his mouth. If the mob found out by his accent that he was a Scotsman, they might 'become insolent'.

In September 1745, it was Edinburgh that was in an uproar of joy. Out at Prestonpans, there was nothing but shock and grief.

7

HERO IN A RED COAT:
THE GALLANT COLONEL GARDINER

WE HAVE AN ETERNITY TO SPEND TOGETHER

If popular opinion dismissed Cope as a bungler, those who opposed the Jacobites found a hero in Colonel James Gardiner, whose estate at Bankton has now been swallowed up by Prestonpans. Born near Linlithgow and educated at the grammar school there, he was a career soldier. This was despite the best efforts of his mother and aunt, who had each sacrificed a husband to Britain's wars in Continental Europe waged under the leadership of the Duke of Marlborough. Mrs Gardiner had lost her eldest son, too, killed on his 16th birthday at the Siege of Namur in 1692.

Despite – or perhaps because of – the deaths of his father and brother, James Gardiner was determined to join the army. He showed early signs of a warlike spirit, fighting his first duel at the age of eight and bearing forever afterwards a scar on his right cheek to prove it. This story becomes more believable after learning that by the age of 14 he had been in the military for several years.

Five years later, when he was 19 years old, he was 'of a party of the forlorn hope' at the Battle of Ramillies, dispatched on a desperate bid to capture the churchyard there from the French. He was shot in the mouth, the bullet passing through his neck to come out to the left of his spine. Left for dead throughout a bitterly cold night, the next morning the young man found a French soldier standing over him with the point of his sword on his chest, ready to administer the *coup de grâce*. A Franciscan friar who was with the swordsman implored him to show mercy: 'Do not kill that poor child.'

James Gardiner was nursed back to health at a nearby convent. He spent several months there, and the sisters grew very fond of him, as he did of them, although he resisted their attempts to convince him he should convert to Catholicism in gratitude for his miraculous escape from death.

It was common at this time for Protestants to believe the worst of nuns and priests, who were frequently lampooned as licentious hypocrites and often featured in pornography. Strong in the Protestant faith though he later became, James Gardiner retained a lifelong respect for the women who had cared for him, often stating that everything he had seen while he had been inside the convent's walls had been conducted with 'the utmost decency and decorum'.

Much to the distress of his mother and aunt, at this stage in his life he himself was a stranger to those virtues and not much interested in religion of any variety. Notoriously foul-mouthed even for a soldier, he was by his own admission also far too fond of casual sexual encounters. He later spoke to a friend of 'that sin I was so strongly addicted to, that I thought nothing but shooting me through the head could have cured me of it'.

Being made aide-de-camp and master of the horse to the Earl of Stair when that gentleman was appointed British Ambassador to the French court in 1714 gave James Gardiner many opportunities to exercise his addiction. He spent much of his twenties in Paris, indulging himself to the full. Never much of a drinker, he was, however, always so sunny-tempered and pleasant that he earned himself the nickname of 'the Happy Rake'.

One evening in Paris in 1719, with an hour to kill before a rendezvous with his current lover, a married woman, Gardiner picked up a book his mother or aunt had 'slipped into his portmanteau' – presumably while he wasn't looking. As he read *The Christian Soldier, or Heaven Taken By Storm* by Thomas Watson, something very strange happened. Twenty years later he told the tale to his friend and biographer, the Reverend Philip Doddridge.

The author of several books and more than 50 hymns, including 'Oh God of Bethel' and the original version of 'Oh Happy Day', which was to become a huge gospel hit 250 years after it was first written, Doddridge described his friend's experience:

> He thought he saw an unusual blaze of light fall on the book while he was reading, which he at first imagined might happen by some accident in the candle. But, lifting up his eyes, he apprehended, to his extreme amazement, that there was before him, as it were suspended in the air, a visible representation of the Lord Jesus Christ upon the cross, surrounded on all sides with a glory, and was impressed as if a voice, or something equivalent to a voice, had come to him to this effect, (for he was not confident as to the very words) 'Oh, sinner! Did I suffer this for thee, and these are the returns?'

This being the eighteenth century and the Age of Reason, even Doddridge, the man of the cloth, felt bound to ask James Gardiner if he hadn't dreamt he had seen Christ. Gardiner was adamant that he had been awake. The vision didn't last long, but it changed his life, sending him off on a voyage of spiritual discovery and a determination to change his ways. He did not keep his assignation with the married woman, and the casual affairs stopped.

This story is only very slightly spoiled by Alexander Carlyle later pouring cold water on some of the details:

> Dr. Doddridge has marred this story, either through mistake, or through a desire to make Gardiner's conversion

more supernatural, for he says that his appointment was
at midnight, and introduces some sort of meteor or blaze
of light, that alarmed the new convert. But this was not
the case; for I have heard Gardiner tell the story at least
three or four times . . .

According to the version Sandy Carlyle got from the horse's mouth –
the colonel liked telling this story – the assignation was at midday, not
midnight. The lady's husband was either a surgeon or an apothecary
and had 'shown some sign of jealousy, and they chose a time of day
when he was necessarily employed abroad in his business'.

At whatever time of day Gardiner experienced his religious
conversion, his friends soon thought he had gone 'stark mad'. He
met their ridicule with good humour, a quality he retained after he
found religion. His Christian belief was a joyous one, his God one
of forgiveness, although he could display the irritating zeal of the
reformed sinner. Even the Reverend Doddridge remarked how his
friend could work religion into every conversation.

It's easy to visualize his junior officers stifling a groan as he bore
down on them with yet another jolly sermon on his lips. His mother,
too, may have smiled ruefully when her son advised her in a letter not
to entertain guests on a Sunday. His concern was that she couldn't be
sure all of them were Christians, whose conversation would give due
reverence to the Sabbath.

On the plus side, he always practised what he preached. In a
sometimes brutal age, he was notable for concerning himself with the
welfare of his officers, his men and the regiment's horses. He made
charitable donations to the poor whenever he could afford to and
was courteous to his fellow man and woman whatever station they
occupied in life. Nor did he set much store on the accumulation of
wealth, saying, 'I know the rich are only stewards for the poor, and
must give an account of every penny; therefore, the less I have, the
more easy will it be to give an account of it.'

He was an early advocate of the swear box, seeking to eradicate in his officers' speech, as he had done in his own, what Doddridge called 'that horrid language which is so peculiar a disgrace to our soldiery, and so absurdly common on such occasions of extreme danger'. While the Reverend's views might lead us to suspect that he himself had never been in a situation of extreme danger, Gardiner had. The money he raised by imposing a fine for every curse went into a fund to provide care and comfort for soldiers who were wounded or fell ill.

It's impossible not to warm to a man who said his wife's only real fault was 'that she valued and loved him more than he deserved'. She was Lady Frances Erskine, daughter of the Earl of Buchan, and she bore him thirteen children, eight of whom did not survive to adulthood. Each death was a tragedy, but the bereft parents took strength from the conviction so incomprehensible to those who cannot share it, accepting the loss of their children as the will of God. Religion occupied as important a place in Lady Frances's life as it did in her husband's.

He was a faithful correspondent whenever his military duties took him away from home. Some of his letters to 'my dearest Fany' can be read today in the National Archives of Scotland in Edinburgh. In one, he tells her that he has dined with Mrs Doddridge; in another he writes of hearing the Reverend Doddridge preach. Almost invariably, the colonel signed off to 'my dearest sweetest Jewel Fany' and sent 'my Love to my children and service to all friends'.

In the summer of 1745, James Gardiner was 57 years old and not in the best of health, the rigours of a military life beginning to take their toll. He remained in command of the 13th Dragoons, one of only two regiments stationed in Scotland at the outbreak of hostilities, and was outspoken in his condemnation of the inadequacy of Scotland's and Britain's defences. As he saw the perilous state of affairs, 'a few thousands might have a fair chance for marching from Edinburgh to London uncontrolled, and throw the whole Kingdom into an astonishment.'

This prediction, based on his knowledge of how many people in Scotland were dissatisfied with the Union with England and disaffected to the London Government, demonstrates that he remained as aware and astute as he always had been. Perhaps because of his failing health, his good humour was beginning to desert him, leaving him morose and gripped by forebodings of doom. He condemned the citizens of Edinburgh for 'spending their times in balls, assemblies, and other gay amusements':

> I am greatly surprised that the people of Edinburgh should be employed in such foolish diversions, when our situation is at present more melancholy than ever I saw it in my life. But there is one thing which I am very sure of, and that comforts me, viz., that it shall go well with the righteous, come what will.

He wrote those words at the end of July 1745, while at Scarborough in an effort to improve his health. On his return, the 13th Dragoons were called to Stirling and then ordered to Dunbar to meet General Cope.

When James Gardiner said his farewells at Stirling Castle to his wife and eldest daughter, Mrs Gardiner broke down, sobbing out her fear that she might be going to lose him. Her husband had invariably comforted her before by reminding her how Providence had always taken care of him. This time he told her not to fear a separation from him because 'We have an eternity to spend together.' Several people who talked with the colonel in the days before the battle recalled that, like his wife, Gardiner seemed to have a sense of foreboding, a premonition of his own death. Sandy Carlyle described him as being 'grave, but serene and resigned', the colonel's religious faith giving him the strength to meet his fate.

Considering his own bravery, Gardiner must have been horribly ashamed that the dragoons under his command had taken part in the infamous Canter of Coltbridge, leaving Edinburgh defenceless against the approaching Jacobites. Walking with Sandy Carlyle in the garden of the manse at Dunbar on Thursday, 19 September, two days before the Battle of Prestonpans, the colonel expressed himself with his customary forcefulness when the young student raised the subject:

> I said, that to be sure they had made a very hasty retreat, 'a foul flight,' said he, 'Sandie and they have not recovered from their panic, and I'll tell you in confidence that I have not above ten men in my regiment whom I am certain will follow me. But we must give them battle now, and God's will be done!'

James Gardiner spent the evening of Friday, 20 September trying to persuade Cope and other senior officers to immediately mount an attack on the enemy, rather than wait for the Jacobite Army to make the first move. He also recommended that the Government cannon be placed in the middle of the line, as far away from the horses as possible. Like too many of the men, they were untested in battle, and he feared the animals would panic at the sound of the big guns. Much to Gardiner's dismay, neither suggestion was taken up. Robert Douglas was a fellow student of Alexander Carlyle's and, like him, one of the pro-Government Edinburgh Volunteers:

> He observed Colonel Gardiner in discourse with several officers on the evening before the engagement, at which time, it was afterwards reported, he gave his advice to attack the rebels, and when it was overruled, he afterwards saw the colonel walk by himself in a very pensive manner.

Gardiner stayed out in the newly harvested cornfield near his house overnight, wrapping himself in his cloak and snatching a few hours' sleep. In the early hours of the morning, he told three of his servants to go home, keeping back only his faithful man-servant John Foster.

When the Jacobite Army attacked at daybreak, almost all of James Gardiner's dragoons turned and fled, only about 15 of them standing their ground. Citing as his authority John Foster's eyewitness account, Doddridge says Colonel Gardiner was shot twice but stayed on his horse, dismissing his injuries as flesh wounds.

When he saw a group of foot soldiers fighting on despite having lost their officer, he cried out, 'Those brave fellows will be cut to pieces for want of a commander,' and rode up to them, shouting, 'Fire on, my lads, and fear nothing.'

As he said the words, he was struck a powerful, swinging blow from a Highlander wielding a scythe. The long curving blade slashed a deep cut in his right arm; Gardiner dropped his sword and was dragged off his horse. Once on the ground, he was struck again, this time on the back of his head. In the chaos, confusion and gun smoke, John Foster could not tell whether the blow had come from a broadsword or a Lochaber-axe, both of which were being used by the Jacobites.

A Jacobite called John MacNaughton, quartermaster of the Perthshire Horse, was later accused at his trial in Carlisle of having struck the fatal blow, although he denied it. Another account attributes it to Samuel Cameron of Kilmallie in Lochaber. He accepted responsibility but maintained until the end of his days that he had acted in self-defence as Gardiner and his horse bore down on him. The animal survived to be ridden by Prince Charles when he entered Derby.

Lying mortally wounded on the ground, the colonel urged John Foster to 'Take care of *yourself*!' When Foster returned to the battlefield almost two hours later, James Gardiner had been robbed of his watch, outer clothes and boots but was still breathing. According to Doddridge, Foster lifted him into a cart and took him to the kirk at Tranent where he died in the minister's bed at eleven o'clock that morning.

Colonel O'Sullivan of the Prince's staff offers an alternative ending to the story. He says that Gardiner died on the mattress of his own bed, which his servants had brought out into the garden of Bankton House. Since it was being used as a field hospital for Jacobite officers, this story sounds as plausible as the other.

Wherever he breathed his last, Colonel Gardiner was buried in the kirk at Tranent on Tuesday, 24 September. Many attended the funeral despite the continued presence of the Jacobite Army in the neighbourhood. It was said that they, too, mourned his death.

The two gunshot wounds and the cuts to his head are not in doubt. General Cope mentions them in his evidence to the board of enquiry, stating he got the information not only from John Foster but also from the minister at Tranent and the surgeon who attended the colonel. Unwell as Gardiner already was, some have questioned how he could have been able to carry on after being shot. Perhaps the adrenalin was flowing along with the blood.

What is also in absolutely no doubt is his courage. James Gardiner went down fighting. The moment of his fall was immortalized by Sir Walter Scott in *Waverley* and captured by William Allan in his painting of the Battle of Prestonpans. The man who was a survivor of so many of Europe's battlefields was cut down no distance from his own front door.

He was killed close by the thorn tree which was the only thing growing in the harvested cornfield. For years afterwards, it was shown to visitors as the place where Colonel Gardiner was struck the fatal blow.

His home, Bankton House, has now been converted into flats. Ten miles south of Edinburgh, and sandwiched between the A1 and the railway line, its bright ochre harling makes it unmissable. His monument stands in front of it, very close to Prestonpans railway station.

A tall and imposing obelisk, it's a hero's memorial. Four magnificently doleful stone lions guard it. They pay eternal tribute to this gallant Scotsman: a husband, father and soldier who, till his dying breath, did his duty as he saw it to God and his country.

8

THE YEAR OF THE PRINCE: TRIUMPHANT AUTUMN AT HOLYROODHOUSE

THEY WERE REALLY VASTLY CIVIL

Charles Edward Stuart would not permit bonfires to be lit or church bells to be rung to mark the victory at Prestonpans. Those who had died or been horribly wounded there had been his father's subjects as much as the men who had fought under his own Standard. Nobody was to be seen exulting in their suffering. He had delayed before leaving the battlefield, visiting the injured on both sides and giving orders that the dead were to be given decent burial. Colonel O'Sullivan described what the Prince said immediately after the battle when urged to rest:

> They then propos'd him to refraish & repose himself, yt he had great need of it; 'no' says he, with a tender hart & in a most feeling way, 'I cant rest until I see my own poor men taken care of, & the other wounded too, for they are the Kings Subjects as well we, & it's none of their fault if they are led on blindly,' upon sch he immediately sent orders, to the neighboring villedges, upon peine of

military execution yt houses & every thing necessary shou'd be provided for the wounded & yt the inhabitants shou'd come with speads & other instruments, to bury the Dead. He spoak to the Chirurgens, first to dress the highlanders, & afterwards to neglect nothing for the others; he neigher wou'd eat or drink until he saw people set about this.

O'Sullivan was partisan, writing his account for the Prince's father and therefore keen to paint his young master in the best possible light, but plenty of other eyewitnesses confirm Charles's concern for the living and regret for the dead.

It was the shell-shocked locals who did the dirty work, of course. Did the sights and sounds and smells of that cornfield's second, bloody harvest of butchered men and horses haunt their dreams and give them waking nightmares forever afterwards?

For the next six weeks, the Prince divided his time between the Jacobite camp at Duddingston and the Palace of Holyroodhouse at the foot of Edinburgh's Royal Mile. When he first arrived there, he was ceremonially escorted into the home of his ancestors by James Hepburn of Keith, a man whose devotion to the Stuart Cause went back to the Rising of 1715.

Four days before Prestonpans, Charles's father had been proclaimed James VIII and III at the Mercat Cross, up the High Street from Holyroodhouse, close by St Giles' Cathedral and the old Parliament House. A huge crowd listened, watched and cheered. As if by magic, all those in Edinburgh who had been against the Jacobites seemed to have faded away.

However, one man who never made a secret of his politics was Duncan Forbes of Culloden. He was still at his Highland home near Inverness and would not be returning to Edinburgh anytime soon. He was, as ever, well informed, as his description of Edinburgh in September and October 1745 demonstrates:

All Jacobites, how prudent soever, became mad; all doubtful people became Jacobites; and all bankrupts became heroes and talked of nothing but hereditary rights and victories; and what was more grievous to men of gallantry, and if you will believe me, much more mischievous to the public, all the fine ladies, except one or two, became passionately fond of the young Adventurer and used all their arts and industry for him in the most intemperate manner.

Less than a week after he took up residence at Holyroodhouse, in a magnificent piece of cheek, the Prince issued a warrant for Duncan Forbes' arrest. From 'Charles, Prince of Wales, and Regent of Scotland, England, France, and Ireland, and the Dominions thereunto belonging', it empowered James Fraser of Foyers to 'seize upon the person of the above-named Duncan Forbes', apprehend him and 'to carry him prisoner to us at Edinburgh, or where we shall happen to be for the time'.

Meanwhile, in Edinburgh, the stunning success of the Jacobite campaign so far was being celebrated. Balls were held at Holyroodhouse, the Long Gallery glorious with men in tartan, velvet and lace, and women in billowing silks and satins, tartan sashes and white roses. Inspired by the white rosebushes at Fassefern, the home of Cameron of Lochiel's brother, this had been adopted as the Jacobite badge. The Prince did not dance, telling his officers he was happy to see them enjoying themselves but that he had other things on his mind.

So did his officers, of course. Enjoyable in themselves, the dancing and flirting were also an important part of Jacobite PR. They gave receptions and organized balls wherever they were. However, more practical measures also had to be taken. That 'where we shall happen to be for the time' indicates that Edinburgh was not to be the Jacobites' final destination. Whether they were to head south or not, supplies were needed: weapons, food, clothes and – as always – shoes, money to pay for the supplies and money to pay the men.

The Jacobite Army prided itself on paying for what it took, both because this was the honourable thing to do and because not doing so was a sure way to antagonize people: not a good move for a Prince hoping to win hearts and minds.

On the other hand, if antagonism towards him and the Jacobite Cause was already there, a heaven-sent opportunity presented itself to show the haughtier Whigs and friends of the Government who were the masters now. The cocky young Jacobite officers who came up against Lady Jane Nimmo at Red Braes Castle near Polwarth in the Scottish Borders tried it – but found themselves facing a formidable adversary.

Lady Jane's husband was the Collector of Excise in Edinburgh and had volunteered to serve with the Government forces. With him away as the Jacobites drew closer to the city, she retreated with her three young daughters and one female servant to the safety of her childhood home. Red Braes was the seat of her brother, the Earl of Marchmont, an MP who spent much of his time in London. When Red Braes turned out not to be so safe after all, Lady Jane kept her brother up to date in a series of letters.

On 30 September 1745, she told him she now knew she 'must expect a visit from the Highlanders 150 of them being sent to Duns to Levy Cess'. This was one of the Jacobites' neater tricks. They were not highwaymen demanding your money or your life; they were collecting taxes due to the lawful Government. Charles Edward Stuart was now the Prince Regent, ruling Scotland as the representative of his father, King James VIII.

Lady Jane was understandably worried by the imminent arrival of these armed tax collectors: 'as we have not heard how they have behaved in other places I know not what to expect.' She did know they would be looking for guns and horses, and also feared Red Braes' neighbours 'would be our greatest Enemys, as it happen'd at the Last Rebellion'. One of her major concerns was that the Jacobite soldiers might destroy Red Braes' painting of the late king. It was far too big for her to be able to hide it.

Despite her natural trepidation, Lady Jane was a woman of courage and character. She'd been brought up that way by her aunt, Lady Grisell Baillie, the estimable lady whose household account books paint a fascinating picture of domestic life in early eighteenth-century Scotland.

Lady Jane's letters to her brother are a mixture of reports of what was going on at Red Braes, requests to be remembered to his wife and children, and snippets of news she has been able to gather about their mutual friends and acquaintances who were fighting the Jacobites. There was, for instance, nothing definite about James Sandilands. She had heard he'd been taken prisoner by the Rebels but did not know whether or not he had been wounded.

The dreaded visit of the Jacobites to Red Braes came on Wednesday, 9 October 1745 when:

> after it was dark bounces in at the Door Some highland Gentlemen with 3 pistols each the first thing they did was to clap a Pistol to Laubrechts breast and demanded Horses and arms. John Hunter mean while rode off with all the Horses. My three daughters had Courage enough to step down Stairs and receive them, Six Gentlemen came up with the Girls after they had Placed Centinels at all the doors and Glengary had drawn up his men upon the Green, they search'd all the House and my Daughters carried the Lights before 'em and kept them as far from the King's Picture as Possible. However they were really vastly Civil and would not go into the Bedchambers.

In between taking Lord Marchmont's horses off to a safe hiding place, the useful John Hunter had 'provided Spirits from Duns for the Common Fellows', but he had nothing suitable for the officers. 'They were extremely Cold and Hungery So he was obliged to produce 6 Bottles of Your Lops. Canary with good will Lest they should have taken it all at once.'

Guided through the house by the Nimmo girls, Lieutenant Robert Grahame of Garvock and his party found 91 old firelocks. A Mr Carre – who, given the joys of Scottish pronunciation, may well have been a Mr Kerr – pronounced them not worth the effort of carrying away, after which the young officers repaired to the fire in the dining room. Despite Lady Jane's reference to Glengarry and his regiment, Robert Grahame was actually an officer in the Perthshire Squadron. Like all cavalry regiments, it had a good conceit of itself, as obviously did he.

For the next two hours, the unwelcome visitors sat round the fire with Jane Nimmo's daughters, eating bread, drinking Lord Marchmont's wine and laughing themselves silly at Johnnie Cope and his headlong flight from the field at Prestonpans.

Lady Jane disapproved of them making fun of Cope and referring to him in such a familiar way, but softened a little when they brought apples out of their pockets and presented them with a flourish to her girls. Just as the Jacobite raiding party arrived, she had received a letter telling her that her husband, the pro-Government volunteer, had 'fallen ill upon the road'.

'In too great distress to mind or care what they did,' she was proud of her daughters for how they coped. 'I believe the children killed them with courtesy,' she wrote.

Politeness all round, then. When Lieutenant Grahame later decided – after a word in his ear from one of those malicious neighbours – that Lady Jane had made a fool of him by hiding the horses, the civility slipped. Brusque letters were exchanged. The 91 firelocks might be old and fairly useless, but he was determined she would send them to him. She was equally determined she would not. She won.

Throughout the Jacobite occupation of Edinburgh, the Castle remained in Government hands under the command of General Guest. In retaliation for being blockaded, he had his gunners terrorize the people living in the Lawnmarket by firing a few cannonballs down the hill. One of them lodged in the gable end of a house at the foot of the modern esplanade and is still there to this day.

Alexander Carlyle and his friends had made sure the guns of the Edinburgh Volunteers had been taken back to the Castle before the Jacobite Army entered Edinburgh. The reserves of Edinburgh's banks had also been stored there for safe keeping, and the banks themselves had closed their doors.

Much of the money which was being collected – including what Provost Cochrane in Glasgow, gritting his teeth, had been forced to hand over after the visit from John Hay – was in Royal Bank of Scotland notes. The Bank of Scotland had been smart enough to withdraw as many of its notes from circulation as it could while the Jacobite Army was heading for Edinburgh.

Disappointingly, the Prince did not relish the thought of taking Scottish banknotes to London and having a stimulating fight over their being accepted as legal tender. He wanted coin, hard cash. His secretary, John Murray of Broughton, therefore called on John Campbell, the cashier of the Royal Bank of Scotland, demanding he exchange the notes for coin. If he did not supply this within 48 hours, 'the estates and effects of the directors and managers should be distressed for the same'.

Campbell said he could not do it. The coin was all in Edinburgh Castle. Well, go and ask for it, said Murray of Broughton. General Guest won't let us in, replied John Campbell. Besides which, the troops in the Castle were still lobbing cannonballs down the High Street.

For their part, the Camerons blockading the Castle were firing their muskets at anyone approaching it. Some of the people on the receiving end of these potshots were taking butter and eggs in for General Guest. This was in deference to his great age and delicate stomach. Although this kindness had been agreed by senior Jacobite officers, nobody seemed to have told the foot soldiers.

Understandably reluctant to be caught in the crossfire, John Campbell 'bespoke a pott of Coffee at Muirhead's' and discussed the situation with the directors of the Royal Bank. None of them wanted their property 'distressed'. This time, a letter to General Guest resulted in their request to enter the Castle being granted. They did so waving a white flag all the way, as well they might. Hostilities did not cease while they were in there, as John Campbell related in his diary:

> During our continuance in the Castle which was from about 9 'till near three a clock ... one Watson a soldier was so courageous as to go down over the Castle wall upon a rope, fire upon the Gardner's house, kill some of the volunteers there, carried off a firelock or two from them, sett the house in fire, returned with these firelocks by his rope into the Castle, where he was received with loud huzzas for his valour.
>
> On his return the garrison was preparing for a sally, but as the men were a-drawing up we got liberty from General Guest to go out again and Captain Robert Mirry escorted us to the gate, where I again raised my white flagg, and with my friends returned to town in safety, landed at my house from whence we adjourned to dine at Mrs Clerks' vintner.

Before he ate, John Campbell exchanged the bags of gold coin for the banknotes, the total sum handed over being £3,076. In his fascinating introduction to the copy of the banker's diary published by the Royal Bank of Scotland in 1995 to commemorate the 250th anniversary of the '45, John Sibbald Gibson argues convincingly that it was this money which financed the Jacobite invasion of England.

He further suggests that John Campbell was by no means reluctant to help provide it. The Edinburgh banker was also a Highland gentleman. In a pretty unequivocal demonstration of where his sympathies lay, he chose, during the period of the tartan ban which followed the failure of the Rising, to have himself painted in full Highland dress.

That's not all. In his portrait, John Campbell stands next to a bag of coins and some paper money, an indication of his profession as a banker. His political convictions as a Jacobite may be inferred not only from his Highland dress but also from other objects depicted in the painting. The tartan ban went hand-in-hand with a disarming of the Highlands, the ownership of weapons becoming illegal. Yet John Campbell is armed with a dirk and a broadsword, and the butt of a Doune pistol and a musket are clearly visible on the table beside him.

It is very clear, too, where the sympathies of Charles Leslie, the editor and publisher of the *Edinburgh Evening Courant*, lay. While the Jacobites occupied Edinburgh, he had to walk down to Holyroodhouse to submit his copy for approval before it was printed, 'having,' as he sarcastically wrote, 'meritoriously incurred their Displeasure by some Paragraphs'.

Quietly seething, Leslie vented his wrath at this censorship by composing a neatly written memorandum in which he named Jacobite collaborators in Edinburgh. Chief amongst these was Provost Archibald Stewart.

Citing the housekeeper at Holyroodhouse as his back-up for the story, Leslie alleged that the provost had given orders for rooms to be got ready for the Young Pretender the day *before* the Jacobites took Edinburgh, when, in theory, nobody knew when or if they would succeed in their efforts. Leslie thought the 'Scandalous Surrender' of Scotland's capital also owed much to the make-up of the so-called meeting where it had been decided not to offer any resistance to the Jacobite Army.

The well-affected citizens being away trying to prevent Edinburgh's fall at the time the meeting was held, the people who had voted for surrender had been 'Smuglers, some Nonjurant Merchants, Common tradesmen and even Street Cadies, Chairmen and the lowest of Ale house keepers'.

Out in the streets, people of a higher social class – Leslie named George Gordon Junior of Gordonbank – had been observed and heard pushing 'the mean People to go and make a Noice'.

It seems likely that this is the same Charles Leslie who later vented his spleen by denouncing people to the English Attorney General, almost certainly the people he mentions in his memorandum. The Attorney General dismissed his evidence, writing that what he had received:

purports to be a List delivered by one Charles Leslie, and there is no evidence transmitted to us against one of the Persons contained in it, Except that of Mr Leslie himself, which from his own account in the List seems to be plain against them.

If the editor of the *Edinburgh Evening Courant* could – more or less – spell, another Edinburgh man implacably opposed to the Jacobites quite gloriously could not.

Patrick Crichton was a saddler and ironmonger in the Canongate, and Laird of Woodhouselee, just outside Edinburgh. *The Woodhouselee Manuscript* is his journal of what went on while the Jacobite Army occupied Scotland's capital.

Forced like Lady Jane Nimmo to admit that some of the 'highland banditti' were 'very civil', he thought others were complete 'hillskipers, scownderalls and poltrowns'. Crichton, too, believed that Provost Stewart was a traitor, and he reserved special venom for the wife of the Prince's secretary and long-time Jacobite plotter, John Murray of Broughton. Directly involved in requisitioning horses and raising money for the Jacobite Army, the beautiful Margaret Murray was the daughter of a good Whig, which only made it all the more disgusting that she had so far gone 'into the spirit of the gang'.

Yet perhaps the worst thing about this 'Polish Italian prince with the oddest crue Britain cowld produce', who had come 'all with plaids, bagpips and bairbuttocks', was that they set 'caterpillars' to guard the gates of Edinburgh. Presumably the Laird of Woodhouselee meant caterans – thieves and freebooters, and a common insult thrown at Highlanders – but it's a lovely image.

In those heady six weeks in Edinburgh in the autumn of 1745, the Jacobites could afford to ignore the mutterers. Everything was going their way, their success thus far quite astounding – and they revelled in it.

John Roy Stuart commissioned artist Allan Ramsay to paint a portrait of Prince Charles. The Palace of Holyroodhouse glittered with the light of hundreds of candles. Highland chiefs and their wives, Lowland lairds and their ladies, and the breathlessly excited young women of Edinburgh danced under the brown-eyed gaze of a Stuart prince and the portraits of his ancestors. For the first time in almost a century and a half, Scotland had a royal court again.

Fortune had favoured the brave. There was every reason to believe it would continue to do so.

9

THE YOUNG ADVENTURER:
CHARLES EDWARD STUART

GOD IS NOT ON THE SIDE OF THE BIG BATTALIONS,
BUT THE BEST SHOTS

As well as prizing skill over sheer force of numbers, Voltaire also said that history is a pack of tricks we play upon the past. Nowhere is this more evident than in the millions of words and libraries of books which have been written about the '45 and the personality and character of the man who led it.

Charles was for a long time portrayed as the Bonnie Prince, the young adventurer celebrated in song and legend, but he can also be seen as the selfish and ruthlessly self-centred user of other people and their loyalty to his family and Scotland, a historical irrelevance. It's certainly easy to read him in an almost entirely negative way. There is plenty of damning evidence.

Take the impulsive nature of the attempt itself. He travelled to Scotland with only a handful of men, without any real help from the French or realistic hopes that such help would be forthcoming. For as long as he possibly could, he concealed that fact from the men and women who risked their lives, homes and families' futures for him.

Take his belief in the divine right of kings, the idea that he and his family had been chosen by God to rule Britain. Or his inability to realize that while some of his supporters were equally convinced of this doctrine, it did not mean the monarch or his son could behave like tyrants. For Scots in particular, the divine right had to go hand-in-hand with the acceptance that the kings and queens of Scotland had always ruled only with the consent of the people.

This is why we speak of Mary, Queen of *Scots* and not Mary, Queen of *Scotland*. This is why the Scottish unicorn, symbol of Scottish royalty, wears a heavy chain around its neck. The monarch's powers are restricted, dependent on the people allowing their ruler to exercise them. Scotland belongs to the Scots, not to any government or ruler.

In theory, Charles Edward Stuart was at pains to emphasize that his vote on the council he held at Holyroodhouse at nine o'clock every morning was just another vote. In practice, his unwillingness to listen to any advice unless it was what he wanted to hear was obvious and sometimes overt. He had more than once to be reminded that free-born Britons could not be treated like slaves.

To be fair, the Prince was not helped by disagreements and personal antipathies between his commanders. The most damaging of these was between Colonel O'Sullivan and Lord George Murray, the latter having joined the Prince at Perth and become his commander-in-chief.

O'Sullivan and Sir John Macdonald, another of the Seven Men of Moidart and a senior cavalry officer in the Jacobite Army, both tell in their accounts of the '45 a curious story about Lord George, whose family seat was at Blair Atholl, north of Pitlochry. A Macdonald woman and a Cameron man came to see Sir John at Perth, the former explaining they were there 'on purpose to warn H. R. H. that Lord George was one of his greatest enemies'.

The story was that Lord George had, a little while before, gathered together some of the Atholl men, telling them they were going to join the Prince. Later, however, he told them they would be joining Cope's army instead. The Macdonald woman said she had known Lord George 'for many years as a scoundrel' and begged Sir John to pass on the story 'because she was convinced, as were many others also, that this man would betray us and would cause the ruin of the party and of his fellow Scots'.

Other people had a quite different view of Lord George, considering him to be an honourable, if short-tempered, man and a gifted military commander. James Johnstone, one of the gentlemen volunteers to the Jacobite Army, was a big fan:

> Had Prince Charles slept during the whole of the expedition, and allowed Lord George to act for him, there is every reason for supposing he would have found the crown of Great Britain on his head when he awoke.

Johnstone was clear also as to what the Prince should have done after Prestonpans, which had made him 'the entire master of Scotland, where the only English troops which remained were the garrisons of the castles of Edinburgh and Stirling'. Since Charles was now Regent of Scotland on behalf of his father, King James, he ought to have concentrated on hanging on to one country rather than trying immediately to conquer another:

> His chief object ought to have been to endeavour, by every possible means, to secure himself in the government of his ancient kingdom, and to defend himself against the English armies (which would not fail to be sent against him) without attempting, for the present, to extend his views to England. This was the advice which every one gave the Prince and, if he had followed it, he might still perhaps have been in possession of that kingdom. He was strongly advised to dissolve and annul the union between Scotland and England, made during the usurpation of Queen Anne by a cabal of a few Scots peers, whom the English court had gained over to its interests by force of gold,

contrary to the general wish of the Scottish nation, all ranks of which, down to the lowest peasant, have ever held this act in abhorrence. Such a step would have given infinite pleasure to all Scotland, and the sole consideration of being freed from the English yoke would have induced the Scots to declare themselves generally in his favour.

John Roy Stuart was another vociferous supporter of the opinion that, first and foremost, Scotland should be secured and held fast. He thought the decision to invade England was the first of many mistakes and that it was madness to leave Scotland without having captured the strategically crucial fortresses of Edinburgh and Stirling castles.

If it had been up to John Roy, James Johnstone and the many other Jacobites – perhaps the majority – who were of the same opinion, Charles would have proclaimed his father king of Scots, revoked the Treaty of Union, called a parliament in Edinburgh and taken full control of Scotland. Wondering what might have happened if these views had prevailed leads inevitably to one of the most tantalizing 'what ifs?' of history.

John Roy Stuart was the only colonel in the Jacobite Army not invited to attend Charles's daily council meetings at Holyroodhouse. This is curious, as he and the Prince had known one another for at least ten years and were good friends. If John Roy was a Catholic, as the evidence strongly suggests, this may have had something to do with his exclusion.

The Prince and at least some of his closest advisers were well aware of how delicate the religious issue was. A Catholic himself, Colonel O'Sullivan thought it advisable that Charles should not be seen to be surrounding himself with Catholics. On the other hand, John Roy himself believed his exclusion resulted from his vehement opposition to the invasion of England.

When the council first discussed this plan, most of its members, especially the clan chiefs, were initially hostile to it. However, the

Prince's determination meant that when the vote was taken, half the council members reluctantly agreed with him, and the proposal was carried. John Roy's vote would have made the difference. Before the vote, so might his persuasive tongue.

Charles wanted London. That he used his faithful Scots, much against their better judgement, in a vain attempt to get there and in an equally vain attempt to inspire the English Jacobites to rise en masse is, for many, another reason to condemn him. After the Battle of Falkirk in January 1746, when the Highland chiefs and his other commanders insisted, against his will, that the Jacobite Army had to retreat to Inverness, the Prince wrote an angry letter to Lord George Murray:

> When I came to Scotland, I knew well enough what I was to expect from my Ennemies, but I little foresaw what I meet with from my Friends. I came vested with all the Authority the King could give me, one chief part of which is the Command of the Armies, and now I am required to give this up to fifteen persons, who may afterwards depute five or seven of their own number to exercise it, for fear, if they were six or eight, that I might myself pretend to ye casting vote.
>
> I am often hit in the teeth that this is an Army of Volontiers, consisting of Gentlemen of Rank and fortune, and who came into it merely upon motives of Duty and Honours; what one wou'd expect from such an Army is more zeal, more resolution, and more good manners than in those that fight merely for pay. Everyone knew before he engaged in the cause what he was to expect in case it miscarried, and shou'd have staid at home if cou'd not face death in any shape.

The ingratitude is monumental. Yet, to quote Joseph Addison, the author of *Cato*: 'Much might be said on both sides.'

To come to Scotland with only a handful of companions in the hope that thousands would rise in his support must have taken enormous courage, determination and self-belief. For a young man in his mid-twenties, it must also have taken guts to argue his case with men old enough to be his father and grandfather.

Maybe staying in Edinburgh and securing Scotland was not an option. Shocked by their defeat at Prestonpans, the Government had finally been galvanized into action. The next army sent against the Jacobites would not be made up of terrified raw recruits but of battle-hardened veterans. They were already being shipped back from the war in Europe. Would England have accepted Scotland reclaiming her independence without a fight?

The Jacobites had to seize the initiative. Marching into England did that. It was the wrong time of year to launch such a move, of course, when autumn would soon be giving way to winter. Then again, expect the unexpected. Be bold. It was in keeping with the whole attempt and with the Prince's character and personality.

There was another crucial consideration. French interest in supporting Charles's campaign was quite naturally bound up with what would be best for France. They wanted England distracted from the wars in Europe and preferably removed altogether from the scene. They had been ready to send an invasion fleet across the Channel in 1744, when the Protestant Wind blew up, and were poised to do the same again in 1745.

The embarkation of the fleet was planned for Christmas, and Voltaire himself had written a manifesto in support of a Stuart restoration. He was a great admirer of Charles Edward Stuart and of the British. He saw Charles as a prince who could inspire the British people to do great things. On the great philosopher's recommendation, the French had sent an unofficial ambassador to the Jacobites: Alexandre Boyer, the Marquis d'Eguilles. When he landed at Montrose in October 1745, it was taken as a promise of French support.

Winning back the crown of Britain for his family was what Charles had been raised for. This was his destiny. He had grown up in the knowledge and belief that he was the Prince of Wales, his younger brother Henry the Duke of York, their parents the King and Queen of the Kingdoms of Great Britain and Ireland and all the dominions pertaining thereto. His father had failed to make those phantom titles a reality. Now it was Charles's turn.

His mother, the Polish princess Clementina Sobieska, died when he was 15, leaving him, his brother and his father bereft and distraught. This was despite James and Clementina's marriage having always been a difficult one, and Clementina herself a rather distant and ethereal figure, inclined to retreat into prayer and fasting.

Writing to his 'Dear Papa', the six-year-old Charles promised that 'I will be very dutiful to dear Mamma, and not jump too near her.' It's rather sad to think of a boisterous and energetic young boy having to promise not to be a boy for fear of disturbing his languid mother.

Charles's father was affectionate towards his jumping boy and his younger brother, Henry. James took great care over their education, although he despaired of his elder son's lack of interest in book-learning and his terrible spelling – but, hey, this was the eighteenth century.

Balancing the books was Charles's gift for languages. While still very young, he mastered English, French and Italian, all in daily usage at his home, the Jacobite court in exile at the Palazzo Muti in Rome. Almost as soon as he made landfall in Scotland in 1745, he made it his business to learn some Gaelic.

He was tall, strong and physically fit, enjoying sport and exercise for their own sake as well as because he was quite consciously in training for the time when he would lead the military campaign to reclaim his father's kingdom. He was a good shot. He also played golf and the violin and, by all accounts, did both rather well. Despite spending much of his life in a state of financial embarrassment, he was a good tipper, too.

He had the common touch, to the extent that he often comes across as being happier in the company of ordinary people than those of a more elevated social class. With them, he could be prickly and haughty. With boatmen, maidservants and his 'brave Highlanders', he seemed more able to relax.

While he was on the run in the Hebrides, often wet, hungry and in deadly danger, his behaviour was impeccable. He ate what food could be got without complaint, and, while sometimes understandably depressed, he did his best to keep everyone else's spirits up. The famous Stuart charm was an enormously powerful weapon. It could sweep the most unlikely people off their feet.

Assembling at Dalkeith, the Jacobite Army began its march south on 3 November 1745. Six days later, they reached Carlisle. It was so foggy that, as O'Sullivan put it, a man could hardly see his horse's ears. When the mist lifted, the guns of Carlisle Castle fired at the Jacobites, who were gathered outside the gates of the city demanding entry. They withdrew and sent a local man in with a letter from the Prince.

In it, Charles called on the citizens of Carlisle to surrender. Surely both sides had no wish to spill English blood? Although some within the doughty border fortress were ready and willing to hold out, this proved as effective an argument as it had been at Edinburgh. Six days later again, the Jacobites found themselves masters of Carlisle.

Stories which had grown arms and legs in the telling were spreading rapidly through the towns and villages in England, their citizens terrified they might be on the route of the advancing Scottish army. Concentrating on the exotic mountain men, the peddlers of propaganda – who included Henry Fielding, author, satirist and co-founder of the Bow Street Runners – had told these now panic-stricken people that the bare-arsed banditti burnt, raped and murdered wherever they went. They were cannibals, too, known to be particularly partial to babies and children.

Colonel O'Sullivan noted that wherever they went in England they seldom saw any children. It soon emerged that worried parents had hidden them away for safety. Cameron of Lochiel had to reassure one woman he was not going to eat her children before she dared bring them out from the cupboard where she had concealed them. The Prince allayed the fears of another terrified mother:

The prince lodged this night in a Quaquers house; being in his room with Sr Thomas & Locheil they heard something groning under the Bed, they cal'd for the woman of the house & asked what yt may be. The poor woman began to cry & begged the prince to spear yt child, yt it was the only one she had of seven; the child was drawn from under the bed. Yu never saw a woman in yt condition; she thought the child wou'd be set upon the Spit, as there was not much to eat in the house, but Sr Thomas, who spoak their language very well, appaissed her, & rassured her, so she told him the whole story.

The other Quaquers hearing this, came to see the Prince, being at supper, & knowing yt the Beer of the house was not of the best, they brought him some of theirs; an Old man goes out & brings him two bottles of his, sets them before the Prince & tells him "thou'l find this better." The Prince drinks it, find it very good, & thanks him most gratiously; the Old man lifts up his hand, as if he was to have given him his blessing – "Thou are not a man, but an angel," with tears in his eyes.

This story is a beautiful illustration of how strong Charles's personal charisma must have been. This kindly member of the Society of Friends was clearly dazzled by him.

Charles was a handsome man, too. Anyone who doubts this should take a look at Maurice Quentin de la Tour's 1748 painting of him, which now hangs in the Scottish National Portrait Gallery in Edinburgh. The man with the warm brown eyes who gazes back out at you when you stand in front of it is attractive, masculine and confident.

Curiously, many modern Scots do their utmost to deny this, denigrating Charles and his physical appearance whenever his name is mentioned. The underlying message of these snide remarks seems to be that he was hopeless in every way and that we Scots must therefore have been hopeless to have followed him. This says rather more about our national crisis of self-confidence and self-esteem than it does about Charles Edward Stuart.

That he knew how to inspire men and women is something else which cannot be denied. The New Spalding Club was a group of gentleman scholars active in Aberdeen during the 1890s. In their *Historical Papers Relating To The Jacobite Period 1699–1750,* editor James Allardyce juxtaposed two speeches. One is what General Sir John Cope said when he addressed the Government army shortly before the Battle of Prestonpans:

> Gentlemen, you are just now to engage with a parcel of rabble; a parcel of brutes, being a small number of Scots Highlanders. You can expect no booty from such a poor despicable pack. I have authority to declare, that you shall have eight full hours liberty to plunder and pillage the city of Edinburgh, Leith, and suburbs, (the places which harboured and succoured them) at your discretion with impunity.

And here is what Charles said to his men:

> The Prince being clothed in a plain Highland habit, docked his blue bonnet, drew his sword, threw away the scabbard, and said, 'Gentlemen, follow me, by the assistance of God, I will, this day, make you a free and happy people.'

James Allardyce made no editorial comment. He didn't need to.

Which one would you rather follow?

10

HOME BY CHRISTMAS: THE FAMILY MEN

ALL THE LADS ARE IN TOP SPIRITS

As might be expected, men on the campaign trail were anxious to hear the news from home and took every opportunity offered to let their families and friends know how they were getting on. As might also be expected, both sides were concerned the other should not worry too much.

Many of the letters sent to and from Jacobite soldiers did not reach the intended recipients. A postman's job – the man very likely to be a boy – during the '45 could be a hazardous one. Knowledge being power, both sides went in for a little tampering with the mail. John Murray of Broughton, the Prince's secretary, gave precise instructions on how to do this. The man he sent to lie in wait for the postie was to tie him up, slap his horse on the rump so it would bolt a few miles down the road, and make off with the bag of letters.

Mail being intercepted made life difficult for both sides. Young Jack Campbell of Mamore wrote to his father from Inveraray on 16 October 1745. There had, he explained, been no point in writing earlier 'as all communication from this country has been interrupted for some time':

As the rebels are still at Edinburg we have no accounts that can be depended on of what is doing there or in England, for as their affairs are in a very bad situation they take great pains to hinder any true account to be sent, especially to the Highlands. On the contrary we are daily entertained here with the most extravagant lyes that ever were heard of. There is not a day passes but we are told of some foreign troops being landed to their assistance, and tho there is not the least truth in these reports the common people believe it firmly throughout all the Highlands ... certainly it is a most unhappy thing that the misbehaviour of a few should have given the Government so bad an opinion in General of all Scotland ...

Telling his father that 'there has been a party of fifty men headed by a madman plundering the country and raising contributions for six weeks past in and about Dunbartonshire', Jack signed himself 'your most obedient Son and Servant'.

One little cache of intercepted mail is hidden away in a brown cardboard box at the Public Record Office in London. It contains letters written by Jacobite soldiers camped at Moffat while they were on their way south on the march into England. The letters and the man carrying them fell into Government hands when he was riding north.

The phrase 'in top spirits' crops up so often in this collection it suggests one of the letter writers offered it to the others as a way of reassuring the folks back home. It's in this bundle of emotion and longing we find the letter of a 60-year-old sergeant in Glengarry's Regiment to his lover, asking after her children and telling her how much he misses her. Duncan McGillis did not make it back to Scotland, so it's all the more poignant that Margaret McDonnell, barmaid at the barracks at Fort Augustus, never received his letter.

The information in those letters which were safely received had to be passed on to other family members. Katherine Hepburn was the daughter of James Hepburn of Keith, the man who had ceremoniously escorted the Prince into Holyroodhouse. Katie was still in Edinburgh a week and more after the Jacobites had left and was anxious to tell her aunt in Aberdeen, her father's sister, the latest news:

> Papa writes us they had crossed Tweed, was all in great health and spirits. They were to be in Carlisle on Saturday night where the whole Army are to join, as it hs been divided in two different parts, because the Country they went through could not provide Meat and Lodging for such a number of men.

The proud daughter and dutiful niece ended her letter on a note of resignation:

> P. S. I hear all the letters are kept up at the Post Office three or four weeks or they be delivered. As they cant read all the Letters they only open the ones to the most suspected persons, and in case there should be any information in the others they dont deliver them till it cant be of no use. So I suppose it will be about Christmas till this comes to your hand. Adiue, My Sisters join me in their Duty to Grandmama and you.

Three days after Katie Hepburn wrote those words to her aunt in Aberdeen, the Reverend Robert Lyon, chaplain to Ogilvy's Regiment, wrote to his sister Cecelia in Perth, telling her that he was with the main body of the Jacobites at Brampton outside Carlisle and 'All as yet goes well, and all your friends and acquaintances are in good health and in full spirits.'

The Post Office throughout the British Isles was well established by the middle of the eighteenth century, but Katie Hepburn believed its postmasters and -mistresses would not undertake to deliver letters sent to and from the Jacobite Army while it was on the move. Robert Lyon offered Cecelia one way of keeping in touch with him.

> P. S. If you meet with any Body going to the Army
> write me your news and direct it to me in Lord Ogilvy's
> Regiment and it will come to hand.

Another phrase crops up in the letters sent and never received from Moffat. Angus MacDonnell was just one of those who told his wife that if the English Jacobites rose he might not even have to draw his sword. He added that in any case he would definitely be home for Christmas – which makes you wonder if all soldiers in all wars have kept their spirits up by thinking that.

Duncan Forbes of Culloden was a prolific letter writer. In his position as Lord President of the Court of Session in Edinburgh, many of these were official, sending and passing on reports to military men and politicians, but there were personal letters, too. On 25 October 1745, he wrote more in sorrow than in anger to the Laird of Pitcalnie. The Laird's son Malcolm, the Lord President's great-nephew, had gone over to the Jacobites. He had been serving in the Government army when he did so, with Lord Loudoun's Regiment, so it's possible he was one of those who changed sides at Prestonpans.

Knowing his impetuous young relative was likely to be hanged for desertion if caught, Forbes saw his defection as an unmitigated disaster:

> I NEVER was more astonish'd, & but seldom more
> afflicted, in my life, than I was when I heard of the
> madness of your son. I cannot conceive of what magick
> he has been prevail'd on to forfeit utterly his own
> honours; in a signall manner to affront & dishonour me,
> whom you made answerable for him; to risk a halter,
> which, if he do not succeed, must be his doom, without
> any other tryall than that of a court martial; & to break
> the heart of an indulgent father, as you are: which, I
> am perswaded, must be ths case, unless he reclaim'd; the
> villains who seduced him, profiting of his tender years &

want of experience, tho' I hope I am a Christian, I never
will forgive; tho' him I will, if he return quickly to his
duty, without committing further folly.

He wrote to young Malcolm, too, asking him to come and see him,
and assuring him he would not try to forcibly stop him returning to
the Jacobite Army. Signing himself 'your affectionate Uncle', he also
wrote: 'I need not tell you that I wish you well.'

Many of the men who wrote letters in 1745–6 and ached so much
for home, hearth and family never did come home again. They left a
legacy in their words of love, care and longing:

Oh a month's rest at home would be a blessing.

Donald Ram desires his father-in-law to hire a lad for
his wife and he desires that his wife would sell the black
cow but if she can't get a good price for her, let her kill
her and be eaten in the house.

Give my kind service to all friends and neighbours.

All the lads are well.

I shall not sleep easy until I see you and the Bairns.

Duncan McGillis, who was never to see his lover, Margaret, or Scotland
again, wrote the most poignant words of all: 'Nothing ails me but the
wanting of you.'

11

Bonnie Prince Charlie Meets Sir Oswald Mosley: The Manchester Regiment

Farewell, Manchester, tho' my heart for you still beats,
Ne'er again will I swagger down your streets

Although he was not in favour of the march into England, James Johnstone did his duty throughout it. Johnstone was now in command of a company within the Duke of Perth's Regiment, whose ranks had been swelled by the considerable number of Government soldiers who deserted to the Jacobites at Prestonpans. Sergeant Thomas Dickson was one of them.

James Johnstone described him as 'a young Scotsman, as brave and intrepid as a lion, and very much attached to my interest'. At Preston on the way south, Dickson offered to go on ahead to Manchester to beat up for recruits.

Johnstone said no, rebuking Dickson 'for entertaining so wild and extravagant a project, which exposed him to the danger of being taken and hanged'. The sergeant went anyway, riding through the night from Preston to Manchester with his mistress and the Regiment's drummer. Johnstone was uneasy rather than angry, although he was irritated that Dickson had carried off his blunderbuss and his portmanteau, presumably leaving his captain without a clean shirt or his razor.

Although surrounded by a hostile mob when he first told the drummer to start beating up, the power of Dickson's considerable personality brought him out on top. The blunderbuss came in useful, too. Swinging round in a continuous circle, the sergeant kept it trained on the crowd. At the same time, he roared like the lion to which Johnstone had compared him, yelling out bloodcurdling threats. If anyone attacked him, his girlfriend or the drummer, he would blow their bloody brains out.

Taking their cue from him, some of Manchester's Jacobites – of whom there were many – found their courage. As they stepped forward, the balance of the crowd shifted in favour of Sergeant Dickson and his unorthodox recruiting party, and the Jacobite Manchester Regiment was born.

Dickson brought Johnstone back a list of one hundred and eighty recruits, his captain 'agreeably surprised to find that the whole amount of his expenses did not exceed three guineas'. Everyone had a good laugh at Manchester's expense, declaring that the city had been taken for the Jacobites by a sergeant, a drummer and a whore.

Although dismissed both then and now as riff-raff and rabble, unemployed and workshy labourers with time on their hands and nothing better to do than seize the chance of making mischief, the Manchester Regiment included many men whose commitment to the Stuart Cause ran deep.

The Regiment's colonel was Francis Townley, who came from a devoutly Catholic and passionately Jacobite Lancashire family. He was a professional soldier, having served in the French Army, earning his spurs during the War of the Polish Succession.

While several of the senior officers and many of the rank and file of the Manchester Regiment were Catholics, the majority of the officers were Protestants. These included brothers Robert, Thomas and Charles Deacon, who were the sons of the non-juring Anglican Bishop of Manchester. Non-jurors were clergymen who maintained their loyalty to the House of Stuart and refused to take the oath of allegiance to George II.

When the main body of the Jacobite Army arrived in Manchester, the supporters of King George and the political status quo retreated into their homes, just as they had in Edinburgh. The Manchester Jacobites had a field day. As in Edinburgh, young women were strongly attracted to the Cause. One of them was Elizabeth Byrom, who wrote it all up in her diary.

'Beppy' to her friends and family, she went out on the street with hundreds of other Mancunians to hear King James proclaimed the rightful king. That night she sat up late with her aunt, stitching blue-and-white St Andrew's crosses. The next day was 30 November, and there were celebrations in honour of Scotland's patron saint and the Scottish visitors. The Manchester Regiment was also officially constituted.

Gazing in admiration at the Prince as he rode through the streets of Manchester, Beppy declared it a 'noble sight'. Wearing her white gown, the colour of choice for a Jacobite lady, she was introduced to him that evening, kissing his hand. After that, she and her friends drank so many toasts to Charles and his father that she got tipsy.

Beppy's father, John Byrom, was a complex and interesting man. He invented a system of shorthand, a useful tool for a man who spent much of his life embroiled in plots and intrigues, and the clandestine correspondence which went along with them. One of these was a sexual adventure: he was for several years the lover of Queen Caroline, wife of George II.

Byrom also composed a famous Jacobite toast – one suitable for those who wanted to hint at where their allegiance lay:

> God bless the King! God bless the Faith's Defender!
> God bless – no harm in blessing – the Pretender!
> Who that Pretender is, and who that King –
> God bless us all – is quite another thing!

In *The Queen's Chameleon,* Byrom's biographer, Joy Hancox, tells a fascinating story which suggests that Charles Edward Stuart's visit to Manchester in 1745 was not his first. The tale comes from the memoirs of one of several men who bore the title and name Sir Oswald Mosley, the first name being a traditional one in that family.

These memoirs were published in 1849 and refer back to a woman, 84 years old in 1815, whose father had been the landlord of Manchester's Bull's Head inn. In his time, the tavern was a favourite watering-hole for the local Jacobites. In the summer of 1744, when his daughter was a girl of 13, she remembered a handsome young gentleman riding in on several occasions from Ancoats Hall, where he was staying with Sir Oswald Mosley.

The handsome young gentleman was interested in the London newspapers, which he read with great concentration. On one occasion, he asked the landlord's daughter to bring him a basin of water and a towel to wash the newsprint off his hands. When she came to take the basin and towel away, he gave her half a crown. The generous tip made a big impression on her.

In November 1745, she was standing at the tavern door watching the Jacobite Army march into Manchester. The Prince passed by – and she recognized the handsome young man who had been so avid a reader of the newspapers the year before.

It's a good story, given extra credence by the evidence of Thomas Coppack, the Anglican chaplain to the Manchester Regiment. When he and other members of the newly formed regiment sat drinking at the Bull's Head at the end of November 1745, they were joined by young Oswald Mosley, son of the house of Ancoats Hall. Had he come to visit a friend as well as show his support? The Prince is known to have made at least one incognito visit to England during his life. It's entirely possible that he made more.

Support for the Jacobites in Manchester was about a lot more than drinking yourself silly through innumerable loyal toasts to the Stuarts. Many in the city could be counted among those who, as people said then, were disaffected to the Government and the House of Hanover.

Manchester had its own issues. It was growing rapidly, as was its textile industry, yet felt itself sidelined and distanced from those who held the reins of power in London.

Hand-in-hand with this went the powerful Jacobite convictions of the officers of the Manchester Regiment. Like many of their Scottish counterparts, their devotion to the Stuarts was inextricably bound up with their religious beliefs. Yet coupled with this almost mystical strand of their political philosophy was straightforward distaste that Old England was now being ruled by a bloody foreigner.

Some people thought Charles Edward Stuart was a bloody foreigner too, of course, seeing little to choose between a usurping German and a half-Italian and half-Polish adventurer. The officers of the Manchester Regiment did not see Charles that way. They believed he was their best and perhaps last hope of protecting and safeguarding hard-won English liberties.

This interesting point of view, that Charles could deliver national and personal freedom, was shared by many of his Scottish supporters. It goes against the grain of the traditional historical view. As with the Scottish Jacobites, and pointing to the association of the English Jacobites with the Tory party, such thinking has dismissed Jacobite political thought as reactionary and right wing.

According to this analysis, the Rising of 1745 and the attempt to restore the Stuarts was the last gasp of the old world. Jacobitism had to be stamped on and stamped out, as Scotland had to stay inextricably bound into the Union with England. Only then could Great Britain steam ahead into the sunlit uplands of the modern age.

Some strands of the Jacobite movement were undoubtedly reactionary, belonging much more to the old world than the new, not least the absolute authority many Highland chiefs wielded over their clansmen and -women. Yet, as the only available opportunity at that time for achieving a groundbreaking political change, the Jacobite movement was a focus for the discontent felt by people of many different backgrounds and with many different aspirations.

The eighteenth century was a fascinating period of transition between the old and the new. In Scotland, the seeds of the Enlightenment were beginning to sprout. Throughout the British Isles, the Industrial Revolution was poised to roar into action, transforming the cities and the countryside. In agriculture, new methods of working on and profiting from the land were being introduced.

In terms of social class, these changes exacerbated old tensions as well as introducing new ones but, after a long and tortuous struggle, led to the democracy and personal freedoms we enjoy today. In their belief that Charles Edward Stuart could deliver such political and personal liberty, it could be argued that the officers of the Manchester Regiment were the forerunners of the political Radicals which the cotton mills and factories of Manchester and Lancashire were later to produce in such abundance.

Apart from the unemployed riff-raff jibe, the private men of the Manchester Regiment have also been dismissed as 'Irish immigrant rabble'. This is an interesting insult. There are many people of Irish descent in Manchester, descendants of those who left their homeland in search of the work to be found in the city's many textile mills. Although this industry took off from the 1760s onwards, the real influx of Irish people happened in the nineteeth century, before, during and after the potato famine.

How many Irishmen and -women there were in the Manchester of 1745 is therefore debatable. It would seem racism and anti-Catholicism were at work, the latter being, of course, a particularly powerful bogeyman in Protestant England at this time. It would seem, too, that these twin prejudices of race and religion have continued to colour attitudes towards the Manchester Regiment. A read-through of its officers' and men's names does not in fact turn up many Irishmen. Instead, we find Henry Bibby, a weaver from Wigan; James Braithwaite, a saddler from Penrith; Thomas Ogden, a weaver from Manchester; and Thomas Warrington, a chair-maker from Macclesfield. James Sparkes, a framework knitter from Derby, joined the Manchester Regiment when the Jacobites occupied his home town. He was later hanged at York.

❖ ❖ ❖

The Jacobites' march into England had seemed unstoppable. In some places, such as Manchester, the welcome accorded to the Prince and his men had been wildly enthusiastic. Yet even the Manchester Regiment did not supply anything like the number of recruits hoped for. At Derby, after heated debate and bitter argument, this lack of support led to the decision to abandon the march on London. The Manchester Regiment turned round and trudged north with everyone else. Although some of these new recruits deserted along the way, around 120 were left behind at Carlisle when Charles and the rest of the Jacobite Army crossed back into Scotland.

The Prince has often been criticized for leaving them to their fate in order to satisfy his vanity by hanging onto one of England's mightiest fortresses. Some argue, however, that Colonel Townley preferred to stay in Carlisle rather than cross into Scotland.

Many of his men were unwilling to leave their native country for the uncertainty of what might await them in Scotland. A handful of them did, including John Daniel, the gentleman volunteer from Lancashire, although he too was reluctant to cross the border, as he later wrote: 'Every thing being now in readiness, we began our march, in order (alas! As it happened) to bid adieu to old England for ever!'

There were also Scotsmen in the short-lived Jacobite garrison at Carlisle. A fair number came from John Roy Stewart's Edinburgh Regiment, although many of them actually belonged to Perthshire and Banffshire.

With no real hope of defending Carlisle against artillery brought in from Whitehaven, the Jacobite garrison surrendered to the Duke of Cumberland on 30 December 1745. The treatment meted out to them was chilling in its cruelty.

The officers were sent to London, while the 300 or so other ranks, including some women and children who had followed the Jacobite Army into England, were locked up in a gloomy dungeon within Carlisle Castle. They were kept there for several freezing January days, shackled and without food, drink or light. There is a stone on one wall of this vault which still today has an unusual shape. The story is that moisture collected there and the prisoners took turns to lick it in an attempt to assuage their thirst.

Subsequently transferred to other prisons, we do not know how many men of the Manchester Regiment died as a result of this maltreatment. Of those who survived, many were among the 1,000 prisoners, again including some women and children, who were transported to the West Indies to work as indentured servants in the plantations there.

More than half the officers of the Manchester Regiment were executed. Eighteen of them, including the chaplain, Thomas Coppack, and seven of the Regiment's eight sergeants, went to the gallows. There was a strong feeling that punishment was even more severe for them because they were Englishmen and so seen as greater traitors than the Scottish Jacobites.

Bishop Deacon lost all three of his sons. Robert died of illness as a prisoner at Carlisle, Thomas was hanged and Charles was transported to the West Indies, dying soon after he got there.

John Daniel and James Bradshaw are the only two members of the Manchester Regiment known to have fought at Culloden. John Daniel escaped; Jem Bradshaw was taken. He was hung, drawn and quartered on Kennington Common in November 1746. Six other members of the Manchester Regiment, including Colonel Townley, Thomas Sydall, Adjutant of the Regiment, Thomas Deacon and Jem Dawson, were executed there in July of the same year. An old, sad story says that Jem Dawson's sweetheart was there and died of a broken heart moments after she witnessed his death.

William Harrison Ainsworth was a nineteenth-century Manchester lawyer who turned to writing, producing 39 novels, all heavily based on historical fact. One of them was *The Manchester Rebels*. In it, he tells the tale of the deaths of Jem Dawson and his sweetheart, and has Colonel Townley mount the ladder to the scaffold with a straight back and a scornful smile.

Ainsworth also has Thomas Deacon, with his dying breath, cry out 'God save King James III!' When Thomas Sydall hears the executioner remark, as he puts the noose over his head, that he is trembling, Sydall indignantly denies it: 'I recoil from thy hateful touch – that is all.' And to prove that his courage was unshaken, he took a pinch of snuff.

The heads of Colonel Townley and Jem Dawson were displayed on Temple Bar in London. Those of Jem Bradshaw and Thomas Deacon were sent to Manchester to be displayed on the Exchange there as both an act of gloating revenge and a vicious warning.

It is recorded that Bishop Deacon went there and stared for a long time at the heads. When a sympathetic bystander asked why he did not weep, he said because he did not mourn for his son, who had died the death of a martyr. Then the bishop took off his hat and bowed to both heads, and every time he passed Manchester's Exchange thereafter, he did the same.

12

THE YEAR OF THE PRINCE: BLACK FRIDAY AT DERBY

WITHIN THREE DAYS' MARCH OF THE CAPITAL

Boost for morale though the new regiment was, the numbers were a mere drop in the ocean. Colonel O'Sullivan had been hoping for one thousand five hundred volunteers from Manchester, ten times more than actually did enlist. He believed that many English people wanted to see a restoration of the Stuarts but feared to commit themselves – especially without the back-up of those conspicuously absent French troops.

Sir John Macdonald felt that appeals should be made to the many Catholics in Lancashire, via letters sent to their priests. He suggested this to Sir Thomas Sheridan, another of the Seven Men of Moidart and former tutor to Prince Charles. Sheridan would have none of it, unwilling for the Prince and his army to have 'anything to do with Roman Catholic priests'. Macdonald considered this attitude foolish in the extreme:

> Catholics should not hide their feelings – or what those
> feelings should be. Namely that the Protestant religion
> should remain the dominant one in England, since it

was established by acts of Parliament, while at the same
time the Catholic religion should have full liberty as in
England Presbyterians and other nonconformists have
likewise.

Macdonald believed openness and honesty would be the best way to
counteract the anti-Catholic propaganda which 'filled the newspapers'
about the Prince and the Jacobites. It was stupid to try to pretend they
had nothing to do with Catholics when the army had 'nearly as many
of them as of Protestants'. Given that many people even now try to
maintain that this was a Catholic army, this is an interesting statistic.

That the propaganda had much impact on those Protestants who
might otherwise have rallied to the Prince's Standard seems unlikely.
Not exactly appealing to deep thinkers, the pamphlets, prints and
broadsides which were the tabloid press of their day attacked the
Jacobites by evoking the spectre of rule from Rome by a despotic
Pope whose shock troops would be sinister priests. Jesuits were the
favourite bogeymen.

Although the burnings of 400 Protestant martyrs during the reign
of Mary Tudor might have still been vivid in the public imagination,
those horrors had happened almost 200 years before. That was then and
this was now. Added to which, many eighteenth-century Englishmen
and -women retained a romantic and sentimental attachment to the
Stuarts. After all, one of the most popular kings ever to sit upon the
British throne had been a Stuart.

Charles II might have famously remarked that Presbyterianism was
no religion for a gentleman. Unlike his brother James, who succeeded
him and lost the throne, Charles had been smart enough and cynical
enough not to embrace the Catholic religion. He was fondly
remembered in the 1740s, as he still is today, as the Merry Monarch,
the encourager of arts, industry and science, hero of the Great Fire of
London, legendary lover of women and friend to all men. As a future
politician might have said, Charles II truly was the People's King.

His great-nephew had inherited all of his charm and seemed as promising in other respects. Except when he rode officially into a town or city, during most of the invasion of England the Prince walked on foot at the head of his men, putting in the same effort as they did and presumably having the blisters to prove it. The London mob – as volatile, unpredictable, brutally sentimental and potentially influential as that of any eighteenth-century city – might well have taken him to their hearts.

By and large the Hanoverians were not an attractive bunch, either in their looks or their personalities. The Stuarts were much sexier: physically attractive, exciting, a little bit louche and at the same time touched by God. John Daniel, the gentleman volunteer to the Manchester Regiment, summed it up beautifully:

> The first time I saw this loyal army was betwixt Lancaster and Garstang: the brave Prince marching on foot at their head like a Cyrus or a Trojan Hero, drawing admiration and love from all those who beheld him, raising their long-dejected hearts, and solacing their minds with the happy prospect of another Golden Age. Struck with this charming sight and seeming invitation *'Leave your nets and follow me,'* I felt a paternal ardour pervade my veins, and having before my eyes the admonition *'Serve God and then your King,'* I immediately became one of his followers.

Yet there was a big difference between looking back longingly to Good King Charles's golden days or wiping away a tear at the sight of the 'golden-haired laddie' – the schmaltz had started even then – and committing yourself to the Stuart Cause. Those who enlisted in the Jacobite Army were risking their lives, their livelihoods and their families' futures. This was not like deciding which way to vote at the next election.

As in Scotland, there may have been Stuart sympathizers who simply felt the House of Hanover was too well established to be unseated. Or that it was not worth the blood which would have to be shed to do it.

Despite the failure of the English Jacobites to rise, by the time the Prince's army reached Derby on 4 December, morale was high and the men were ready for action. James Johnstone watched them crowding into cutlers' shops 'quarrelling about who should be the first to sharpen and give a proper edge to his sword'.

Derby did not supply many recruits either, but the welcome given to the Jacobites was remarkably cordial. They seem to have earned this by demonstrating their famous civility. They might requisition your horses or ask if you could spare 'a brace or two of good pistols', but they did it with a disarming smile and never entered any ladies' bedchambers uninvited.

Of course, if you knew they were coming, and even if your absent master was suspected of having Jacobite sympathies – or maybe because he did – you might hide the best horses, as was done at Kedleston, the home of Sir Nathaniel Curzon. A Dr Mather wrote to Curzon's son to tell him what happened:

> You will guess how the stables were furnish'd when I tell you what they took, viz., the two old brown mares, Miss Glanville, and out of the Coach Horse Stable, Old Bully. (There were a set left in the latter, tho' the best of them were put out of the way and others put in their stead, as was done with the rest, expecting a visit.) They went away with these saddled and bridled, and the Pistols, and that was all. They wou'd drink very little, and gave so little disturbance that my Lady and half the family knew not of their having been in the House till Morning.

The news that the advancing Jacobite Army was in Derby, only 120 miles away, sent London into a spiral of panic. Shops and theatres closed, and there was a run on the Bank of England. Cunning as foxes, its directors and cashiers worked out a strategy to stem the flow of outgoing funds. First, they planted their own agents in the crowd of clamouring customers. When these agents presented their notes and demanded coin in return, they were paid in sixpences so the transaction would take as long as possible. They then went out one door and back in the other, elbowed their way to the front and presented more notes, preventing the genuine customers from removing any money from the bank.

Government troops were being mobilized to defend the capital, but if Hogarth's *March to Finchley* is to be believed, they were strolling rather than marching, dallying with their doxies all the way. As many among the civilian population still felt a tug of loyalty towards Charles Edward Stuart as the Prince of the old royal house, so did many in the military. Rumours abounded of Jacobite sympathies among Government officers – and they and the men under their command were in a position to take action. Had they done so, the balance of power might well have tipped in favour of Charles Edward Stuart and the Jacobites. Many on both sides believed these soldiers might rather have gone over to the Prince than fight under the command of his cousin several times removed, the Duke of Cumberland. Called back from the ongoing conflict in Continental Europe, King George's son was now in charge of the war against the Jacobites.

Well-off Londoners were packing up and hiding their valuables. There was a rumour that King George himself had two yachts stowed with treasures waiting at Tower Quay, ready at a moment's notice to carry him and the Royal Family to the safety of Holland. The Duke of Newcastle, principal Secretary of State, shut himself away in his house, considering his options.

Yet on the very day Newcastle was perhaps wondering if he should spend more time with his family, the Jacobites were marching back to Scotland, having taken the agonizing decision to turn around. A council of war was called on the morning of Thursday, 5 December, meeting in Derby's Exeter House. All the colonels were present this time, including John Roy Stuart, and the atmosphere was tense.

Lord George Murray spoke first, calling it as he saw it, as he always did. The English Jacobites had not risen, nor the Welsh under Sir

Watkin Williams Wynn, as had been hoped for. The French had sent no troops to help take London. Thousands of Government troops now stood ready to defend the city, in two or perhaps even three separate armies. If the Prince's army was to give all of them battle, Jacobite casualties were likely to be heavy.

The Scots were far from home. They would undoubtedly suffer more losses on a hurried and forced retreat; it would be far better to make an organized and disciplined withdrawal now. In Lord George's opinion, this was the only sensible option.

There was a long silence. Then the Prince spoke, beginning to discuss the order in which the regiments of the army would line up the following day for the march south. Lord George interrupted, angrily reminding him no decision had yet been made that they were going to march south.

The Prince turned to the other members of his council. The Duke of Perth and Jacobite Colonel Ranald MacDonald of Clanranald, son of the chief of that title and himself known as Young Clanranald, agreed with him. The others agreed with Lord George. Lords Elcho and Ogilvy were particularly warm in their support for the retreat. Charles brought out what he thought was his trump card, the news that Lord John Drummond, brother of the Duke of Perth, had landed in Montrose with a regiment of Scots and Irishmen in the French service. To Lord George, that was another reason for going home. They could rendezvous with Lord John's Regiment and make a stand in Scotland.

Charles lost his temper. Lord Elcho said that the Prince used 'very Abusive Language' against him, Lord George and Lord Ogilvy, accusing them of betraying him. The Prince argued passionately that if they could only get to London, he would be welcomed with open arms. The English and the Welsh Jacobites would rise en masse, and on this great wave of popular support the Stuarts would be restored to the throne. Men such as the Duke of Newcastle would declare their support and other influential figures would follow.

When pressed, Charles admitted to his war council that he had no promises of support from any Jacobites south of the border or west of

Offa's Dyke. The council members were horrified, and the meeting broke up in acrimony.

Lobbying through the day by the Prince did not bring many round to his way of thinking. A second meeting of the council called that evening started with Lord George assuming the retreat had been decided and outlining his plans for it to be executed as efficiently as possible. If they had to fight a Government army on the way, so be it, but the focus would be on getting back to Scotland as quickly as possible. The powerful clan chiefs agreed with him.

Forced to accept the decision, Charles was nevertheless devastated by it, saying 'I shall summon no more Councils, since I am accountable to nobody for my actions but to God and my father, and therefore I shall no longer ask or accept advice.' Colonel O'Sullivan summed up the Prince's feelings:

> but a Young Prince, yt sees himself within three days, or at utmost four days, march of the Capital, where if he was once arrived, wou'd in all appearance restor the King, cou'd not relish the word of retrait, & really he wou'd not hear yt word from the beginning, he had an avertion to the word it self, but finding every body almost of yt opinion was obligded to consent. I never saw any body so concerned as he was for this disapointmet, nor never saw him take any thing after so much to heart as he did it.

Dr Robert Mather added some more snippets of information, when he wrote to Sir Nathaniel Curzon's son about the horses and pistols being taken:

> They listed Sparkes, the fishing-tackle-man at Derby, but sent him back from Ashburn as too great a rogue to keep with them. He fell to plundering at Bradley, so He will probably be hanged.

Which is exactly what happened to the unfortunate Mr Sparkes, who as well as being the 'fishing-tackle-man' also apparently moonlighted as a framework knitter. Dr Mather had another story about Miss Glanville, the old brown mare he had mentioned earlier in his letter. When the Jacobite Army marched out of Derby, the horse was seen 'dancing among them with a Highlander on her back', who cried in delight that this one was going to 'gollope, gollope, this will gollope!' Did her new rider know she was called Miss Glanville, or did he give her a new name?

Although some stragglers from the Jacobite Army were 'killed by the country people', the retreat was carried out swiftly and efficiently, despite the terrible weather, frequent bombardments of torrential rain and freezing sleet. The men in charge of the baggage train had a particularly hard time, bumping carts along rough and rutted roads.

Although it was the Jacobites who now feared ambushes, these did not materialize. Sir John Macdonald was relieved but surprised by this:

> It seems that the English army is not acquainted with what is called guerrilla warfare. We only saw some of their militia on horseback on the hill tops watching our march and being very careful to keep out of shot, even by a single soldier.

They were, however, being pursued, the Duke of Cumberland by now hot on their heels. John Roy Stuart and his Edinburgh Regiment formed the rearguard, protecting the baggage train and scooping up any stragglers. As Cumberland caught up with them, several skirmishes and running battles ensued.

At some point in the various melees, at or near Lowther Hall, a few miles north of Shap Fell, John Roy lost his servant, his targe and one of his pair of Doune pistols. What became of the servant is not known, but the shield and pistol can be seen today in Aberdeen's Marischal Museum.

The fighting culminated in what was to become the last military engagement fought on English, as opposed to British, soil. Now officially relegated to the status of a skirmish, locally they still prefer to call it the Battle of Clifton Moor. It was fought on a dark winter's afternoon along narrow country lanes lined with hedges, not ideal terrain for either side. The Edinburgh Regiment provided back-up to the soldiers fighting under Lord George Murray, the Jacobite commander-in-chief. The Appin Stewarts, Angus MacDonell of Glengarry and Cluny Macpherson and their men were also in the thick of the fight, which lasted for about half an hour.

The Jacobites lost 12 men and inflicted casualties of about 50 dead and wounded on their opponents, mainly troopers from Bland's Regiment. Although the Jacobites then retreated, both sides claimed Clifton as a victory.

Angus MacDonell of Glengarry did not live long to celebrate it. Despite surviving Clifton and, a month later, the Battle of Falkirk, he was accidentally shot in the streets of Falkirk shortly after that battle by a Highland soldier cleaning his gun.

Inconclusive it might have been, but the engagement at Clifton and the disinclination of Cumberland to follow them into a snowy Scotland gave the Jacobite Army the breathing space it needed to head north, cross the border and get back home.

After brief sojourns at Dumfries and Hamilton, the next stop on the itinerary was Glasgow.

13

THE PRINCE, THE PROVOST & THE TWELVE THOUSAND SHIRTS

OUR VERY LADYS HAD NOT THE CURIOSITY TO GO NEAR HIM

Andrew Cochrane must have watched the advance guard of the Jacobite Army ride into Glasgow on Christmas Day 1745 with real trepidation. When the emergency had begun, his concern had been that Glasgow was full of essential supplies, an irresistible sitting target for an army on the march.

After the comings and goings of the past autumn, with the demands for money and goods, there was now a history of mutual and bitter antagonism between the city and the Jacobites. Once again, it was John Hay who played the heavy. After it was all over, Cochrane wrote again to MP Patrick Crawford in London:

> On the 25th December, about one forenoon, arrived the vanguard of the Highland army, and with them John Hay, late a writer, now a minister, kinsman to a certain great man, who had undertaken to be our scourge and persecutor. He came to the clerk's chamber, where the Magistrates and some of the principal inhabitants were, and made us a long harangue on our late rebellion and

appearance in arms, by marching a battalion to Stirling, and concluded that his H---ness was resolved to make us an example of his just severity, to strike a terror into other places. We did all we could, consistent with our duty, to soften him, and applied to some of the chiefs who arrived that night with a column of the army.

Frustrated by Glasgow's continuing defiance of him and by how it had continued to 'show too much Zelle to the Government', Charles threatened to sack the city. He would let his army loose to plunger and pillage as they pleased. This was not the Bonnie Prince's finest hour.

It was Donald Cameron of Lochiel who stayed his hand. Lochiel had close family and business connections with Glasgow. In 1743, he had placed an order for a large quantity of tartan cloth with one of the town's weavers, helping fuel the rumours of an impending Rising. Everything a clan chief should be and often was not, Lochiel was a humane man who cared deeply for his clansmen and -women, and felt responsible for their well-being. They, in return, looked up to him. Now he showed that care and concern for the people of Glasgow.

It's a strongly held tradition in Glasgow that, in gratitude for Lochiel having saved the city from being sacked, the bells of the Tolbooth at Glasgow Cross should ring out whenever he or any of his descendants came to town. This tradition has been observed in modern times.

Although Lochiel had prevented a violent sacking of the city, a peaceful plundering was to take place instead. According to Provost Cochrane, the men who billeted themselves in pubs and private houses did not pay for their accommodation. This was unusual for the 'we pay our way' Jacobite Army.

Cochrane might have been trying to paint them all in as bad a light as possible, or he might have been telling the truth. After the long walk home, they may have felt they were entitled to be fed and watered, and provided with clean sheets and a soft bed free, gratis and for nothing in this city which had stood so stubbornly against them.

They were certainly in no mood to be crossed, as the next demand made on Provost Cochrane showed. The unwelcome visitors wanted 6,000 cloth jackets, 12,000 linen shirts, 6,000 pairs of shoes, 6,000 blue bonnets and 6,000 pairs of tartan stockings, plus a sum of money which the provost does not specify.

Presumably pausing only to reel back, strike their foreheads with the backs of their hands and ask incredulously *how* many shirts, Glasgow scrabbled around trying to gather together as much as they could of the Jacobites' list of demands. Angry though they were, the citizens of Glasgow were terrified that if they didn't show willing the sacking would be back on the agenda.

Having put the fear of God into the Glaswegians and got what he wanted from them, the Prince now switched to a charm offensive. It did not go down well. Or did it? Falling over backwards, as usual, to prove Glasgow's loyalty to King George after the scary men in tartan were safely away Cochrane wrote to everyone he could think of, maintaining that not even 'the meanest inhabitant' had accorded Charles Edward Stuart the slightest amount of respect, or even taken an interest in him:

> Our very ladys had not the curiosity to go near him, and declined going to a ball held by his chiefs. Very few were at the windows when he made his appearance, and such as were declared him not handsome. This no doubt fretted.

Once more, the good provost seems to be protesting too much. Despite their resentment at the demands made of them, Glaswegians have always enjoyed a good show, and a good show was what the Prince and his men put on for them. It was all great street theatre.

Despite Cochrane's denials, a few members of the Jacobite Army were Glaswegians. One of them was Andrew Wood, described as both a shoemaker and a gentleman. He had been with the Prince in England, a member of John Roy Stuart's Edinburgh Regiment. He probably found that hard to live down when he got home.

Charles personally presented Andrew Wood with his captain's commission, probably at the Shawfield Mansion on the Trongate, where he had taken up residence. This beautiful building was the home of Mr Glassford, one of the foremost of Glasgow's Tobacco Lords. A plaque at the foot of what used to be his garden and is now Glassford Street marks where his house once stood.

Provost Cochrane's denial that any local ladies went to that 'ball held by his chiefs' is also suspect. Another strong local tradition has it that they did, naming one in particular. She was Clementine Walkinshaw, who was to become Charles's long-term mistress and the mother of his only acknowledged child.

Distracted though he might have been by dallying with Clemmie, Charles took particular care to dress with great elegance while he was in Glasgow, and to make sure the locals saw him and his army. Sharp as tacks, more than one eagle-eyed Glaswegian spotted that when the Prince put on a show of strength by reviewing his troops on Glasgow Green, the men marched down one street and up another in order to appear a larger force than they actually were.

There's another account from an anonymous eyewitness of how Glasgow reacted to the invasion of the 'Hieland raggymuffins':

> Like other young people, I was extremely anxious to see Prince Charles, and for that purpose stationed myself in the Trongate, where it was reported he would pass. He was holding a muster of his troops in the Green; and when it was over, he passed on horseback at the head of his men, on his way to his head-quarters. I managed to get so near him that I could have touched him with my hand; and the impression which his appearance made upon my mind shall never fade from it as long as I live. He had a princely aspect; and its interest was much deepened by the dejection that appeared in his pale countenance and downcast eye. He evidently wanted confidence in his own cause, and seemed to have a

melancholy foreboding of that disastrous issue which ruined the hopes of his family forever.

The Jacobite Army left Glasgow on 3 January 1746, taking a printing press and two magistrates as hostages to ensure the city's future good behaviour. Within a week, Provost Cochrane was fielding demands coming from the Government side.

Jack Campbell, Glasgow's MP, future 5th Duke of Argyle and now serving the Government as the dashing Colonel Jack of the Argyle Militia, wrote from Dumbarton to ask that the 40 kettles he wanted be a little bigger than the sample Cochrane had sent him. If the knapsacks he had ordered weren't 'made of calves' skin such as soldiers always have', Cochrane was to proceed no further with them. The young Colonel Jack at least finished his letter with 'I am sorry to give you so much trouble.'

Glasgow's sacrifice was soon to be counted in more than kettles, shirts and bonnets. In the middle of January 1746, the Glasgow Regiment lined up at Falkirk to face the Jacobites in battle.

14

REPORTER IN RHYME:
DOUGAL GRAHAM, THE BELLMAN
OF GLASGOW

FIRST THEN, I HAVE AN ITCH FOR SCRIBBLING

Many men wrote about their experiences during the '45, in letters home, journals, succinct official reports, longer narratives and books. Many expressed themselves in verse, pouring out into poetry the emotions aroused by armed and bloody combat and the experience of being a fugitive hunted down like a wild animal in your own country. Only one wrote a complete *History of the Rebellion* in rhyming couplets.

Dougal Graham was that soldier – or was he? He claimed in the preface to his book to have been an eyewitness to most of the 'Movements of the Armies, from the Rebels first crossing the Ford of Frew to their final defeat at Culloden'. This has led many writers to assume he was a volunteer in the Jacobite Army.

His name does not appear in the records of the Jacobite Army to be found in *No Quarter Given: The Muster Roll of Prince Charles Edward Stuart's Army, 1745–46*, but this proves very little, as omissions are inevitable. Nor would the muster roll of any Jacobite regiment include the camp followers who went on the march into England, such as wives and children, prostitutes and traders in other commodities who saw a potentially lucrative business opportunity.

In 1745, Dougal Graham was 21 and working as a chapman, a pedlar who went around the country selling ribbons, pins, shoe-laces and cheaply produced books known as 'chapbooks'. In size, these were more like booklets or pamphlets. It was from the chapman that ordinary people bought romances, tales of the heroes and heroines of old – the life of William Wallace was a perennial favourite – sermons, almanacs, broadsides, the prophecies of Peden, Cargill and Thomas the Rhymer, and poems. Criss-crossing Scotland as these travelling salesmen did, they also brought news and gossip about what was happening in the here and now.

The interesting conclusion which can be drawn from this is that enough working-class Scots could read to make the sale of chapbooks worthwhile. Those who had the skill might also have read them aloud to their families and neighbours. There was clearly a thirst throughout Scotland for news, information and thrilling tales of romance and adventure. Nothing new there, then.

Sometimes people terrified themselves by what they read. A group of women in Port Glasgow were thrown into terrible distress after reading a book bought from a pedlar of the prophecies of Peden. One of these foretold that the people of Scotland would suffer untold woes in the year 1744 and that the Clyde would run red with blood. A year out because of the Protestant Wind, perhaps? And if the Clyde itself did not run red, burns, pools and wells at Prestonpans, Falkirk and Culloden famously did.

It seems likely that when the Rebellion started, Dougal Graham saw an opportunity to make both money and his name by carrying on his existing profession and keeping his eyes and ears open. A Victorian historian of Glasgow wrote of 'an old man who knew Dougal well, that he was only a follower of the army, and carried a pack with small wares'. Dougal Graham could have set off, perhaps on horseback, with his pedlar's pack, which he could replenish out of his takings along the way. It would have been an ideal occupation for a man like Dougal, a smooth-talking salesman with a keen interest in his fellow man and woman, and the world about him.

He certainly did his research. He cannot have been present at every incident of which he writes, but all the well-known stories of the events of 1745–6 feature in his *History*. He also got his book out into the marketplace as quickly as any contemporary reporter's account of a modern war, as an advert in the *Glasgow Courant* of 29 September 1746 demonstrates:

> That there is to be sold by James Duncan, Printer in Glasgow, in the Saltmercat, the 2nd shop below Gibson's Wynd, a Book Intitled, A full, particular, and true Account of the late Rebellion in the Year 1745 and 1746 beginning with the Pretender's Embarking for Scotland, and then an Account of every Battle, Siege, and Skirmish that has happened in either Scotland or England.

This book and his subsequent writings were to bring Dougal fame and fortune, or at least a comfortable living. He became one of the characters of Glasgow and a successful businessman, surmounting humble beginnings and physical deformity to do so. He was born in 1724 in what was then the village of Raploch (now part of Stirling) and may have grown up, as a brief nineteenth-century biography of him puts it, in 'the quaint village of Campsie'.

In the parlance of his own times, Dougal Graham was 'humphie backit'. In addition to the hunchback, he had a growth on his chest and never grew taller than five feet. His brain, however, was razor-sharp. Intelligent and quick-thinking, he was a dab hand at the repartee and a master of the witty one-liner – and he knew how to market his work.

The advert he placed in the *Glasgow Courant* in September 1746 ends with a proud boast: 'The like has not been done in Scotland since the days of Sir David Lindsay.' He evokes the name of the author of *Ane Satyre of the Thrie Estaitis* for exactly the same purpose as a modern publisher asking an established writer to endorse a new writer's work.

The *Courant* advert informs eager readers that the book costs fourpence but discreetly suggests there may be a bulk discount for booksellers and packmen if they go directly to the printer or Dougal Graham himself. This implies he was already enough of a 'kent' face for everyone to know where to find him. If he wasn't already living in Glasgow before he went off on his adventure with the Jacobites, as he seems not to have been, he may have gone there to buy the chapbooks he hawked around Stirlingshire.

Although the evidence suggests that his *History of the Rebellion* sold thousands of copies, no first edition of it has survived. Chapbooks were not made to last. In 1752, he published a second edition, describing himself as 'Dougal Graham, merchant'. He had by now become the publisher and printer of his own works. Like a modern author writing straight onto a computer, he composed directly onto the printing press, 'at once spinning thought into typography', without first writing his verses by hand.

By this time he was living in Glasgow and had become the city's unofficial Poet Laureate, recording current events in his trademark rhyme, although he also wrote prose. George Caldwell, a publisher and bookseller in Paisley, was always keen to get hold of Dougal's works to offer to his customers:

> A' his books took weel, they were level to the meanest
> capacity, and had plenty o' coarse jokes to season them.
> I never kent a history of Dougal's that stuck in the
> sale yet.

The Scottish literati of the time looked down on him, of course, as their modern counterparts still do on any writer who tells a rattling good yarn, writes something readers want to read and is appreciated by ordinary people. One reviewer dipped his quill in vinegar: 'This is a sorry performance.' Dougal got his revenge in sales. *History of the Rebellion* went to three editions in his lifetime and at least eight after his death.

He has been much appreciated by scholars and historians ever since. One of them was Mr McVean, 'the antiquarian bibliophile of the High Street'. Another was Sir Walter Scott, who found the *History of the Rebellion* fascinating, especially in the details it records which are not to be found in other accounts of the '45. Robert Burns was also a fan of Dougal's work, particularly its often bawdy humour.

Despite his success, Dougal Graham had no great conceit of himself. One of his other books, *John Cheap, the Chapman,* is thought to be autobiographical. If it is, the picture he paints of himself is most definitely warts and all:

> John Cheap, the chapman, was a very comical short thick fellow, with a broad face and a long nose; both lame and lazy, and something lecherous among the lasses; he chused rather to sit idle than work at any time, as he was a hater of hard labour. He got the name of John Cheap the chapman, by his selling twenty needles for a penny, and twa leather laces for a farthing.

The titles of some of his later publications would now be considered very politically incorrect. Take *The Comical Sayings of Paddy from Cork, with his Coat button'd behind.* Or, in the splendidly long-winded style of eighteenth-century titles, *Grannie McNab's Lecture in the Society of Clashing Wives, Glasgow, on Witless Mithers and Dandy Daughters, who bring them up to hoodwink the men, and deceive them with their braw dresses, when they can neither wash a sark, mak' parritch, or gang to the well.*

Throughout his life, Dougal responded in writing to current events, as when road tolls were first introduced to Scotland in the mid-1760s. 'Turnimspike' was a song designed to be sung to the tune of 'Clout the Cauldron' – whatever that was. Dr Charles Mackay, a student of Dougal's works, has left us an eloquent commentary:

Turnimspike, or Turnspike, is ludicrously descriptive of the agonies of a real Highlander at the introduction of toll gates, and other paraphernalia of modern civilisation, into the remote mountain fastness of his native land. Long after the suppression of the Rebellion, great consternation was excited in Ross-shire, by the fact that a sheriff's officer had actually served a writ in Tain. 'Lord, preserve us!' said a Highlandman to his neighbour, 'What'll come next? The law has reached Tain.'

Dougal's works also received the ultimate accolade of being among those most frequently shoplifted. A bookseller by the name of Motherwell complained bitterly about this:

There are a number of infamous creatures, who acquire large libraries of curious things, by borrowing books they never mean to return, and some not unfrequently slide a volume into their pocket, at the very moment you are fool enough to busy yourself in showing them some nice typographic gem or bibliographic rarity. These dishonest and heartless villains, ought to be cut above the breath whenever they cross the threshold. They deserve no more courtesy than was of old vouchsafed to witches, under bond and indenture to the Devil.

Dougal Graham himself was regarded as an infamous creature by some in his own time. When he applied for the post of Glasgow bellman, they objected on the grounds of his involvement with the Jacobites. The appointment was in the gift of the Glasgow magistrates and, following Provost Cochrane's gallant efforts – no Jacobites in Glasgow, sir – they were not keen on the connection.

Mr Caldwell, the Paisley bookseller, offered an explanation of how Dougal Graham got the job he wanted, maintaining that the would-be bellman told the magistrates he had been pressed into Charles Edward Stuart's service. This excuse rather contradicts another one Dougal made, that at the time of the outbreak of the '45, as Caldwell was later to put it, 'he was naething mair than a hafflins callant that scarcely kent his left hand frae his richt, or a B frae a bull's fit.'

Be that as it may, Dougal Graham got the job as 'skellat' bellman. The unusual word simply means that he gave out the news of the day, while the 'mort' bellman announced who had died. In his official uniform of tricorne hat, long red coat, blue breeches, white stockings and buckled shoes, Dougal walked around Glasgow ringing his bell and giving out useful information. He might let everyone know there were caller herring freshly landed at the Broomielaw this morning, or list the departure times of the stagecoaches which regularly left the Black Bull and the Saracen's Head inns. His bell tolled closing time at these and other hostelries, too. The bellman also searched for 'wander'd weans' whose distraught mothers had been unable to find them. He was popular with children – at only five feet tall, he wasn't much bigger than many of them – and there was usually a crowd of them around him when he rang his bell.

He died in 1779, when he was in his mid-fifties, but the memories and tales of his wit lived on for many years afterwards, as did his chapbook stories and his *History of the Rebellion*. It's a highly detailed and comprehensive study of what happened in 1745–6, and it begins by giving the historical background:

> In the year se'enteen hundred and forty one,
> An imperious and bloody war began,
> Amongst kings and queens in Germanie,
> Who should the Roman Emperor be.
> French and Prussians did jointly go,
> The Hungarian queen to ovethro';
> But British, Hanoverians, and Dutch,
> Espous'd her cause, and that too much.
> From year to year, the flame it grew,
> Till armies to the field they drew.
> At Dettingen and Fontenoy,

Did many thousand lives destroy.
And then the French, they form'd a plan,
To animate our Highland clan,
By sending the Pretender's son
To claim Great Britain as his own;
Which drew the British forces back,
And made the German war to slack.

Beautifully summed up, and it scans not too badly either. Not all of his poetry does, and some of his rhymes are less successful than others:

His MANIFESTOES, also spread,
Which for the Scots, great favour had;
How that the Union, he'd dissolve,
And the tax from Malt, Salt and Coal:

What's interesting is that he confirms many of the less well-known stories of the Rising, including, for example, the tale of 'Swethenham of Guise's foot' being released on parole. Did a clansman in MacDonald of Keppoch's Regiment tell the funny little pedlar that tale one night around the campfire on the march into England?

Dougal also tells stories which other people don't. There's one about bands of robbers 'in tartan dress'd from top to toe' going around demanding horses and money from people, which recalls Colonel Jack Campbell of the Argyle Militia's letter to his father telling him that a 'madman' and his gang had been stravaiging about Dunbartonshire demanding money with menaces. The Prince's men got the blame for such raids, but, according to Dougal, these were opportunist thieves rather than soldiers of the Jacobite Army. Dougal mourned the death of Colonel James Gardiner as a good Christian and a good soldier, and his description of the run-up to Prestonpans has a certain poetic charm, followed though it is by a grim eighteenth-century pun:

Then tidings came in from Dunbar,
Of Gen'ral Cope's arrival there
But twenty miles from Ed'nburgh east,
Which made them all take arms in haste.
On the east side of Arthur's seat,
They rendezvouz'd both small and great,
And call'd a council what to do;
For ten miles east they had a view
Of all the coast to Aberlady,
And so for battle made all ready.

Although they did for quarters cry,
The vulgar clans made this reply,
'Quarters! You curst soldiers, mad,
It is o'er soon to go to bed.'

He mentions, too, a prediction made by Thomas the Rhymer, that one day the area around Prestonpans would be the site of a terrible battle fought in the early morning, as indeed it was. According to Dougal, both Merlin and the Venerable Bede had also predicted this.

His words describing the exhausted Jacobite Army marching into Glasgow paint a picture as vivid as it is humane:

Their count'nance fierce as a wild bear
Out o'er their eyes hang down their hair,
Their very thighs red tanned quite;
But yet as nimble as they'd been white;
Their beards were turned black and brown,
The like was ne'er seen in that town,
Some of them did barefooted run,
Minded no mire nor stony groun';
But when shav'n, drest and cloth'd again
They turn'd to be like other men.

The Battle of Falkirk brings us back to 'Brave col'nel JACK, being then a boy, His warlike genious did employ'. Dougal also covers the Prince's wanderings after Culloden in some detail, including the part played in his rescue by Flora MacDonald, and the hangings of the Jacobites in the aftermath of the Rising. Since these reprisals happened between September and November 1746, they cannot have formed part of the first edition of *History of the Rebellion,* which had only been published in September of that year.

It seems unlikely that Dougal Graham was present at those executions which took place in London. He makes an easy but basic mistake when writing about them, having them take place at Kensington. In fact they were carried out south of the Thames, at *Kennington.* Might he, though, have actually attended the executions at Carlisle in person? The distance from Glasgow is only 100 miles and he already knew the way – and he writes of them with real horror:

> Of these poor souls at Carlisle,
> Whose execution was so vile,
> A wooden stage they did erect,
> And first, half strangl'd by the neck,
> A fire upon the stage was born,
> Their hearts out of their breasts were torn
> The privy part unspared was,
> Cut off, and dash'd into their face,
> Then expanded into the fire;
> But such a sight I'll ne'er desire,
> Some beholders swooned away,
> Others stood mute, had nought to say,
> And some of a more brutish nature,
> Did shout *Huzza,* to seal the matter,
> Some a mourning, turn'd about
> A praying for their souls, no doubt
> Some curs'd the butcher, Haxam Willie,
> Who without remorse used his *gullie,*

> And for the same a pension got,
> Thus butchering the *Rebel Scot*.

After that, it's no surprise that Dougal issued the following warnings to his fellow countrymen:

> My dear Scots-men, a warning take
> Superior pow'rs not to forsake,
> Mind the Apostle's words, of law and love,
> Saying, *All power is giv'n from above.*
> 'Tis by will of heav'n kings do reign,
> The chain of Fate's not rul'd by men.
> Every thing must serve its time,
> And so have kings of Stewart's line.

> And those who trust in France or Spain,
> Are fools if e'er they do't again:
> Witness poor Charlie and the Scots,
> What have they got but bloody throats?

On the alleged treachery of Lord George Murray, he writes wisely, too, of human nature:

> For there is never a Battle lost, but the Commander gets
> the Blame, and when one is won, the Commander gets
> all the Praise, as if the Soldiers had done nothing; And
> it is further observed, after the loss of a Battle it is the
> cry of the Public and the run-away Soldiers, WE ARE
> SOLD, WE ARE SOLD.

Because Dougal published his first edition of *History of the Rebellion* so quickly, he had to be careful what he said. Showing overt sympathy for the Jacobite soldiers and criticizing the Government troops could have had him arrested for sedition. By the time he published the third edition, in 1774, he could be more frank. As he wrote in his preface, Charles's Cause was now well and truly lost, and the Duke of Cumberland had 'gone to the house of Silence'. Therefore Dougal Graham could write of the cruelty of the Redcoats in the aftermath of Culloden and the consequent suffering of so many Highlanders, men, women and children, who'd had nothing to do with the Rebellion.

In the third edition, he also emphasized that he had done his research, including reading what the celebrated Monsieur Voltaire had written about the attempt of 1745, which may have helped Dougal set the historical scene and place the Rising in its European context. Of course, he himself had an advantage over Voltaire in that he had his own eyewitness observations to rely on. He had written his *History* for the ordinary man and woman in the street and for himself, to satisfy his 'itch for scribbling', and now offered this 'brat of his brain' to the public – and the public loved it.

15

WITH GOD ON OUR SIDE: PISKIES, PAPISTS & PRESBYTERIANS

BY THE ASSISTANCE OF GOD, I WILL, THIS DAY, MAKE YOU A FREE AND HAPPY PEOPLE

Both sides in the '45 believed, of course, that God was on their side. The loyal oath sworn by the men of the Duke of Perth's Regiment went like this:

> I solemnly promise and swear In the Presence of Almighty God That I shall faithfully and diligently serve James the Eighth King of Scotland England France and Ireland against all his Enemies foreign or domestick And shall not desert or leave his service without leave asked and given of my officer. And hereby pass from all former alledgeance given by me to George Elector of Hannover. So help me God.

As every regiment in the Jacobite Army had its surgeon, so it also had its chaplain, who was given captain's status. Some regiments had more than one, an interesting indicator of the varied religious make-up of the men who followed Charles Edward Stuart.

Cameron of Lochiel's Regiment had three padres: the Reverend John Cameron of Fort William for the Presbyterians, the Reverend Duncan Cameron of Fortingall for the Episcopalians and Father Alexander Cameron, a Jesuit, for the Catholics. Alexander Cameron was also Cameron of Lochiel's brother.

When Alexander had first converted to Catholicism, it came as quite a shock to his Presbyterian family. It was an even bigger shock when he became a priest, and a Jesuit at that: Christ's shock troops. Father Cameron himself was happy to admit that in his youth he had been a bit 'wilde'.

At the time, and sometimes even today, the '45 was presented as a Protestant–Catholic struggle. The unlikely assertion is made that if Charles Edward Stuart had been successful, Britain would now be a Catholic country. Charles was indeed a Roman Catholic, raised in a Catholic country by devoutly Catholic parents. His father, James, put his faith before regaining his lost crown. At various points in his life, most specifically when Queen Anne died in 1714, it's very possible that if he had been prepared to renounce the Catholic religion, the Stuarts would have found themselves back on the throne. However, James could never bring himself to follow the example of the pragmatic and Protestant Henri of Navarre, who declared Paris to be worth a Mass and so became king of France.

Charles was not nearly so devout a Catholic as his parents. Lord Elcho famously said that his religion was 'to seek'. In 1750, the Prince even made a secret visit to London where, in the church of St Mary's in the Strand, he was received into the Protestant Church of England. Although he later returned to the Catholic Church, he was beside himself with rage and grief when his brother Henry became a Cardinal, believing the Stuart Cause's identification with Catholicism had contributed hugely to the failure of the '45. With Henry now a Prince of the Roman Catholic Church, Charles saw his chances of ever becoming Prince of Wales vanishing into the mist.

Charles's willingness to convert in 1750 begs the question as to why he did not do so in 1745 or before. The answer is that converting at that time would have had negative as well as positive effects on his Cause. He was hoping for support from France, a Catholic country. His father would have been both furious and heartbroken if his son had left the Catholic Church, and, at that time, James was a very powerful figure in his son's life. Charles's Catholic supporters in Britain, some of them men and women of high social status and potential influence, might also have turned against him.

There is another important point. Full of youthful idealism, the Prince may have thought his often-repeated guarantees of religious freedom for all would be enough to reassure those Protestants who worried about restoring a Catholic monarch. In his relaxed attitude to religion, he was light years ahead of the monarch and the government he sought to overturn.

Roman Catholics in eighteenth-century Britain were treated as worse than second-class citizens. They were seen as the enemy within, owing their primary allegiance not so much to God as to an Italian Pope, French priests and Spanish Jesuits. In 1701, the Act of Settlement made it impossible for the king or queen of Great Britain to be a Catholic or marry a Catholic. This law remains on the statute books today.

Even before that, in 1700, the Scottish Parliament had passed stringent laws which not only allowed the authorities to arrest any man suspected of being a priest, but also made it illegal for individual Catholics to attend Catholic church services. They were also banned from inheriting or even renting land and property, and were required to send their children to Protestant schools.

Being thrawn Scots as well as Catholics, they found ways around these laws. In country areas in particular, most Protestants and Catholics managed to rub along together without too much friction. Be that as it may, the priests who rode around Scotland – incognito, in ordinary clothes and never to be addressed as 'Father' for fear of giving the game away – were running enormous personal risks. If found or reported to have been saying Mass, or celebrating marriages, baptisms and funerals according to Catholic rites, they could be banished. If they returned to Britain, they could, in theory, be sentenced to death.

Their flock made up only a very small part of the Scottish population, between 2 and 3 per cent, and was widely scattered into the bargain. This was long before the waves of migrations of Irish Catholics to Glasgow and the west of Scotland. At the time of the '45, Scotland's Catholics were to be found keeping their heads down in the Borders, Galloway, the western Highlands and Islands, the central Highlands and upland Aberdeenshire and Banffshire.

Many of their descendants have discreetly kept the faith into our own times. In particular, the ornate Catholic churches and beautiful little chapels of north-east Scotland can take non-Catholic Scots by surprise. One of the most moving relics of the days of persecution is the seminary at Scalan, in the breathtakingly lovely and still remote Braes of Glenlivet. They trained what were called 'heather priests' there. After Culloden, the Redcoat garrison at nearby Corgarff Castle burned the place down. It was later rebuilt and is now permanently open to visitors of all faiths or none who choose to make the pilgrimage.

There is no doubt that Catholics in both Scotland and England had high hopes of what the restoration of the Stuarts would mean for them, or of how closely their faith intertwined with their politics. Looked at in the wider context, however, the Catholics were only one group among many who found in the Jacobite Cause a focus for their discontent with the status quo.

The church most strongly associated with the Jacobites was the Episcopalian. You could hardly be the latter without being the former. Because so many of them had remained faithful to the Stuarts, they refused to take the loyalty oath to the Hanoverian succession. This made them non-jurors, and, like the Anglican non-jurors in England, they too were persecuted.

Throughout the '45, Episcopalian meeting houses were ransacked and wrecked by Redcoat soldiers. Considering that the Episcopalians and the established Church of England were so close together in terms of doctrine and style of worship, this is more than a little ironic. Given how much the Episcopalians suffered because of their loyalty to the House of Stuart, it's also rather sad that their church is so often in Scotland today referred to as the English church.

The Church of Scotland, on the other hand, was as closely bound up with what was then called the Protestant Succession as the Episcopalians were with the Stuart Cause. Some Presbyterian ministers even took to the battlefield on the Government side, most notably at the Battle of Falkirk. Many more thundered fire and brimstone sermons from their pulpits at Jacobites, Catholics and Episcopalians. Charles Edward Stuart was a 'Pope-bred princeling' who had 'suck'd in malice with his milk' and stood at the head of 'banditti, thieves, robbers' and 'ragged ruffians of the north and savage mountaineers'.

Church of England clergymen spat out this vitriol, too. Some published their interminably long sermons as pamphlets, so that their dire warnings of the dangers posed by these malevolent Catholics might reach a wider audience than their own congregations. Consciously or not, the perceived external danger posed by the Jacobites was a great way of keeping people in line. Sitting round the campfire might at times be uncomfortably hot, but there were goblins and demons circling out there in the darkness, waiting to pounce.

The Duke of Cumberland issued a proclamation soon after Culloden telling lurking Jacobites that they should surrender themselves and their weapons to their nearest Church of Scotland minister. Yet despite keeping an inquisitive eye on their Jacobite neighbours before, during and after the event, many Presbyterian ministers refused to supply lists of those either well-affected or disaffected in their neighbourhood. Many, to their eternal credit, hid Jacobite fugitives and helped them to escape. Among those were the Reverend Lumsden and his wife, of Towie in Aberdeenshire.

When Charles Gordon of Blelack and his friend Jonathan Forbes managed to make it to Towie, the Lumsdens hid them for some time in the attic of the manse. Comments were made about the amount of food the household was going through. Mrs Lumsden blithely blamed it on the two pigs she was fattening for market. When the maids complained of seeing shadows in the night, she terrified them with tales of ghosts.

Another Charles Gordon, skulking near his home at Terpersie near Alford, was flushed out by a Redcoat patrol. They frogmarched him to the local minister and demanded he confirm Gordon's identity. The minister declined to cooperate. The soldiers then took him to his own home. His small children came rushing out, happily shouting 'Daddy! Daddy!', and thus unwittingly sealed their father's fate.

When it was all over, many Catholic priests were arrested and some were treated very brutally, although only one man of the cloth was tried for treason and hanged. The Reverend Robert Lyon was, of course, an Episcopalian.

16

BARDS & BROADSWORDS: THE BATTLE OF FALKIRK

DOWN THEY CHARGE, UNHESITATING, SWORDS EAGER HEADS TO SEVER

In a telling illustration of the interesting times through which they lived, two of Scotland's greatest Gaelic poets fought on opposite sides during the '45. In their mother tongue – the language of the Garden of Eden – they were Alasdair MacMhaighstir Alasdair and Donnchadh Ban Mac an t-Saoir. The English versions of their names are Alexander MacDonald and Duncan Ban MacIntyre, respectively.

Alexander MacDonald was in his mid-forties in 1745. A Clanranald MacDonald and cousin to the famous Flora, he was one of the first people to greet Charles Edward Stuart when he landed on the Scottish mainland on the shores of Loch nan Uamh in July 1745. So as to draw no undue attention to himself, the Prince was dressed very plainly that day. Unaware to whom he was speaking, it took one of Alexander MacDonald's clansmen to give him a black look before 'he began to suspect he was using too much freedom with one above his own rank'.

Charles obviously didn't mind the familiarity. He appointed Alexander MacDonald his Gaelic tutor and gave him the first military commission that he issued during the campaign. MacDonald served throughout the campaign as a captain in Clanranald's Regiment.

He was writing political verse well before Charles arrived. His '*Oran Do'n Phrionnsa*' ('A Song to the Prince') celebrates that longed-for event. Translated into English by John Lorne Campbell, it reads:

> O, hi ri ri, he is coming,
> O, hi ri ri, our exiled King,
> Let us take our arms and clothing,
> And the flowing tartan plaid.
>
> Joyful I am, he is coming,
> Son of our rightful exiled King,
> A mighty form which becomes armour,
> The broad-sword and the bossy shield.
>
> He is coming o'er the ocean
> Of stature tall, and fairest face,
> A happy rider of the war-horse,
> Moving lightly in the charge.

MacDonald wrote many more songs in the same vein: joyous, lively and bloodthirsty. In '*Oran Nuadh*' (or 'New Song'), he called for genuine commitment, not mere gestures:

> Let slashing, clashing blades of steel
> Answer skirl of chanters;
> When you've set the headlong rout,
> Far and wide re-echo
> Whistling blows, which smite to sever
> Bodies clean asunder;
> To flight they'll take in panic-spate,
> And ne-er again turn on you.
> There's many a man who'd drink the health
> Of our rightful ruler,

Provost Andrew Cochrane
of Glasgow. (Author's collection)

Contemporary map of the Battle of Prestonpans from
the *Gentleman's Magazine* of 1745. (Author's collection)

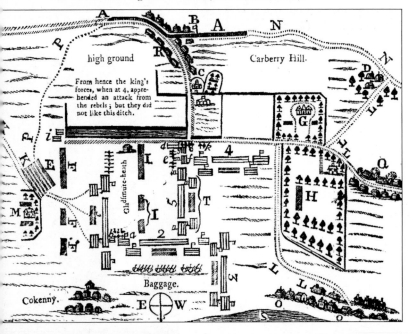

Reverend Alexander Carlyle.
(© The MacBean Collection,
Aberdeen University Library)

'The Battle of Prestonpans and
the Death of Colonel Gardiner'.
(© The MacBean collection,
Aberdeen University Library)

Colonel Gardiner's Monument and
Bankton House. (W.R. Totterdell)

John Campbell, cashier of
The Royal Bank of Scotland.
(Reproduced by kind permission
of The Royal Bank of Scotland
Group © 2008)

Bonnie Prince Charlie entering
the ballroom at Holyrood House,
with Cameron of Lochiel to his
right and Lord Pitsligo to his left.
(The Royal Collection © 2008,
Her Majesty Queen Elizabeth II)

John Roy Stuart's flintlock Doune pistol.
(© University of Aberdeen)

Dougal Graham, Skellat Bellman of Glasgow.
(Courtesy of Aberdeenshire Libraries
and Information Service)

Sir Stuart Threipland's medicine chest.
(Royal College of Physicians of Edinburgh)

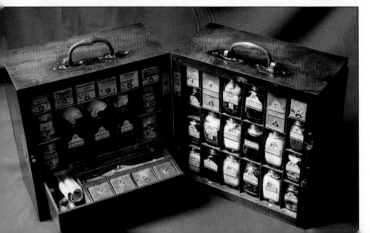

'Colonel Jack', John Cambell of
Mamore, later 56th Duke of Argyle.
(Author's collection)

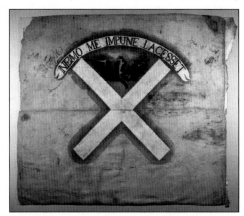

Angus Banner.
(Dundee Art Galleries and Museums)

ebell Gratitude', a contemporary
nt showing the death of Captain
ossett. (Courtesy of the Trustees
the National Library of Scotland)

Ranald MacDonald.
(© The MacBean Collection,
Aberdeen University Library)

Ranaldo MacDonald
de Bellfinlav in Benbeculâ, in Prœlio Cullodino (Ætatis
suæ 18) multo vulnere saucio, nudato, sub dio circiter horas
22 restabat; sed tandò humanitate (tunc temporis admodò
singulari) cujusd. Jacobi Hamilton, Hiberniensis, Vicarij de
Legione Cholmondlyacâ salvo evasit, d. vulneratos
Comilitones (referrîs tremisco) consultò lnactatos. Miserri-
mè jugulatos undig. videbat; adeò ut contaminata effet terra
cœlibo! Monst——Horrend:——Ingens.

Duncan Forbes of Culloden, Lord
President of the Court of Session.
(Author's collection)

Execution of MacDonnell of Tirnadris and other
Jacobite prisoners at Carlisle. (Author's collection)

Francis Farquharson of Monaltrie.
(Courtesy of the Trustees of the
National Library of Scotland)

Captain Andrew Wood's Halfpenny.
(In a private Scottish collection)

The above is a piece of the Prince's Garter. The ribbon on which he wore the order of the Garter. *see back of title-page.*

32. 6. 18

The above is a piece of that identical Gown, which the Prince wore for four or five Days, when he was obliged to disguise himself in a Female-dress, under the Name of Bettie Burk. A swatch of the said Gown was sent from Mrs McDonald of Kingsburgh according to her promise. See Vol. 1st, page 152.

The above is a piece of that identical Gown-string, which the Prince wore about him, when in the Female-dress. The above Bit I received of Miss Flora MacDonald's own Hands, Thursday, Nov 5th 1747, when I saw the [....] & had it about me. *Robert Forbes [....]*

The LYON in Mourning: Or,

A Collection (as exactly made as the Iniquity of the Times would permit) of Speeches, Letters, Journals, &c. relating to the Affairs, but more particularly the Dangers & Distresses, of

Vol: 3d.

Uimodo parebat subjecta Britannia Regi, Sactuti : terris, orbe vagatur inops!

1747.

Frontispiece of *The Lyon in Mourning,* Vol. 3.
(Courtesy of the Trustees of the National Library of Scotland)

The Culloden Memorial. (Author's photograph)

Smashing his wineglass on the hearth,
Cursing the usurper;
But honour now lives more in deeds
Than drinking toasts unnumbered,
A gill of blood shed on the moor
Excels wine drunk in gallons.

There were plenty of 'whistling blows' at the Battle of Falkirk, a subject which also exercised Duncan Ban MacIntyre's pen. He went there as part of the Argyle Militia, persuaded to stand in for his landlord in return for a cash payment and the loan of that reluctant gentleman's broadsword. When MacIntyre came home after the militia had been disbanded and claimed his fee, it was refused on the grounds that he had lost the sword.

Never annoy someone who has a way with words. Inspired to get his revenge by writing his first song, Duncan Ban complains of having had no leadership at the battle and declares: 'Ne'er again shall I go forward, / To the Whiggish King's assistance.' He has a go at his landlord, too – and his rotten sword.

Mighty iron with small edge to it,
That describes the sword completely,
It was pliant, starting, notchy,
And its neck was curved and crooked;
I was bruised on my thigh-side
After carrying it while marching,
Heavy as a pile of alder,
Woe to him who asked 'twere lucky.

Despite the unlucky sword, and unlike many on the Government side, Duncan Ban MacIntyre had the good fortune to survive the Battle of Falkirk.

The lead-up to the Jacobite victory at Falkirk was unpromising. After they left Glasgow on 3 January 1746, the Jacobite Army spent a few fruitless weeks trying to capture Stirling Castle. Given that this fortress sits on a sheer volcanic rock high above a flat plain – that's why they built it there – the enterprise was more or less doomed to failure.

Nor did it help that the engineer in charge of the operation was spectacularly incompetent. James Johnstone was one of many who offered a sarcastic summing-up of this Frenchman of Scottish extraction. A Chevalier of the Order of St Louis, no less, his name was Mirabelle de Gordon:

> It was supposed that a French engineer, of a certain age and decorated with an order, must necessarily be a person of experience, talents, and capacity; but it was unfortunately discovered, when too late, that his knowledge as an engineer was extremely limited, and that he was totally destitute of judgment, discernment and common sense. His figure being as whimsical as his mind, the Highlanders, instead of Monsieur Mirabelle, called him always Mr Admirable.

The stalemate at Stirling did the Jacobite Army's morale no good. Men were beginning to desert, sloping off home when nobody was looking. Edinburgh was once more in Government hands and thousands of troops were marching north to defend it, making the logical assumption that the Jacobites would try to recapture the Scottish capital. To prevent this, the Duke of Cumberland had called on the services of the ruthless general known as Hangman Hawley. Notorious for meting out harsh punishment to deserters from his regiment and soldiers under his command who had been found guilty of other breaches of military discipline, until he came north of the border it was his own men he strung up.

Determined to take the fight to the enemy and end the siege of Stirling Castle, Hawley marched out of Edinburgh. The Jacobites marched to meet him, which they did at Falkirk. As at Prestonpans, both sides did a considerable amount of manoeuvring before it all began. Alerted at three o'clock on the morning of 17 January that the enemy's drums were beating, Sir John Macdonald described what happened next:

> It was decided to march on the enemy, Lord George at the head of the Highlanders on the heights leaving the high road to Edinburgh on the left and came to a halt with his right resting on a small wall on a heather moor opposite the town of Falkirk and on his left the enemy's camp, who were quietly remaining in their camp until they saw us on the moors. Then they moved towards the town of Falkirk, and came towards us, crossing a ditch between the two armies, their cavalry on the left in front of the infantry. The cavalry rode up the slope in good order ready to charge our right, then composed of Macdonalds who waited for them, kneeling on one knee till they were within pistol shot, then firing their volley, attacked the cavalry sword in hand, and it fled by the right across our front line, receiving the whole of its fire. This charge took place before our second line was formed. Suddenly the Highlanders of the front line attacked and beat the enemy. (I could not well see this manoeuvre on account of the inequalities of the land.) At the same time our second line, consisting of Lowlanders, smitten apparently with terror took to flight. I therefore quitted the cavalry which would not listen to orders, to go and rally a large body of our people going off on the right. I met Sulivan and together we managed to halt them and bring them back.

The manoeuvre which Sir John could not see because of the lie of the land was vividly described, as ever, by James Johnstone:

> The Highlanders . . . discharged their muskets the
> moment the cavalry halted and killed about eighty
> men, each of them having aimed at a rider. The
> commander of this body of cavalry, who had advanced
> some paces before his men, was of the number. The
> cavalry closing their ranks, which were opened by our
> discharge, put spurs to their horses and rushing upon
> the Highlanders at a hard trot, breaking their ranks,
> throwing down everything before them and tramping
> the Highlanders under the feet of their horses. The
> most singular and extraordinary combat immediately
> followed.

Horribly, this 'singular and extraordinary combat' involved the Highlanders knifing the horses in the belly with their dirks before grabbing at the animals' riders, pulling them down by their clothes and stabbing them, too.

Because of this, Falkirk is notable as one of the few battles where infantry attacked cavalry rather than the other way around. Johnstone believed this ferocity was what defeated the Government forces, although he acknowledged that the high wind and heavy rain in which the battle was fought also had something to do with it.

In a grim foreshadowing of Culloden, where the men of the Jacobite Army had sleet driving into their faces, at Falkirk it was the Government soldiers who were face-on to the wind and rain. The pans of their musket also became waterlogged. Although they tried to adjust their position to compensate for the direction of the stormy weather, the Jacobites adjusted theirs in return.

Trying to determine what was going on, two opposing commanders moved forward and found themselves no distance apart. Each recognized the other, perhaps because they had both served in the British Army or perhaps because they'd had an encounter with one another at Prestonpans. One was John Roy Stuart. The Government officer rejoiced in the name of Shugborough Whitney. Sadly for him, he was not destined to rejoice in anything for very much longer.

'Ha!' called Whitney, 'Are you there? We shall soon be up with you!'

John Roy growled back in return: 'You shall be welcome when you come, and by God, you shall have a warm reception!'

A few moments later, Whitney was dead. Whether John Roy struck the fatal blow is not recorded.

Falkirk was a messy battle, both sides ending up with their ranks in complete confusion. In the driving rain and descending darkness, Donald MacDonell of Tirnadris, the hero of High Bridge, found himself captured by a group of Government officers who had failed to persuade their men to remain on the battlefield and were debating what to do next. As at Prestonpans, many of the soldiers under their command had simply turned and run. These included the soldiers of an English Redcoat regiment led by Scotsman and Highlander Sir Robert Munro, who abandoned their colonel to his fate. His brother Duncan was also killed.

In the midst of this horror of violence and storm, the men of the Glasgow and Paisley militias *did* stand their ground. At least 19 of the Glasgow men died, while a dozen of the militia men were wounded and a dozen more taken prisoner. These figures would have been higher but for the compassion of Andrew Wood of the Jacobite Army, the young shoemaker who had recently received his captain's commission from the Prince. He saw several of his friends and neighbours safely through the Jacobite lines and on their way home to Glasgow.

As darkness fell on the sodden battlefield, the confusion grew worse. It was quite some time before the Jacobite Army realized it had, in fact, won, the Government troops having abandoned the field. At about half past seven that evening, the Prince's army walked into Falkirk as the victors. It was the second defeat the Jacobite Army had inflicted on Government troops, and the humiliation was not to be forgotten.

A few days after the battle, Dr William Leechman, a professor at Glasgow University, sent a very polite letter to Lord Pitsligo asking him to intervene on behalf of four young men who had been taken prisoner at Falkirk: two Church of Scotland ministers and two divinity students. They had, Leechman wrote, only been spectators and had taken no part in the fighting. Acknowledging that they should have had more sense, the professor asked Lord Pitsligo if he could help return them safely to their friends and their congregations. In a P. S., Leechman passed on Mrs Leechman's 'most respectful Compliments to your Lordship'. They also asked to be remembered to 'our agreeable Guest and friend Mr Forbes', so if he and Lord Pitsligo had been billeted upon them while the Jacobite Army was in Glasgow over Christmas and New Year, relations must have been cordial. Given what we know of Lord Pitsligo's character, it's very possible that he backed up Cameron of Lochiel when he persuaded the Prince not to sack Glasgow.

Someone was, however, telling lies. At least one of the young ministers had not gone to Falkirk merely to watch the battle as a spectator. He had raised a militia from his parishioners at Beith and ridden at the head of it. Although they were stood down at Glasgow, the Reverend went on to Falkirk with every intention of fighting there on the Government side.

Lord Pitsligo's reply to the professor has been lost. He may well have been prepared to help the young ministers, but at least one of them released himself, escaping from his Jacobite gaolers after they locked him up in Doune Castle, north of Stirling. He was there with John Home, Alexander Carlyle's friend and fellow volunteer to Edinburgh's College Company, who had also gone to Falkirk as a volunteer to the Government forces. The young minister, only 23 at the time, was John Wotherspoon (also spelled Witherspoon). He was later to become one of the founding fathers of Princeton University and a signatory of the American Declaration of Independence.

Lord Pitsligo certainly responded to a request for help from another minister, the Reverend James Robb of Kilsyth. The clergyman was diplomatically away from home when 'my house had the Honour of such a Lodger for a night'. However, he used the connection of Lord

Pitsligo having stayed under his roof to plead for one of his parishioners, who had been taken prisoner by the Jacobites because they wrongly believed him to have stolen one of their horses. Alexander Forester was a Kilsyth man who 'kept the best public house upon the road and is known to several of your people who have a kindness for him'. Lord Pitsligo wrote back to say he would do what he could.

Despite their victory at Falkirk, the Jacobites decided to retreat north. It was the Highland chiefs who insisted on this, and their decision was questioned then as it continues to be questioned now. They argued that their men would go home whether they were given permission to or not and that it made sense to secure Inverness and make a stand on their own home ground.

To many, the failure to capitalize on the victory at Falkirk and retake Edinburgh remains one of those inexplicable Jacobite mistakes. James Johnstone always maintained the Government did not win the war so much as the Jacobites lost it.

Always preferring to travel light, the Jacobites abandoned much of the contents of the baggage train at Falkirk, including most of those shirts, jackets and stockings Glasgow had been forced to come up with. For the sake of his blood pressure, we have to hope Andrew Cochrane never found out.

Although the Prince ordered that Shugborough Whitney and the Munro brothers should be brought into Falkirk and buried in the graveyard, the rest of the dead were shown no such respect. The lashing rain which accompanied the battle was still pouring down 24 hours later when James Johnstone was dispatched with a sergeant – he does not tell us whether this was the redoubtable Thomas Dickson – and 20 men from the town back up the hill to the battlefield, with orders to bury the bodies and gather up the cannons which the Government troops had left behind in their haste and confusion.

It was another miserable night, windy as well as wet, and it was soon to become more unpleasant still, for man and beast alike:

The sergeant carried a lantern, but the light was soon extinguished, and by that accident we immediately lost our way and wandered a long time at the foot of the hill among heaps of dead bodies, which their whiteness rendered visible notwithstanding the obscurity of a very dark night. To add to the disagreeableness of our situation from the horror of this scene, the wind and rain were full in our faces. I even remarked a trembling and strong agitation in my horse, which constantly shook when it was forced to put its feet on the heaps of dead bodies and climb over them. However, after we had wandered a long time amongst these bodies, we at length found the cannon.

Along with Alexander MacDonald and Duncan Ban McIntyre, there was – at least – a third poet and songwriter at Falkirk. Ferocious in battle, John Roy Stuart could write ferocious words, too, but also those expressing the deepest of regrets. He was thinking of Culloden when he wrote of 'the white bodies that lie out on yonder hillsides', but he could as easily have been describing Falkirk.

The memory of still and silent white bodies haunted the imaginations of many men, as the reaction of his horse to the dead of Falkirk on that rain-swept night was to haunt James Johnstone for the rest of his long life.

17

LANCETS, SCALPELS & GOLF BALLS: THE MEDICAL MEN

COULD I BUT GET MY INSTRUMENTS . . .

The muster roll lists 14 men who were officially attached to their individual regiments in the Jacobite Army in the role of either surgeon or physician, and other sources greatly increase that number. Lord Pitsligo, for example, took along his own doctor, John Cruickshank of Fraserburgh. How Dr Cruickshank's other patients coped during his long absence on the campaign trail is not recorded, although we can probably guess they did not do so uncomplainingly.

The most famous Jacobite doctor was Archibald Cameron, brother to Cameron of Lochiel. Both sides in the conflict benefited from Dr Archie's medical skills, kindness and compassion. These were deployed right from the start of the hostilities. He treated the wounds of the Royal Scots who were so terrifyingly attacked at High Bridge by the 12 men and a piper under MacDonell of Tirnadris.

Captain John Scott of Scotstarvet was impressed, not having expected to be cared for at all by the wild mountain men. It was great PR for the Jacobites, especially when Captain Scott's own side, metaphorically speaking, shot itself in the foot by refusing to send out its own surgeons to tend to the Government soldiers wounded in the ambush.

The medicine of the time was not as primitive as might be thought. Although we might now grimace at the thought of expecting a child with a cold to sleep with a dead dormouse on his or her chest, many plant-based remedies well known in the eighteenth century still exist today, either in their herbal form or transformed into modern drugs. For example, a cure for headache was to prepare an infusion of willow bark, the original basis for aspirin. Inoculation against smallpox was well known and widely practised, especially in the Highlands.

There were travelling charlatans talking up their own somewhat dubious pills and potions, and the term 'quack' was in common use. In country areas especially, many people doctored themselves and their families. Good housewives would have a comprehensive medicine chest, as would many Church of Scotland ministers, ministering to their flocks' bodies as well as their souls.

There was a class distinction between surgeons and physicians, as some of the latter may think there still is. The physicians saw themselves as superior to mere sawbones. This may be why one medic in the Jacobite Army described himself as a 'gentleman surgeon'.

Surgery was pretty basic, largely due to the lack of any effective and predictable anaesthesia. This was a century before Sir James Young Simpson's wife came back into her dining room in Queen Street in Edinburgh's New Town, thinking it was time the gentlemen joined the ladies, and found her husband and his friends under the table. They weren't drunk but knocked out by chloroform, acting as their own guinea pigs to see how it would work.

Some operations were routinely performed. Trepanning was a procedure in which a hole was drilled into the skull to relieve pressure on the brain. Arms and legs too badly injured in accidents to be saved and which were threatening to turn gangrenous were amputated. Kidney and gallstones were excised. Mastectomies because of breast cancer were performed; later in the eighteenth century, the novelist Fanny Burney was one of those who endured such a procedure. All of these operations were carried out while the patient was fully conscious. Surgeons therefore had to be quick both in making cuts and in making decisions. Two doctors on the Government side at Prestonpans took one of those quick decisions, surrendering themselves so as to be able to help their injured comrades.

Too late for the battle but finding 23 wounded Government officers in a house near his own, these were the men Sandy Carlyle volunteered to help in whatever way he could. He knew one of them, Alexander Cunningham, 'afterwards the most eminent surgeon in Dublin', and surgeon to Ligonier's Dragoons during the '45. Unfortunately, neither Cunningham nor his colleague William Trotter, surgeon to Hamilton's Dragoons, had their medicine chests or their instruments. Those had been in the baggage train, which was now either somewhere on the battlefield or in the hands of the Jacobite Army.

Cunningham indicated one young Redcoat officer called Captain Blake. Slumped unconscious in an armchair, to Sandy Carlyle he looked to be on the point of death. On the chest of drawers next to him lay part of Blake's skull, 'two fingers' breadth and an inch and a half long'. Horrified, Sandy cried out that there was surely no hope for the man. Cunningham contradicted him, saying: 'The brain is not affected, nor any vital part: he has youth and a fine constitution on his side; and could I but get my instruments, there would be no fear of him.'

Volunteering to go and look for the missing medicine chests and instruments, Sandy was given a guard by the Jacobite Captain Stewart, a man who was 'good-looking, grave, and of polished manners'. The guard took him to Cameron of Lochiel. He, too, was courteous, ordering a soldier to help the student in his search. Although it was fruitless, by the time Sandy Carlyle returned, Cunningham and Trotter had been supplied with instruments by a local surgeon. All the casualties had their wounds dressed, and 'Captain Blake's head was trepanned, and he was laid in bed.'

Amazingly, Blake was up and dressed a few days later, well enough to invite Sandy to have a glass of wine with him. After expressing his surprise – 'Captain Blake, are you allowed to drink wine?' – the two young men 'drank out the bottle of claret'.

More than 50 years later, seeing Blake's name and address in a letter to a newspaper, Carlyle wrote to him. Blake wrote back, extending an invitation to his home in George Street, Westminster, 'where he hoped we would uncork a bottle with more pleasure than we had done in 1745, but to come soon, for he was verging on eighty-one'.

There is a second and wonderfully gruesome postscript to this story. When the *Gentleman's Magazine* subsequently noted the death of Captain Blake's daughter, it recorded that she had always worn a distinctive necklace. Set all round with diamonds, what hung from its chain was the piece of her father's skull hacked away from the rest of it at Prestonpans. *Souvenir de la guerre.*

Some doctors and medical students came out from Edinburgh to help tend the wounded at Prestonpans, too. One of the latter was Alexander Wood, just 20 years old at the time, and tall and lanky. In later life, he was to become Lang Sandy Wood, held in high esteem by his patients and his colleagues. He is allegedly the first man in Edinburgh ever to use an umbrella, the sensation of the 1780s.

One of the qualified doctors who went out to Prestonpans was Alexander Monro, the first generation of a medical dynasty. He, his son and his grandson, all named Alexander, dominated medical teaching at Edinburgh University for 150 years. They were known successively as Monro *primus, secundus* and *tertius.*

In September 1745 the concern of the first Alexander Monro was to get the wounded taken to the new Royal Infirmary, which had opened its doors only a few years before. It was a state-of-the-art facility, if still not quite finished. One of its very modern touches was a staircase wide enough to allow patients to be carried to the upstairs wards in sedan chairs.

Although a friend of the Government and supporter of the political status quo, Alexander Monro, like Charles Edward Stuart, made no distinction between Jacobite and Redcoat wounded. Many Jacobite soldiers also shared these feelings. They could fight as viciously as wild dogs, but once the battle was won they were more likely to take prisoners than finish off their defeated adversaries. Written evidence of this can be found in *The Lockhart Papers*. This collection of the extensive correspondence of Jacobite agent Sir George Lockhart also includes this eyewitness account of Prestonpans and its aftermath:

> I observed some of our private men run to Port Seton for ale and other liquors to support the wounded. And as one proof for all, in my own particular observation I saw a Highlander supporting a poor wounded soldier by the arms 'till he should ease nature and afterwards carry him on his back into a house and left him sixpence at parting. In all which we followed not only the dictates of humanity but the orders of our Prince in all.

In contrast, when the Jacobites left Edinburgh, and the garrison in the Castle sallied forth to retake it, some Redcoats are said to have rampaged through the wards of the new Royal Infirmary tormenting Jacobite soldiers recovering from wounds sustained at Prestonpans.

It comes as a surprise to learn from the doctors who, over the years, have naturally taken an interest in their Jacobite counterparts that the men who were wounded at Prestonpans were less likely to have suffered serious injuries if they had been on the business end of a broadsword, which were well known for inflicting wide but not deep cuts. Although these bled profusely, they usually left the internal organs unscathed. It was the sharpened scythes and Lochaber-axes which had sliced off heads and arms and legs that did the real damage. Serving your time in the army or navy was a traditional training ground for surgeons, giving them intensive experience of a wide variety of wounds. Dealing with the wounded of Prestonpans must have proved a steep learning curve.

Another of the well-known doctors on the Jacobite side was John Rattray, whom the *Oxford Dictionary of National Biography* describes as a 'golfer and physician'. The order in which these twin passions are placed is not insignificant. Born at Craighall Castle, Blairgowrie, he was the son of the Episcopalian Bishop of Dunkeld. Rattray's second wife was Mary Lockhart of Carnwath, who had two brothers fighting in the Jacobite Army. John Rattray played golf – rather a lot, it would appear – at Leith Links, and was prominent in the Company of Gentlemen Golfers, which drew up the first-ever rules of golf. In 1744, Rattray won the first-ever Open, making him 'captain of the goff', his trophy a silver club. He was unable to defend his title the following year due to the little local difficulty of what some people sarcastically referred to as the 'scuffle' at Prestonpans.

Asked to lend his medical skills to the Cause, Rattray came out to the battlefield with George Lauder, another surgeon. Both men subsequently accompanied the Jacobite Army into England and back north to Inverness, Rattray becoming on the way one of the Prince's two personal medical advisers.

The Prince's other adviser was Dr Stuart Threipland of Fingask, later Sir Stuart Threipland. His younger brother David, briefly a member of a Jacobite cavalry regiment, was killed at Prestonpans. Although he spent some time in exile in France after Culloden, Dr Threipland later returned to Edinburgh, had a successful medical practice and became a leading light of the medical establishment. Throughout the '45, he travelled with a medicine chest which it is believed the Prince gave him. It is today one of the treasures of the Royal College of Physicians of Edinburgh.

George Lauder later stated that he and Rattray had been kidnapped by the Jacobites after Prestonpans and pressed into service as army surgeons. When he made this statement, however, he was trying to get them both out of trouble, so it should be taken with a large pinch of salt.

There is no ambivalence in his description of the Herculean task which he and Rattray faced at Prestonpans. One thousand Government officers and men were prisoners, and many of those had sustained horrific and multiple wounds. There was Captain Poyntz, 'who had one very dangerous wound in his hand and five in his head'. Lieutenant Disney 'had his hand cutt of with a Sword and a shot in his shoulder, and must have dyed with loss of Blood in a very short time without assistance'.

A young Mr Bishop, whose father, Captain Bishop, had been killed in the battle, had 14 wounds. Lauder operated on him, dressed his wounds, gave him medicines – as he did to many others – without any hope of being paid for them. He 'even found him Lodgings, Nurses and Money for his Subsistence, he being an orphan destitute of Friends and Money'.

On the day of the battle and in the days which followed it, Lauder, Rattray and their six student apprentices treated three hundred men, operating when necessary, dressing wounds and amputating limbs which could not be saved. They were assisted by Hugh Hunter, who was the surgeon to Lord Loudoun's Regiment in the Government army.

They were also visited in Edinburgh by another paroled Government officer. He was Colonel Halkett of Lee's Regiment, and, after expressing his thanks for the care being taken of his men, he asked for a favour: could Lauder come with him to their camp, about seven miles from Edinburgh, where the young surgeon of Lee's Regiment was facing an agonizing dilemma?

There were three or four men whom he thought needed amputations, but he felt he did not have the experience necessary to make that irrevocable decision. He also doubted his ability to perform the operations. Lauder went out to see the young surgeon and the soldiers under his care, decided that the amputations were not required, brought the men into Edinburgh and saw that they were taken care of until they recovered from their wounds.

At the Battle of Falkirk, Lauder showed the same care and compassion, looking after Captain Fitzgerald and Captain Halley of the Redcoat Munro's Regiment. Not only did he treat their wounds, he also insisted that, for the sake of their health, they must not be taken along with the Jacobite Army as prisoners on its retreat north, effectively winning the Redcoat officers their liberty.

Cameron of Lochiel sustained a minor wound at Falkirk, a musket ball hitting his heel. As his brother Archie was helping him, he too received an injury. Elsewhere on the wind-lashed battlefield, two other brothers were in a similar situation. The Cameron brothers made it safely away. The Munro brothers did not.

Dr Duncan Munro was another Edinburgh surgeon and another supporter of King George, as was his brother. Sir Robert Munro of Foulis was a soldier in command of one of the English regiments which fought at Falkirk. Duncan had gone along to be on hand if his brother were to be wounded.

Their fears were not unfounded. When his men broke and ran, leaving their colonel to his fate, Sir Robert was viciously attacked by six Highlanders at once. Over 60 and famously fat, it seems likely that they recognized him and immediately targeted him as a fellow Highlander fighting, as they saw it, on the wrong side. Robert and Duncan Munro were cousins of Duncan Forbes of Culloden. Robert's son Harry wrote a couple of days later to let the Lord President know what had happened:

> I think it my duty to acquaint your Lop of the deplorable situation I am in. The Engagt. Between the King's troops and Highlanders on Thursday last, w'in a mile of Falkirk, proves to me a series of woe! There both my dear father & uncle Obsdale wer slain! The last, your Lop knows, had no particular business to go to the Action; but, out of a most tender love & concern for his Brother, cou'd not be dissuaded from attending him, to give assistance if need required.
>
> My father, after being deserted, was attacked by six of Locheal's Regt, & and for some time defended himself with his half Pike. Two of the six, I'm inform'd, he kill'd; a seventh, coming up, fired a Pistol into my father's Groin; upon wch falling, the Highlander wh his sword gave him two strokes in the face, one over the Eyes & another on the mouth, wch instantly ended a brave Man.
>
> The same Highlander fired another Pistol into my uncle's breast, & wh his Sword terribly slashed him ... My father's Corpse was honourably interred in the Church-

yd of Falkirk by direction of the E. Of Cromertie & the McDonalds, all the Chieffs attended his funerals.

Despite being buried with respect in the kirkyard in Falkirk, their deaths, especially that of the unarmed non-combatant Dr Munro, were considered by the opponents of the Jacobites as a war crime and an atrocity.

A few doctors and physicians died in captivity. Others were captured and condemned but then acquitted. Whether their status as healers helped secure their release is not clear. James Stratton of Berwickshire was captured while acting as surgeon to the short-lived Jacobite garrison at Carlisle. One of those medical men who was acquitted, at his trial it was said that although he had not carried arms, he was as a surgeon 'a party to levying war'.

Dr Archibald Cameron, Cameron of Lochiel's brother, escaped capture after Culloden but was betrayed on a covert trip back to Scotland. In 1753, he was tried and hanged in London for his part in, as he wrote, 'what they term *Rebellion*'. Imprisoned in the Tower of London, he complained that he was not allowed pen, ink or paper, 'not even the use of a knife with which I might cut a poor blunted pencil that had escaped the diligence of my searchers'. He wrote with the blunt pencil anyway, on a few scraps of paper, anxious to set the record straight before he died, and gave what he had written to his devoted wife, Jean. Interestingly, he confirms the speculation about his brother having saved Glasgow from being plundered by the Jacobite Army, giving himself some credit, too:

> My brother and I did service to the town of Glasgow, of which the principal gentry in the neighbourhood were then, and are to this day, very sensible, if they durst own the truth. But that might be construed as disaffection to a Government founded on and supported by lies and falsehood.

He immediately goes on to say that he saved Kirkintilloch from a similar fate, his brother's men being 'justly incensed against it for the inhuman murder of two of Lady Lochiel's servants', a story which does not seem to be recorded elsewhere.

Dr Archie's devotion to his Prince was undimmed. Charles remained affable, courteous and courageous. As one of his aides-de-camp, the doctor declared that the allegation of an order issued to the Jacobite Army the day before Culloden to give no quarter to their enemies was a 'most unjust and horrid calumny' put about 'by the rebels under the command of the inhuman son of the Elector of Hanover, which served as an excuse for the unparalleled butchery committed by his orders in cold blood after the unhappy affair of Culloden'.

The day before his execution, Archie Cameron wrote to his eldest son. It's a letter filled with love and a father's last words of advice, enjoining the boy to serve God, his King, his Prince and his country, and to care always for his mother, brothers and sister. His pencil was so blunt he had to break off in the middle of sending his 'love and dying benediction to my children, affection to my brother's children, best wishes to all my friends, and hearty compliments to all my good acquaintance and ...' That's where the letter finishes.

He had no money to leave his son, but he sent him his steel shoe-buckles along with a verbal message that even if he'd had gold buckles he would not have sent them, for he had worn the steel ones while he was skulking with the Prince: 'For as steel is hard and of small value, it therefore an emblem of constancy and disinterestedness.'

Archie Cameron was hung, drawn and quartered at Tyburn, which occupied the site at the end of Oxford Street where Marble Arch now stands.

The doctor was the last martyr to the Jacobite Cause.

18

GENTLEMEN, TAKE NO NOTICE! ROBERT STEWART OF GLENLIVET

HE ACKNOWLEDGED THAT HE WAS BEGINNING TO FEEL 'A LITTLE WEAK'

While the bulk of the Jacobite Army marched into England at the end of 1745, other detachments of it had held onto northeast Scotland. Despite the heavy snows of the winter of 1745–6, the Jacobite line in Aberdeenshire was a shifting one.

With a few notable exceptions, such as James Moir of Stoneywood, who came out for the Prince, by and large Aberdeen was for the Government and Aberdeenshire was for the Jacobites. At the end of September 1745, it had been John Hamilton, factor to the Duke of Gordon in Huntly, who marched into Aberdeen and proclaimed King James VIII and III the rightful king. When the Provost of Aberdeen declined to drink James's health, John Hamilton threw the glass of claret he was proffering in the provost's face. One of those left behind in England to garrison Carlisle three months later, he was to pay dearly for his moment of triumph.

Out in Aberdeenshire, Jacobite sentiment was strong. Many of the country people were Episcopalian, a good number were Catholic and the farmers bitterly resented the Malt Tax. Imposed by the London

Government after the Union, it was a perennial source of discontent throughout Scotland. The fishing villages around the Buchan coast were considered to be Jacobite to a man – and woman.

A letter from a Government spy complains bitterly about women spreading information useful to the rebels. If a troop of soldiers came into Strathbogie – present-day Huntly – at six o'clock at night, writes the anonymous correspondent, the Jacobites in Peterhead would know about it by eight o'clock the following morning. The Aberdeenshire women were well organized. When a piece of news was received, each would pass it on to two friends who would head off in different directions to spread it further. Clearly exasperated, the spy mentions 'Barbara Strachan, the Jackobite, post mistres off Buchan', whose job made it easy for her to traverse the countryside passing on information: 'Thers not one place of it all she travels not once a-week, when business is throng.'

Not everyone in Aberdeenshire was well-inclined towards the Jacobites. Cosmo, the 3rd Duke of Gordon, declared himself for the Government, but his attitude was highly ambivalent. It's hard to resist the conclusion that, like Lord Lovat, he was sitting firmly if uncomfortably on the fence, waiting to see which way the wind would blow. His brother Lord Charles Gordon was actively involved on the Government side, while their younger brother Lord Lewis Gordon threw his lot in with the Prince:

> O, send Lewie Gordon hame,
> And the lad I daurna name!
> Though his back be at the wa',
> Here's to him that's far awa'!

Unfortunately, reality falls sadly short of the romantic image of the dashing young Lord Lewie, just 20 years old at the outbreak of hostilities. Being Jacobite in sentiment could be a long way from being prepared to take the huge risks involved in leaving your family and going for a soldier. Lord Lewie was incensed, and not a little embarrassed, by the difficulties he encountered while raising his regiment.

Any hopes ordinary men might have had of keeping their heads down until it was all over were shattered by his recruitment tactics. He himself wrote, chillingly, 'We have been obliged to use great threatenings', and, indeed, 'Come with me or I'll burn your cornfield' must have been a powerfully persuasive threat to a farmer struggling to make a living and feed his family. It's one still remembered with a shudder by some descendants of those farmers today.

At the end of December 1745, Lord Loudoun, commander of the Government troops in the north of Scotland, sent a force west and south from their base in Inverness in an attempt to retake Aberdeen, Aberdeenshire and Banffshire. The MacLeods, led by their chief, who had declined to support the Prince, marched through Cullen, Banff and Oldmeldrum. A detachment of pro-Government Munros, Grants and Mackenzies came by Keith and Strathbogie, successfully forcing the two Jacobite garrisons there to retreat to Aberdeen.

Led by Captain George Munro of Culcairn, a professional soldier, Lord Loudoun's troops met up with the MacLeods at Inverurie. The surrounding countryside being largely Jacobite, Culcairn was scared of losing men if he sent out patrols. His knowledge of Jacobite movements was therefore non-existent.

To add to his woes, Lord Loudoun had seriously underestimated the strength of the Jacobite garrison in Aberdeen. Over a thousand men marched out of the city at nine o'clock on the morning of Monday, 23 December. One column, commanded by Gordon of Avochie, approached Inverurie along the King's High Road through Kintore and another led by Lord Lewie Gordon crossed the Don to make a flanking movement, approaching the town from the east.

It was a high-risk strategy. Both Jacobite detachments might have to ford a river in full view of the enemy – Lord Lewie and his men the Urie, and Gordon of Avochie the Don. It was always a vulnerable position in which to put yourself. If this pincer movement were to work, surprise and timing would be crucial.

Jacobite organization was magnificent. Patrols and scouts were everywhere, ensuring that the enemy remained unaware of the approaching danger. At Kintore, the minister was arrested and houses along the main road were occupied to prevent any word being sent to Inverurie.

MacLeod of MacLeod and Munro of Culcairn were taken completely by surprise when the shout went up that a large Jacobite force was advancing down the hill from Keith Hall, behind Inverurie. MacLeod and Culcairn were positioned just outside the town, slightly to the north and west of the small but steep man-made hill known as the Bass of Inverurie, halfway between the Urie and the Don. Only now did they realize that their enemies were approaching the fords of both rivers.

While the Redcoats tried, fruitlessly, to decide which ford to attack, Lord Lewie's French adviser, Major Cuthbert, took the initiative. With a group of chosen men, he waded through the icy waters of the Urie and took up a position in the shelter of the Bass and the nearby churchyard. It was four o'clock on a winter's afternoon, and daylight was fading fast. Accurate shooting was difficult.

Gordon of Avochie and around 60 of his men came across the Don and joined up with Lord Lewie and Major Cuthbert. The two Jacobite detachments then advanced, shooting as they went. Their enemies were forced to retreat. They went right through Inverurie, Old Rayne and Huntly, not stopping to rest till they had crossed the Spey. The engagement had lasted less than 20 minutes, and Aberdeenshire and Banffshire were once more in Jacobite hands.

A little less than two months later, after the Prince's army had taken the fateful decision at Falkirk to head for Inverness, the Jacobites chose to leave Aberdeen. They did so just as the weather began to close in again. John Daniel, the gentleman volunteer from Lancashire, gives us a graphic description of how bad conditions were:

> When we marched out of Aberdeen, it blew, snowed, hailed, and froze to such a degree, that few Pictures ever represented Winter, with all its icicles about it, better

than many of us did that day; for here men were covered with icicles hanging at their eyebrows and beards; and an entire coldness seizing all their limbs, it may be wondered at how so many could bear up against the storm, a severe contrary wind driving snow and little cutting hail bitterly down upon our faces, in such a manner that it was impossible to see ten yards before us. And very easy it now was to lose our companions; the road being bad and leading over large commons, and the paths being immediately filled up with drifted snow.

Anyone who knows the A96 Aberdeen to Inverness road and the Glens o' Foudland – still to be dreaded in a warm car in snowy winters today – will immediately get the picture.

John Daniel and his horse made it through because he remembered he had a bottle of spirits in his riding-coat pocket. He drank some, and it warmed him up just fine. On the point of finishing it off, he thought of 'my poor horse, which seemed to be in as bad a situation as myself, being one of a delicate and tender breed'. He knew his mount 'could drink beer', so he poured some of the spirits into his hat, diluted it with a handful of snow, and presented it to the beast. It did them both the world of good.

As the Prince and his men drew nearer to Inverness, Lord Loudoun retreated north to Dornoch, and Lord President Duncan Forbes took himself off to Skye. Old Fort George, on the hill by the river Ness where Inverness Castle now stands, was besieged by the Jacobites and fell. A Frenchman helping to blow the castle up afterwards was clearly of the school of Mr Admirable, the incompetent engineer who had failed to help the Jacobites capture Stirling Castle. The Frenchman at Inverness, wondering why a charge had not gone off, bent over it at exactly the wrong moment, and went with it to kingdom come. Although the trip up into the air and back down to earth gave his dog a gammy leg for ever afterwards, it survived the explosion.

Fort Augustus was also besieged and also fell, while Fort William withstood a siege which lasted weeks and was not taken. The redoubtable Sergeant Molloy was, however, persuaded to surrender Ruthven Barracks. He did so with considerable dignity and only after he had negotiated and been guaranteed humane treatment for his men.

At Moy Hall, the home of the equally redoubtable 'Colonel' Anne Mackintosh, yet another variation on the famous 12-men-and-a-piper trick saved Prince Charles from a much larger Government force led by Lord Loudoun, again trying and failing to get the better of the Jacobites.

Meanwhile, Lord Pitsligo was acting as Jacobite Governor of Elgin in Morayshire, trying, as he always did, to be fair to everybody. As the Prince's army was by now running short of just about everything, horses, carts and oatmeal were being requisitioned from wherever they could be found:

> There are fifteen horses more sent from this place today
> . . . which is such a burden upon this Country that a
> great many of the Farmers will be incapacitated from
> tilling their ground and their familys consequently
> reduced to Beggary. I'm sure it was allways the Prince's
> intention (since hardships must be) that none should
> suffer beyond their proportion.

When Cullen House on the Moray coast was plundered by the Jacobites, Lord Pitsligo was mortified. The troop of soldiers sent there was supposed only to bring in some supplies from the estate but decided to take revenge on the house's owner, the Earl of Findlater, who was most definitely a friend of the Government. They rampaged through the house, stealing what they could easily carry away and wrecking what they couldn't. Mirrors were smashed, feather cushions and mattresses were ripped open, their contents strewn on the floor, and all the dust and feathers were mixed up with 'jelly and marmalade and honey and wet and all sorts of nastiness'.

Worried that the entire Jacobite Army would get a bad name or that there might be revenge attacks on the homes of the Prince's supporters, Lord Pitsligo wrote to Sir Thomas Sheridan, one of Charles's closest advisers:

> As this unlucky affair will make a noise over all the world, I would humbly suggest that the Prince should testify his dislike of such proceedings in some publick Declaration. I have this moment spoke with a Servant of Lord Findlater's who tells the dammages are far beyond what I imagine, for there is hardly a bit of Glass left in the windows.

Sheridan wrote back the next day to say that of course the Prince 'is concern'd at any damage done in a country which he came not to oppress but set free', but that unfortunate things happen in war.

The Duke of Cumberland and his army arrived in Aberdeen on 27 February 1746, ten days after the Jacobites had left it. The hostile weather shut them in there for six weeks. Cumberland stayed in the Guest Row, in the building behind present-day Union Street now known as Provost Skene's House. He and his men used their time in Aberdeen well, practising a new bayonet drill.

This involved ignoring the enemy soldier standing straight in front of you and instead thrusting your bayonet diagonally at the man standing to his left. He would be holding his targe in his left hand and have his sword arm upraised, thus leaving the right-hand side of his body unprotected.

The technique required absolute trust in your comrades, whom you had to hope and pray were covering your own vulnerable left side. Rehearsed over and over again in Aberdeen, this new drill was to have devastating consequences for the Jacobites at Culloden, although perhaps as much because it fostered trust among the Redcoats as for its effectiveness.

When the snow began to ease off towards the middle of March

1746, the Duke of Cumberland sent out a scouting party. In response, the Jacobites in Strathbogie thought it wiser to retreat to the place which the Hanoverian General Bland spelled 'Forcoborse'. Following his quarry to Fochabers was likely to be more successful with some local help. Captain Alexander Campbell, leading 70 of his own men and 30 riders of Kingston's Light Horse, found the assistant minister at Cairnie Kirk, halfway between Huntly and Keith, more than willing to act as a scout.

The minister, who was also a Campbell, suggested hiding the troop of soldiers along the Cairnie burn, 'that being a very hollow burn with a good deal of planting in it' – which it still is today. If the minister came back pursued by Jacobites, the Campbells and the cavalrymen would be in an ideal position to mount an ambush.

The Reverend Campbell found no immediate sign of the Jacobite Army, allowing the Government troops to advance to Keith. They entered the town in the early morning of 19 March, waking up the inhabitants by breaking windows and looting shops. It did not take the Jacobites long to get wind of what had happened. It's more than likely that someone, furious at the plundering, slipped quietly out of Keith that misty morning and headed for Fochabers.

Later that day, the Jacobites decided to send a party of about 50 men back to Keith. Most of them were from John Roy Stewart's Edinburgh Regiment, which included quite a few Banffshire men, perhaps newly raised from the local area. The officer in charge of the expedition was Captain Robert Stewart of Glenlivet, a man who was very much on home territory. Accompanied by a small troop of cavalry, they marched openly towards Keith. A few miles before they reached the town, however, they veered off to the east, crossed the Isla and skirted the town in a wide arc. All of this was designed to make it look as though they had come in from the direction of Huntly and thus were not foes but friends.

Midnight was striking as they approached the town – and their ruse was successful. On being challenged by the Campbell sentry, Robert Stewart answered without hesitation: 'We're friends, Campbells.' The sentry, greatly relieved, approached them with a broad smile and told them he was glad to see them. He was sure the enemy was close at hand.

He was immediately seized, flung to the ground and held there. 'Make a sound,' he was told, 'and you'll get a dirk through your heart.' Captain Stewart led his men to the churchyard, where the main body of the Campbell militia was encamped. Forty-five years before, the infamous James Macpherson, who went so rantingly to his death after playing a tune on his fiddle below the gallows tree in Banff, had been captured here in Keith kirkyard.

The shooting started, the Campbells returning fire vigorously from the windows of the old kirk. 'Yield, or die!' yelled Robert Stewart. A few minutes later, twisting round to check the positions of his men, he was struck by a musket ball. It passed right through him, entering his left shoulder and coming out at the right.

Dismayed, his men lowered their weapons. 'Gentlemen,' Captain Stewart said briskly, 'take no notice!' The shooting went on for about half an hour before the Campbells surrendered. The skirmish at Keith, however, was not yet over.

The Jacobite cavalry had surrounded the town, a much smaller place then than it is now, and was fighting a desperate action against the dragoons of Kingston's Horse. Fearing they were about to be overpowered, Jacobite Major Nicholas Glasgow sent an urgent plea for help to the kirkyard.

Ignoring his wound, which was bleeding profusely, Robert Stewart immediately led some of his party down the street. There was a short, sharp engagement which ended disastrously for the Redcoats, with nine of them killed and the rest captured, along with their thirty horses.

Stewart lined the prisoners up two abreast, with his own men guarding them on either side, and prepared to march them back to Fochabers. Only then did he acknowledge that he was beginning to feel 'a little weak'. His wound may well have saved his life, as it prevented him from being at Culloden.

Some of the Campbells managed to escape and hide down by the Auld Brig of Keith. Next to it there is an enormous stone slab which even today could conceal a dozen men. Under the stone, there is a large cavity which is said to lead to caves which run backwards under the old toll-road, the present-day A96. The spot was always known afterwards as the Campbells' Hole.

The front line had been redefined yet again, but General Bland was philosophical, saying, 'I hope we shall soon have our revenge with interest.'

Culloden was less than a month away.

19

THE YEAR OF THE PRINCE: BITTER SPRING

OUR MEN ATTACKED WITH ALL THE FURY IMAGINABLE

As Jacobite Governor of Elgin, Lord Pitsligo had to field bad-tempered demands for safe conducts from people at whose tables he had probably dined and to whom he was very possibly related. Anne, Lady Innes, wrote to him nine days before Culloden demanding to know why she was being refused a pass to go to Aberdeen. Her health was such that she felt the need to 'retire from amidst these unhappie Confusions'. Since she was prepared to give him her oath that she would not tell the Government commanders anything about the Jacobite forces, she could not understand why Lord Pitsligo would not permit her to travel. He answered her frankly but in his usual gentlemanly fashion:

> To deal openly with your Ladyship, I did hear you had declared your intention of going to Aberdeen, which would not be permitted in any army, and accordingly I thought it was required of me to hinder your journey. But now that you are pleased to assure me in the most binding terms that you are to give no Intelligence, I

shall no longer oppose it. This, I reckon, will serve for a
Pass the length of Speyside, my Commission extending
no farther . . .

The next day, Lord Pitsligo received a letter from Lord John
Drummond, telling him the Duke of Cumberland had spent the
previous night at Oldmeldrum. Had he perhaps been aware when he
granted Lady Innes her pass that it might all too soon not be worth
the paper it was written on?

Two days later, he was sent word from Fochabers that he and
the men stationed at Elgin had to be ready to move at 'a moment's
warning' – which, indeed, they did, decamping that very same day
through Forres and on to Nairn.

The Duke of Cumberland was right behind them. He and his
'vermine of Red Quites' crossed the Spey unopposed. Why the
Jacobites did not attempt to prevent them from doing so has often
been debated. There were plans to guard the fords, but they came
to nothing, perhaps because the river was very low. If it was easy to
cross, then the soldiers could come over quickly in large groups and
would not be in the vulnerable position they would have occupied
had the river been high and flowing fast. Cumberland recorded that
he 'only lost one Dragoon and 4 women drowned'.

The duke was relaxed enough to rest his men at Garmouth
overnight before marching on to Nairn. As the Government army
came in at one end of the town, the Jacobite rearguard were leaving
it at the other. Cumberland stayed in Nairn, and his army set up
camp.

The Prince had made his base at Culloden House, just outside
Inverness. In his choice of headquarters, there must have been an
element of getting his own back on the Lord President, Duncan
Forbes of Culloden, who had done so much to organize the effort
against him. Orders issued by Charles to all his officers 'civil and
military' are worded in a somewhat ambivalent way:

> These are requiring you to protect and defend the House
> of Colloden and furniture from any insults or violence
> that may be done by any person or persons, except such
> Orders as are issued by us. Given at Inverness, 28th Feb.
> 1746. By His Highness's Command.

It seems Charles reserved the right to 'insult' Culloden House if he saw fit.

The two armies were now only twelve miles apart. All that remained was to choose a time and a place. It was Colonel O'Sullivan who selected the ground, a piece of high moorland up the hill from Culloden House. One of the things he liked about it was the moor road which ran through it and is still there today, albeit now covered over. Battles were usually fought on or near a road: it made it easier to run the cannons in.

Lord George did not like the ground at all, not so much because it was very marshy in places as because it was flat and featureless, and he thought it would allow the Government troops to use their cannons to 'anoy the Highlanders prodigiously before they could possibly make an attack'. His opinion was shared by many in the Jacobite Army. This may be why Lord George's suggestion of a night march and surprise attack on Cumberland's camp at Nairn was, at first, greeted with enthusiasm. The Prince's army had, after all, most successfully surprised the Government army at Prestonpans.

The Jacobite Army set off at seven o'clock in the evening of Tuesday, 15 April, leaving fires burning in their own camp so the ships in the Royal Navy flotilla which had just dropped anchor out in the Moray Firth would suspect nothing. The night march ended in failure in the small hours of the following morning. It was dark and wet and men kept getting lost in the woods, the army not making the progress it had to if it was to reach Nairn before daybreak.

After a series of furious arguments between Charles and his colonels, the attempt was abandoned. All it had achieved was to exhaust men who were already weary and hungry. The Prince himself rode into Inverness when he returned from the night march to see what provisions could be got, but in the twenty-four hours before the battle was finally fought, most of the rank and file had been issued with a ration of one biscuit and some not even that.

Later that morning, on Wednesday, 16 April 1746, the Marquis d'Eguilles, French Ambassador to the Jacobites, asked if he might speak with Charles in private. When they were alone together, d'Eguilles threw himself at the Prince's feet and begged him not to give battle that day. Half the men had gone off to Inverness in search of something more to eat than that one biscuit. The Marquis suggested they retreat to Inverness, get the men fed and rested, and take Cumberland on the next day. When d'Eguilles found he could not change the Prince's mind, he returned to his own lodgings in Inverness to burn his papers.

No formal council of war was held at Culloden House, but opinions were expressed. Lord George, MacDonald of Keppoch and Cameron of Lochiel liked neither the chosen ground nor the idea of giving battle when the men were so tired and hungry, but the Prince was determined. The choice was soon taken out of everyone's hands.

A man who had fallen asleep in the woods on the way back from Nairn and been abruptly roused from his slumbers rushed in with the news that the Duke of Cumberland and his army were approaching and had been sighted a mere four miles away. Duncan Forbes' household staff, obeying the laws of Highland hospitality even under these most difficult of circumstances, were about to serve the Prince and his officers a midday meal – a roast side of lamb and two chickens. Charles had angrily rejected the food, as Colonel O'Sullivan reported:

> 'Eat,' says the Prince, 'I can neither eat nor rest while my poor peoples are starving,' & imediatly gave orders to get meat of one kind or other for the men, who were in great need of it. All hands were at work to distribute among them proportionably what there was, liberty given to kill Cows, wch the Prince wou'd give bills for;

necessity has no law, on those occasions, but poor people
they had not time to dresse their Victuals.

Charles flung himself out of Culloden House into the chilly April
day, ordering the bagpipes to play so the men lying asleep in the
surrounding fields would hear the call to arms. Riders were sent to
Inverness to gather up anyone who might be there. James Johnstone
was one of them.

After the failure of the night march, he had gone back to his
lodgings, the only thought in his head to get some sleep. He was out
of luck. When he 'had already one leg in the bed', he heard 'the drum
beat to arms and the trumpets of the picket of Fitzjames sounding the
call to boot and saddle'.

Meanwhile, the Prince had ridden up onto the moor and was
moving among the men beginning to line up there. He reminded
them of their great victories at Prestonpans and Falkirk. Telling them
they had the same swords now as they did then, he asked one man to
hand him up his blade. 'I'll answer this will cut off some heads & arms
today,' Charles said before returning it to its owner. 'Go on my Lads,
the day will be ours & we'll want for nothing after.' He himself was
carrying a pair of silver-mounted pistols and a leather targe decorated
with a silver head of Medusa.

John Daniel, the gentleman volunteer from Lancashire, estimated
when he watched the Redcoats advance 'like a deep sullen river' that
there were around 11,000 of them to 4,000 Jacobites. The National
Trust for Scotland in their visitor centre at the battlefield quotes the
numbers at 7,500 and 5,500 respectively, but other authorities dispute
those figures, putting the Government army at 9,000 and the Jacobite
at 5,000.

John Daniel was proud to be carrying 'a curious fine standard',
which he had acquired at Falkirk from Colonel Gardiner's leaderless
dragoons. Its motto read, '*Britons, strike home!*' He clearly found this
entirely appropriate. After all, apart from a handful of Hessians on the
Government side and the French and Franco-Scots on the Jacobite

side, the men lining up across the moor road in both armies were indeed Britons.

As he approached the Jacobite lines, the Duke of Cumberland briefly stopped his own troops and made a short speech, addressing them as 'Gentlemen and Fellow-Soldiers':

> I have but little Time to address myself to you; but I think proper to acquaint you, That you are instantly to engage in the Defence of your King and Country, your Religion, your Liberties, and Properties; and thro' the Justice of your Cause, I make no Doubt of leading you on to certain Victory. Stand but firm, and your Enemies will soon fly before you.

The Government soldiers did stand firm, and, because of where they chose to do so, they moved the fight forward from where the Jacobites wanted it to be. This deprived them of what had been seen as the protection of the stone dykes on either side of their line. These enclosed the fields belonging to Duncan Forbes' estate.

The epicentre of the battle has long been thought to be around the cairn which now commemorates it. Recent investigation by Dr Tony Pollard and his team from Glasgow University's Centre for Battlefield Archaeology and the physical evidence they found moves it closer towards the modern visitor centre, on the rise above the dip of the Well of the Dead. This is where the fighting was at its most intense.

The battle started shortly after one o'clock with an exchange of artillery fire. Some people described as 'gentlemen from Inverness' had come out to view the event as spectators, reportedly even carrying picnic baskets with them. It wasn't an ideal day for eating out of doors: bitterly cold with wintry showers. In any case, when a few cannonballs thudded into the ground in front of the would-be voyeurs of death and injury, they beat a hasty retreat.

Although it was the Jacobites who opened fire, the Government artillery was far superior. Among it were two batteries of three coehorn mortars apiece. Lighter than other cannons, they could be lifted and repositioned to deadly effect as a battle developed. They also fired up and over, so could be placed behind troops who would keep their gunners safe from attack.

Terrible damage was done to the Jacobite front line as the men there stood waiting for the order to advance. It never came. Lachlan MacLachlan, a young aide-de-camp to the Prince, had his head taken off by a cannonball on his way to deliver it.

As the Jacobites had edged forward and come through and beyond the dykes which should have protected both flanks of their army, their front line had stretched out and opened up. There were shouts of 'Close up! Close up!' John Roy Stuart's Edinburgh Regiment, initially stationed in the second line, moved forward to help plug the gaps.

Unable to bear the punishing bombardment any longer, the right wing of the Jacobite Army surged forward and charged. They were led from the centre of the front line by Alexander MacGillivray of Dunmaglass at the head of the Clan Chattan regiment that his cousin, Anne, Lady Mackintosh, now famously known as 'Colonel' Anne, had raised. The Camerons, Stewarts of Appin, Frasers and the Atholl Regiment were also heading across the field, as was Francis Farquharson of Monaltrie and the men of Braemar and Deeside.

As they ran forward through artillery fire, swirling smoke and sleety rain, they swerved to the right, probably to avoid boggy ground and find firmer footing beside the moor road, which also curved to the right. This made it difficult for the men of the Atholl Regiment to fire their muskets, for fear of hitting friends rather than foes.

Those who were not felled by gun and artillery fire and made it to the Government front line flung themselves in a great mass against the regiments on its left wing, inflicting heavy casualties on the men of Barrell's Regiment. One who survived described the horror of it:

> It was dreadful to see the enemies' swords circling in the air, as they were raised from the strokes! And no less

> to see the officers of the army, some cutting with their
> swords, others pushing with the spontoons, the sergeants
> running their halberds into the throats of the enemy,
> while the soldiers mutually defended each other, and
> pierced the heart of his opponent, ramming their fixed
> bayonets up to the socket.

Cameron of Lochiel was drawing his sword from his scabbard to attack Barrell's when he was hit by grapeshot in both ankles. Two of his faithful clansmen carried him out of danger.

To the right of Barrell's Regiment stood the men of Sir Robert Munro's Regiment, who had broken at Falkirk. At Culloden, they stood their ground, but the force and fury of the Highland charge was so great the Jacobites succeeded in pushing through them to the Government second line. At this point, the Jacobites found they had been outflanked. From their right, they were being shot at by the men of James Wolfe's Regiment, which had been moved forward and around from the Government second line for that purpose.

Although it may be questionable how effective the much-practised bayonet drill could be in such a melee, General Huske was heard to bark out an order to 'Give 'em the bayonet!' Surrounded and trapped, it's estimated that 700 Jacobites were killed in a few minutes by the guns and bayonets of the Government soldiers.

Many had been shot down before they reached the Government front line. Clan Chattan was slaughtered. Alexander MacGillivray of Dunmaglass fell, never to rise again, by the Well of the Dead. Those who survived retreated back across the field.

Back there, another outflanking manoeuvre was being put into action. The Campbells of the Argyle Militia had been ordered to demolish the stone dykes of the Culwhiniac enclosure on the right wing of the Jacobite Army to allow mounted dragoons to ride through them. It was the Campbells who emerged from them first, rushing out to attack the fleeing clansmen.

They were unaware that they were also taking on the experienced marksmen and French Army officers of the Royal Ecossais, the troops who had landed at Montrose in November 1745 under the command of Lord John Drummond. They rode to the rescue of the Jacobite foot soldiers, covering them and allowing many to get away in safety. Again, archaeological investigation of skulls found on the battlefield shows that several of the Campbells coming through the breach in the stone dykes were shot between the eyes. Colonel Jack Campbell of the Argyle Militia wrote to his father from Inverness that night:

> I have just time to informe you that we have gain'd a compleat victory over the rebels. The main body of my corps was order'd as a guard for the baggage by which means I had no oppertunity of seeing the affair distinctly and must therefore differ writing particularly till another oppertunity. Part of our men were engag'd and behav'd incomparably well amongst whom Ballimore was kill'd and Achnaba dangerously wounded.

The death of Colin Campbell of Ballimore had been foreseen a few days before by a 'half-witted' Campbell clansmen who was reputed to have the second sight. 'What,' he asked, 'can be the reason that my captain has a stream of blood running down his brow?' Ballimore is said to have heard of his question and laughed it off.

A handful of heroes from John Gordon of Avochie's Strathbogie Battalion, men from Huntly, Banff and Fochabers and the countryside in between, did not leave the field but stayed where they were, firing from behind a dyke to cover the retreat of others. They were set upon by the Redcoats and 'killed to a man'.

Over on the left wing of the Jacobite Army, the fight was also raging. James Johnstone was there, momentarily stunned when his friend Donald MacDonald of Scotus fell dead beside him. Clan chief MacDonald of Keppoch died, too, the spot now marked by a small memorial stone.

The Irish Picquets, professional soldiers from the Irish Brigade of the French Army, covered the retreat of Keppoch's fleeing clansmen and lost 100 of their own men in the process. A group of Jacobite gunners stayed at their post behind another of the stone walls enclosing the Lord President's fields. Four cannons and three coehorn mortars were moved in to attack and annihilate them.

Although James Johnstone tells a story of a troop of Government cavalry clearing a path to allow a group of Highlanders to leave the field, other horsemen cantered after fugitives and cut them down. Kingston's Horse took their revenge for being humiliated at Keith, their General Humphrey Bland later commended by Cumberland for having 'made a great slaughter'.

Realizing victory was theirs, the Redcoat infantry advanced across the field, killing many of the wounded Jacobites where they lay. One of the Government soldiers later described himself and his comrades as looking 'like so many butchers', their white gaiters stained red from the blood they were splashing over each other.

One who escaped their attention was Ranald MacDonald of Belfinlay. Not long after the battle had ended, he saw a coach with ladies in it. As it passed, the coachman 'made a lick at me with his whip as if I had been a dog'. One of the women in the coach was the Countess of Findlater, whose house at Cullen had been plundered by the party of Jacobites of whom Lord Pitsligo had been so ashamed. Thanks to the humanity of a Captain Hamilton in the Government army, Belfinlay lived to tell the tale – but before Hamilton rescued him, the young man lay all night in agony on the freezing field.

Satisfied with what had been achieved within the space of an hour, the Duke of Cumberland sat down to eat a late lunch on the large boulder which now stands at the crossroads just east of the battlefield. He had observed much of the action from there, and it has been known ever since as the Cumberland Stone. Some of us will remember being encouraged by our fathers and mothers to spit on it.

Some people now work very hard to convince themselves and the rest of us that at Culloden, more Scots fought for Cumberland than for Charles Edward Stuart. This remarkable idea does not stand up to scrutiny or, indeed, five minutes' concentrated thought.

The current party line is that the '45 was not the last battle between Scotland and England – Auld Enemy 1, Auld Caledonia 0 – but the final act of a Scottish – and British – civil war. In which case, it would be interesting to know where the Englishmen in the Jacobite Army were. Apart from the Manchester Regiment and, at Culloden, John Daniel, Jem Bradshaw and – perhaps – some of the deserters from Prestonpans, they're not there.

Curiously, many who advance this point of view are latter-day Jacobites, their sympathies entirely with the Prince and his men. They usually also assert that the Scots in the Government army were Lowlanders. Undaunted by the facts, this neat theory presents the '45 as a struggle between noble, doomed Highlanders and quisling Lowlanders failing to support the Stuart Cause in favour of kowtowing to English masters for the sake of the main chance and advancement within an ever-more powerful Great Britain. According to this scenario, the souls of the Highlanders rose above such cynical materialism.

The argument that more Scots fought on the Government side than on the Jacobite stems from the presence of Scottish regiments within the Government army. Of the twenty-two regiments that the Duke of Cumberland commanded on the day, four were Scottish: the Scots Fusiliers, Lord Mark Kerr's 11th Dragoons, the Royal Scots and the Campbell Argyle Militia, led by Colonel Jack. (Although led by a Scotsman, Munro's Regiment on the Government side, still bearing the name of Sir Robert, who had died at Falkirk, was an English one. As was often the custom in those days, it was known by the name of its colonel. Three months on, and with the British Army at full stretch, his successor as their commander had not yet been appointed.)

Despite its name, the Royal Scots may not have contained as many Scotsmen as might be thought. Wedded though we are now to the concept that a regiment recruits from a specific geographical area, this was not the case in the eighteenth century. Regiments beat up for recruits wherever they were stationed. The evidence of Colonel

Gardiner's letters to his wife shows that he and his nominally Scottish regiment, for example, were stationed at various times in different towns in various parts of England. Furthermore, in the period before Culloden, the Royal Scots had been on an extended tour of duty in Ireland. Colonel Dick Mason, curator of the Royal Scots Regimental Museum in Edinburgh Castle, believes that in the mid-1740s there were probably many Irishmen within the regiment's ranks. At this time, of course, Ireland, both north and south, was ruled over by the British monarch.

Cumberland had other Scotsmen under his command, largely officers serving with English regiments, although this cuts both ways. It's an unscientific form of analysis, but it does seem unlikely that Captain Norton Knatchbull of the Scots Fusiliers was one of the Kirkintilloch Knatchbulls; likewise Lieutenant Guildford Killigrew of Lord Mark Kerr's 11th Dragoons.

All the Redcoat officers – English, Scottish, Irish or Welsh – were at Culloden because they were professional soldiers and it was their duty to be there. The political opinions they held privately were another matter. There were rumours that several of them – and not only the Scottish officers – were secretly more inclined towards the House of Stuart than the House of Hanover. Even the aged General Guest at Edinburgh Castle had been suspected of having Jacobite tendencies.

In this connection, Cumberland's decision to initially set Colonel Jack Campbell of Mamore and his Campbell clansmen to guard the baggage train, well behind the Government lines, is interesting. The duke may have felt that a locally raised militia would not be as effective in a full-scale battle as a regiment of regular soldiers. Or, given that he never really trusted Scots, he may not have wanted to run the risk that the Campbell clansmen would be tempted to go over to the other side. Despite traditional clan enmities, there were a good many Campbells within the ranks of the Jacobite Army.

With the exception of the Irish Picquets and the Franco-Scots, that 5,000-strong army was overwhelmingly Scottish. If we do the sums for the four Scottish regiments within the 9,000-strong Government army – albeit having to assume the numbers in each were similar – we come up with a figure of 1,350 Scots: around 15 per cent of the total. We then have to make another assumption, although it seems a fair one: that the Scottish officers in English regiments were more than balanced out by the Irish private men in the Royal Scots. With around 5,000 Scotsmen in the Jacobite Army, then, and 1,350 on the Government side, the arithmetic of the claim that more Scots fought against Charles Edward Stuart than for him simply does not add up.

The neat theory that the '45 in general and Culloden in particular was a struggle between noble, doomed Highlanders and Englishmen aided and abetted by quisling Lowlanders also does not hold water for two reasons: first, substantial numbers of Highlanders weighed in on the Government side, and second, there were numerous Jacobite supporters in the Lowlands and elsewhere.

The forces ranged against the Jacobites included the men in Lord Loudoun's Regiment, the Black Watch and the Independent Highland Companies. (These local militia were first raised to police the Highlands shortly after the Stewarts were deposed back in 1688. Duncan Forbes of Culloden and Lord Loudoun did much to encourage their activities in support of the Government during the '45.) The chiefs of the MacLeods and the MacDonalds of Skye, who had declined to support the Prince, both commanded their own pro-Government companies. There were Munros and Grants who supported the Government side, too, carrying out policing actions and assisting in the hunt for Charles Edward Stuart and other prominent Jacobites after Culloden. Again, the private politics of the men may well have been anti-Government and pro-Jacobite, as in the case of Gaelic bard Duncan Ban MacIntyre. When it came to hunting the Prince and those other fugitives, many in these militias showed, as Sir Alexander MacDonald of Sleat put it, that they 'felt a certain delicacy' about fighting or persecuting their own relatives and friends. Then again, there were others who used their positions in the militias to settle scores arising from inter-clan rivalries, grudges and disputes.

On the other side of the conflict, there were Jacobites to be found outwith the Highlands, notably in the Orkney Islands and scattered throughout southern Scotland. These were not only the gentlemen volunteers. Although they more than did their bit, they were not a huge group in terms of numbers, as the men of Angus, Aberdeenshire and Banffshire were. Geographically, much of this area might be in the north of Scotland but culturally it is and was Lowland. Indeed, the Jacobite Army referred to this 20 per cent of their fighting men as the 'Lowland Regiments'. As historian Henrietta Tayler put it: 'It takes a real Scot to know that Aberdeen is Lowland!'

In the reprisals which were soon to be taken against the Jacobites and the communities from which they came, Aberdeenshire, Angus and Banffshire were not excluded. A proclamation was read in churches throughout Aberdeenshire: 'Wherever arms of any kind are found, the house, and all houses belonging to the proprietor, shall be immediately burnt to ashes.' And if any arms were discovered underground, 'the adjacent houses and fields shall be immediately laid waste and destroyed'.

These threats were carried out in many places. Despite that, the year after Culloden, a Government spy filed a report to his political masters, saying, 'Tho' the people of Aberdeenshire are all quiet at home', they were 'as much disposed to rebellion as ever'.

All that was yet to come. Having finished his lunch, Cumberland moved on to the next task. Out on the moor, at least 2,000 men lay dead. Estimates put the Government fatalities at 50, although, again, there is some debate about this. The estimates of 1,500 Jacobite dead are considered more reliable.

At four o'clock that afternoon, the duke led his victorious army into Inverness.

20

THAT OLD WOMAN WHO SPOKE
TO ME OF HUMANITY:
DUNCAN FORBES OF CULLODEN

WHEN THIS AFFAIR BLOWS OVER, AS I HOPE IT SOON WILL . . .

Dr John Rattray, the Edinburgh surgeon who had treated the wounded after Prestonpans and subsequently marched with the Jacobites as one of the Prince's two personal physicians, had been on the abortive march to Nairn. Exhausted after its abandonment, he went back to Inverness and threw himself 'upon the top of a bed'.

He woke up only after the Battle of Culloden had started. Hurrying towards the sound of gunfire, he met Sir John Macdonald, one of the Seven Men of Moidart. Reining in his horse, Sir John issued an impassioned warning:

> For God's sake, Mr Rattray, go not, for they are hewing
> down all before them, and are giving no quarters, and
> it is not possible you can be safe. You had therefore best
> return with me to Inverness, for as I am a French officer
> I have nothing to fear, and I am to give myself up as
> their prisoner. And as you attended the army only as a

surgeon, you have as little to fear, and therefore you may
deliver yourself up with me.

Sir John was wrong: Rattray had a great deal to fear. Standing in the
streets of Inverness, he was passed by a Redcoat officer he knew, Lord
Cathcart. Cathcart looked at him and shook his head, saying, 'Mr Rattray,
I am sorry to see you there; I am afraid it will go hard with you.'

The Government officers who followed Cathcart into Inverness
thought so, too, and they were much more hostile. 'Damn' you, Sir,'
one of them said, 'we know who you are, the Pretender's physician. If
anyone hang, you shall.'

Rattray and his colleague Lauder both ended up being flung into
the Old High Church of Inverness, on the site now occupied by
Leakey's Bookshop, crammed in with other Jacobite prisoners. It's
from here we get the chilling story that 'all their instruments and
everything that could be useful to the wounded were carefully taken
from them'. The two surgeons were distraught, surrounded by injured
men who gazed at them with pleading eyes and begged for help, but
able to do very little for them.

Jem Bradshaw of the Manchester Regiment, who had fought at
Culloden under Lord Elcho, confirmed this story in the speech he
gave from the scaffold before his execution:

> I was put into one of the Scotch kirks together with a
> great number of wounded prisoners who were stript
> naked and then left to die of their wounds without the
> least assistance; and tho' we had a surgeon of our own, a
> prisoner in the same place, yet he was not permitted to
> dress their wounds, but his instruments were taken from
> him on purpose to prevent it; and in consequence of
> this many expired in the utmost agonies.

Bradshaw also used his dying speech to passionately deny the claim
that the barbarities of Government troops in the aftermath of Culloden

were in response to a Jacobite order to show them no mercy. He called it a 'wicked malicious lie, raised by the friends of usurpation in hopes of an excuse for the cruelties committed in Scotland, which were many more and greater than I have time to describe'.

It's impossible not to compare the mercy the Jacobites showed to their enemies with the heartless cruelty meted out to them after Culloden. Those among them who had a French commission were treated very differently. The Marquis d'Eguilles wrote home to his 'cher papa': 'Nous sommes prisoniers de guerre, mais traités à l'angloise [sic], c'est-à-dire, très-bien. La ville d'Inverness est notre prison.'

There was as yet no Geneva Convention, but there was an understanding that prisoners of war should be treated in a humane way. The French and Franco-Scottish prisoners were allowed to move about Inverness, and the wounded among them, as the Marquis wrote to the French Foreign Office, were being treated by Monsieur Barret, a French surgeon.

The Duke of Cumberland went so far as to give d'Eguilles 1,000 guineas for the subsistence of the Frenchmen. The Marquis also noted that the duke's secretary, Sir Everard Falkener – the Frenchman impressed to find they had a mutual friend in Voltaire – was treating the French officers with great politeness. The Marquis d'Eguilles was relieved that he and his compatriots were being treated well, or, as he had put it, 'in the English way'. The English way was to be entirely different when it came to those regarded as Scottish Rebels. They were to be treated as less than human. It took great courage to run the gauntlet of the English soldiers who were 'hewing down all before them', let alone think of trying to help any wounded men left alive on the battlefield. Yet three women did.

Anne Leith, a young widow from Aberdeenshire, went out to Culloden with her friend Mrs Stonor and a maid known only as 'Eppy' on the very afternoon of the battle. With their baskets full of bandages, the three women did what they could for wounded and dying Jacobites. In the days and weeks which followed, Anne Leith went round the cellars and churches and makeshift prisons in Inverness with more bandages and as much bread as she could buy. She got herself arrested but kept on doing it. A few brave souls in Inverness matched her courage.

One was the Provost of the Highland burgh, John Fraser, and his predecessor in that office, John Hossack. When they ventured to suggest to Hangman Hawley and General Huske that the treatment of the defeated might be more humane, they were evicted. One of Hawley's officers kicked John Hossack downstairs and out into the street.

Another who spoke up for humanity was Duncan Forbes of Culloden, Lord President of the Court of Session and friend, par excellence, of the British Government and the British state. In 1745 he was a widower of 57, a fond and affectionate father to his only son, and desperately worried about Scotland. Convinced that the country's future progress and development would be best served by remaining in the Union with England, he also passionately believed that prosperity would bring Scotland lasting peace.

A lawyer to trade, his position as Lord President of the Court of Session gave him power and authority far beyond the legal sphere. The Secretary of State for Scotland at the time was the Marquis of Tweeddale. His Edinburgh home was in Tweeddale Court at the foot of the Canongate, but he spent much of his time in London, leaving the day-to-day administration of Scotland in the hands of the Lord President and other senior legal officers and members of the nobility.

Duncan Forbes also divided his time between two homes, his elegant mansion on his estate at Culloden and his Edinburgh home at Musselburgh. He had a good intelligence service wherever he was, dispatching discreet people who listened more than they spoke to bring the news back to him. After the debacle of what might have become the '44, when the Protestant Wind wrecked the French ships waiting to sail to Scotland, he was well aware of the renewed rumours circulating at the beginning of 1745, that Charles Edward Stuart was planning a landing in Scotland.

The Rebellion of 1715 had touched Duncan Forbes both professionally and personally. Despite being a rising young lawyer, he had rejected the request to conduct the prosecutions of those found guilty of treason afterwards. He was a humane man and also believed the rigorous punishments he was likely to be involved in handing down would be counterproductive. In this, as in so many other things, he was to be proved right.

By the time of the '15, he was already a young widower and a single parent, his wife Mary Rose of Kilravock having died within a year or two of their marriage. They were childhood sweethearts and a large stone still to be seen and sat on in Culloden Woods is traditionally said to be where he proposed to her.

When Mary died, Duncan's mother stepped into the breach. Mary Innes was a strong-minded woman who loved her family dearly. Sadly, she died when Duncan's son was only six or seven. His father wrote to a female friend: 'Tomorrow my aged mother will be buried. If you saw my little destitute brat, you'd at once love and pity him.'

The funeral of Mary Innes did not go entirely according to plan. In an age of heroic claret drinkers, Duncan Forbes and his brother John more than earned their place. Receiving family and friends at Culloden House that morning, so much wine was drunk it was only when the mourners arrived at the kirkyard that they realized they'd left the coffin and the much-lamented Mary Innes back at the house.

The same woman friend to whom Duncan Forbes wrote about his son's grief at losing his grandmother was concerned that he drank too much. Reminding him that in a flirtatious moment he had once told her he was all hers, she told him to take better care of her property. A few days before his 'justly honoured' mother's death, he told his friend she hadn't quite got it right:

> I never said more than that I was as much thine as I was
> my own, thus thou canst not pretend to more than one
> half of me, and I do assure you that as I have been no
> more than half drunk since I saw thee, I took a special

care that my own half of myself should be drunk while
yours remained in perfect sobriety.

For Duncan Forbes, a different kind of liquid refreshment posed huge dangers. This was a 'vile drug' and a 'contemptible beverage' – and it was tea that he had in his sights. Although his spluttering condemnation of this innocuous drink sounds comical to modern ears, there was a serious side to his complaint. There was a tax on tea, unless, of course, you bought it from one of the free-trading gentlemen who dropped anchor in secluded coves all round the Scottish coast. Huge amounts of revenue were being lost.

The Lord President was concerned that people should pay their taxes because the money was needed to help foster trade and industry. He was directly involved with the project which, in 1729, invited 21 French weavers to come to Edinburgh to teach the locals how to make cambric. Where those weavers once lived and worked and handed on their skills is now Picardy Place in Edinburgh's New Town.

Picture, then, his horror when his dream of a productive, prosperous and peaceful Scotland was shattered by the arrival of Charles Edward Stuart. Using his many contacts, Forbes had done his utmost in the run-up to the '45, when everyone knew something was afoot, to persuade people not to throw in their lot with the Jacobites. Lord George Murray, the commander of Prince Charles's army, was one of them. The Lord President and Lord Lovat were also friends.

Duncan Forbes was equally active once battle commenced. Working in Inverness with Lord Loudoun, he helped raise and organize the pro-Government militias. Despite his stern and sincere disapproval of those who supported the Prince, after the defeat at Culloden he was deeply concerned by the maltreatment of the prisoners.

In this, he was out of step with the Duke of Cumberland, Hangman Hawley and many among the British Army's senior command. 'That old woman who spoke to me of humanity' is how Cumberland described him. When Forbes continued to remonstrate, mentioning 'the laws of the country', Cumberland's reply was blunt: 'The Laws of the Country, my Lord? I'll make a brigade give laws, by God!'

This interchange is reported in *The Lyon in Mourning,* the unashamedly Jacobite compilation of evidence put together by another member of the Forbes clan, Episcopalian Bishop Robert Forbes. There is no record of a family relationship between him and the Lord President.

The Bishop repeats a conversation he had with 'an honest Whig' who said the cruelties perpetrated by the Redcoats under Cumberland and others would be the best recruiting sergeant the supporters of the House of Stuart would ever have. Whether this honest Whig really existed or was a device for Bishop Forbes to tell his tale might be open to doubt. What is clear is the respect felt by Bishop Forbes and many other Jacobites for Duncan Forbes of Culloden, who got very little reward from his own side for the huge effort he put in to maintain the status quo.

Apart from begging the Duke of Cumberland to show mercy to the defeated Jacobites, Duncan Forbes asked for only one personal favour for a personal friend. The Lord President loved his golf, so much so he would even play when there was snow lying on the links at Musselburgh. At the same time as Dr John Rattray was the captain of the Company of Gentlemen Golfers, Duncan Forbes was the secretary. Forbes asked Cumberland to free his golfing friend. When Rattray said he wasn't leaving Inverness without his colleague George Lauder, Forbes asked Cumberland to let him go, too. Although the two of them were arrested again once they returned to Edinburgh, and subsequently taken to London and held prisoner there, they were released for good six months later.

Duncan Forbes did not live long after the Battle of Culloden, dying at the beginning of December 1747. It is deeply ironic that the name of his home has become synonymous with the barbarous cruelty towards his fellow Highlanders which so distressed this humane man.

Like Colonel Gardiner of Prestonpans, his death was mourned as much by his enemies as by his friends. Friend and foe alike said they knew what Duncan Forbes had died of: a broken heart.

21

You Have Killed Your Prince:
Roderick Mackenzie

He chose to die with sword in hand

Inverness was a terrible place to be in the vicious days which followed Culloden. One description of the horror comes from a young Scotsman called David Calder, who was a gentleman volunteer with the Government army, serving under Lord Loudoun. Loudoun and his men had not made it to Culloden. Fearing that his father, Benjamin, might have heard otherwise, David wrote to him from Inverness a week after the battle to reassure him that his son was safe and well. David Calder also told his father that he was 'heartily sorry for the Gentlemen of our Country that has been so foolish as to Concern in this unluckie rebellion'. Quietly but clearly distressed, the young man also commented on the treatment being meted out by the victors to the vanquished: 'Nothing is seen amongst us but continuell processions of prisoners and wounded, all meeting houses destroyed, dead bodies exposed to dogs and ravens, none allowed to burry them.'

One of the first things Cumberland did was to root out the deserters from the Government forces who had gone over to the Jacobites at Prestonpans and elsewhere. This was summary justice at its most brutal. Gibbets were erected in the streets of Inverness, and 36 men were hanged. One of them was Malcolm Forbes of Pitcalnie, the great-nephew of Duncan Forbes. The Lord President's prediction that the young man would find himself a halter had been all too accurate.

As Malcolm Forbes swung from the gibbet, an English officer thrust his sword into the body, declaring that 'all his countrymen were traitors and rebels like himself' – and a Scottish Redcoat officer took extreme exception to what he had just said. This man drew his sword and demanded satisfaction for the insult to his country. At this point, the dispute flared up to include everyone else around them. James Johnstone heard the story while he was on the run after Culloden:

> whilst they fought, all the officers took part in the quarrel
> and swords were drawn in every direction. At the same
> time, the soldiers, of their own accord, beat to arms and
> drew up along the streets, the Scots on one side and the
> English on the other, beginning a very warm combat
> with fixed bayonets.

Only when someone sent for the Duke of Cumberland to smooth the ruffled feathers of the Scotsmen under his command did this Scottish–English conflict stop.

In the following days and weeks, the hundreds of Jacobite prisoners crammed into the gaol, the High Kirk and every other lockable space in Inverness were shipped south. The officers and a few of the private soldiers were to be tried for treason. Many more of the latter were to be transported to the West Indies to work as indentured servants. This was to be the fate of almost 1,000 Scots, including around 50 of the women and children who had followed the Jacobite Army into England and not made it back.

Cumberland was quite clear in his own mind that Jacobite prisoners must not be left in Scottish prisons or tried in Scotland. His fear was that their fellow countrymen would be too lenient with them. As

Duncan Forbes of Culloden and Provosts Fraser and Hossack had learned, 'leniency' was not a word in the duke's own vocabulary.

This 'horrid and unnatural Scotch Rebellion' had to be stamped on with all the force at his command. There was a war going on in Europe and he wanted to get back to it, although it would be a handsome feather in his cap if he could capture Charles Edward Stuart before he left North Britain and its troublesome inhabitants. Government patrols fanned out across the Highlands and Islands, looking everywhere for Charles. They called it the 'summer's hunting'.

Roderick Mackenzie – Rorie to his friends and family – had been in the Jacobite cavalry, serving in the elite Lifeguards under Lords Elcho and Balmerino. In his mid-twenties, he was tall, blond and handsome. The same age and physical build as the Prince, he bore a slight facial resemblance, too.

Skulking in Glenmoriston after Culloden, Rorie Mackenzie came face to face with a troop of Redcoats. Faced with a hellish choice, he raised his sword and fought, preferring a quick death to imprisonment, trial, almost certain condemnation and the prolonged and brutal agony of being hung, drawn and quartered.

Outnumbered as Rorie Mackenzie was, the outcome was inevitable. Yet he snatched one triumph from the jaws of death. With his dying breath he called out an impassioned reproach to the Government soldiers who had ended his life: 'You have killed your Prince!'

Standing looking down at the dead body, the Government soldiers could not be sure if they had or not. None of them had ever seen the Prince. What they did know was that there was a £30,000 reward on Charles Edward Stuart's head – and they took that literally. They buried Roderick Mackenzie's body near where he had fallen, but they cut off his head first, put it in a bag and carried it to Fort Augustus.

Alexander MacDonald of Kingsburgh was a prisoner there at the time, accused of having given succour to the enemy by helping the Prince as he fled from the Western Isles to Skye. A Redcoat officer came to him and asked if he would recognize the head of the Young Pretender if he saw it. Kingsburgh replied that he would, adding –

with a nervous joke – as long as it was still attached to Charles's body. The officer then asked if he would recognize it if it wasn't attached. Did an uncomfortable pause then ensue, both men finding it difficult to meet the other's eyes?

When Kingsburgh told the English officer he doubted he would recognize the head without the body, the man went away and no more was said. The nightmarish story does not end there. The head was pickled in spirits to preserve it and taken to London, in the hope that some imprisoned Jacobite might be persuaded or coerced into identifying it. To whom it was presented for such identification is not recorded. Imagining the possible scenarios sends a shiver down the spine, as does wondering what eventually happened to this now gruesome relic.

This story seems always to have been well known in the Glenmoriston area, one of the many tales handed down from one generation to the next in the tradition of the Highlands. Despite that, Bishop Robert Forbes, compiler of *The Lyon in Mourning*, was still unsuccessfully trying to get the exact details 13 years after that death and hideous decapitation in Glenmoriston. The Bishop was told by one of his correspondents that Roderick Mackenzie's mother and sisters were still living in Edinburgh, but no letter to or from them appears in the *Lyon,* his collection of accounts and eyewitness reports of the events of 1745–6.

Versions of the story set down in writing much later state that Roderick Mackenzie had been a student at Edinburgh University and that his father was a goldsmith. The Incorporation of Goldsmiths of the City of Edinburgh does have a record of a Roderick Mackenzie in 1726. The Roderick Mackenzie of the Glenmoriston story is described in the muster roll of the Jacobite Army as a 'Timber merchant. Fisherow'– which could be the famous Fisherrow in Musselburgh.

James Johnstone tells the story in his memoirs, with evident admiration for Roderick Mackenzie's bravery and quick wits. As two young Edinburgh gentlemen in the Prince's army, it's very likely that they knew one another. Johnstone does not say whether he heard the story while he was on the run after Culloden or whether he was told it many years later. Judging by Bishop Forbes' requests for information, it does appear to have been doing the rounds. There is at least one contemporary written source. Dougal Graham, the Glasgow Bellman, told the story of Roderick Mackenzie's death like this:

> Rod'rick MacKenzie, a merchant-man,
> At Ed'nburgh town had join'd the Clan,
> Had in the expedition been,
> And at this time durst not be seen,
> Being sculking in Glen-Morriston,
> Him the soldiers lighted on,
> Near about the Prince's age and size,
> Genteely drest, in no disguise.
> In every feature, for's very face,
> Might well be taken in any case,
> And lest he'd like a dog be hang'd,
> He chose to die with sword in hand,
> And round him like a mad-man struck,
> Vowing alive he'd ne'er be took:
> Deep wounds he got, and wounds he gave,
> At last a shot he did receive,
> And as he fell, them to convince,
> Cry'd, Ah! Alas! *You've kill'd your Prince:*
> *You murderers and bloody crew*
> *You had no orders this to do.*

It goes on in the same vein for another 20 lines, ending with a couplet which stands comparison with the work of the late, great William Topaz McGonagall himself:

> And ere that he was really dead,
> They forthwith did cut off his head.

When the road through Glenmoriston was widened ten years ago, great care was taken to preserve and then move the cairn which was erected there in Rorie Mackenzie's memory. On the other side of the road, steps lead down from a lay-by to his grave, which is well marked. Many today still make the pilgrimage to visit both it and the cairn.

It may not only be wishful thinking on the part of latter-day Jacobites to believe that Roderick Mackenzie's gallantry in his last seconds of life were not in vain. For a time, the search for the Prince did relax. Then it started up again with a vengeance.

22

THE QUIET MAN: NEIL MACEACHAINN

THE WORST PRETENDER HE'D EVER SEEN

Neil MacEachainn was by Charles Edward Stuart's side during much of his wandering through the Hebrides in the weeks and months after Culloden. Neil himself had not been in what he called 'the misfortunate battle of Culloden' or otherwise involved with the Jacobite Army, but he met up with the Prince and his companions when they came in a rowing boat on a wild night from Arisaig to Roshinish near Benbecula.

The local schoolmaster, Neil was a well-educated man. He had studied at the Scots College in Douai near Paris, although this does not necessarily mean that he was destined for the priesthood. Catholic Scots, barred from studying at any of the universities in their homeland or England, sometimes used this route to access higher education.

The young dominie often called himself Neil MacDonald, the MacEachainns being a sept of the Clanranald branch of that clan. It could be useful, too, in these dangerous times to have a *nom de guerre* or two up your sleeve. As far as the British Government was concerned, helping the Prince after the defeat made you as guilty of 'levying war against the King's Most Excellent Majesty' as any soldier in the Jacobite Army.

Neil MacEachainn may have chosen to risk his life for Charles Edward Stuart when he had not chosen to join his army simply because chance gave him the opportunity to help. Many people sheltered and helped other fugitives to escape. Even people unconvinced by the Cause baulked at handing over their fellow countrymen to the rigours of English justice.

The suggestion has been made that Neil MacEachainn might have been a French agent. The French were certainly very keen to get the Prince out of Scotland, as they eventually did. Whether he was working for the French or not, Neil did play a pivotal role in Charles's escape over the sea to Skye with Flora MacDonald. Neil liked to portray himself as a simple country boy, but he was a lot more than that.

He provided the Prince with a hiding place at Corradale in South Uist, where Charles stayed in safety for almost a month. Neil's admiration for the Prince shines through the account he wrote of the time he spent with him. He praises Charles's 'top spirits' and his confidence that the Cause was not yet lost. It would seem that, in this, Charles was taking comfort from another kind of spirit:

> It was wonderful how he preserved his health all the time
> . . . He took care to warm his stomach every morning
> with a hearty bumper of brandy, of which he always
> drank a vast deal; for he was seen to drink a whole bottle
> of a day, without being in the least concerned.

The Prince loved to sit on a convenient stone in front of the house in Corradale with his face turned up to the sun. When Neil suggested he might be in danger of giving himself a headache, Charles cheerfully told him to mind his own business. He knew what was good for him, and 'the sun did him all the good in the world'.

Given the defeat at Culloden and its associated horrors, it's perhaps not surprising that Neil describes Charles as being up in the clouds at one moment and down in the dumps the next. He improved his mood by dancing, whistling a reel to himself for accompaniment. It must have been quite something to watch 'the lad who was born to be King' whirling and birling in the sunshine outside a wee cottage in the Outer Isles.

One day Charles amused himself by taking potshots at a school of whales which swam in close to the beach. Convinced he had killed one of them, he ordered Neil, a strong swimmer, to strip and go and haul the whale ashore. Neil himself seems to have been an early conservationist, or perhaps he was just kind-hearted. Referring to himself in the third person, he writes: 'Neil, in obedience to his orders and to humour him, began to strip very slowly till he saw the whale which had received no hurt out of sight.'

Initially imagining every ship he saw was a French vessel come to rescue him, Charles soon began to despair of that ever happening. Somehow he was going to have to find a ship to take him away from Scotland. Neil was dispatched to ask Alexander MacDonald of Boisdale if he would help. Boisdale was the man who told Charles when he first landed to 'Go home, sir.' He might now have thought himself justified in saying 'I told you so', but he agreed to come and see him.

Boisdale found Charles and some others still sleeping it off, 'very much disordered by the foregoing night's carouse'. His Prince's fondness for the bottle was clearly beginning to bother Neil MacEachainn, but Boisdale joined in, and 'he and the other gentlemen were very busie and very hearty taking their bottle'.

The news that hundreds of members of the pro-Government Skye Militia had landed on Barra and were soon to be reinforced by hundreds more under the dreaded Captain Fergusson gave the drinkers a sharp reality check. Boisdale was the first to come to his senses, realizing the Prince had to be moved. As he was trying to arrange that, he was arrested. He was taken to London and kept prisoner there for the next year but then released.

Two ladies stepped into the breach: Boisdale's wife and Lady Clanranald, whom everyone called Lady Clan. Although her husband was ostensibly a friend of the Government, he helped, too. So, despite being a captain in the Skye Militia, did one Hugh MacDonald, and he had a stepdaughter called Flora.

Charles went personally to ask for Flora's help, taking with him Felix O'Neil, a young man of Irish extraction, born in Rome, and who had served in both the French and Spanish armies before joining the Prince. Neil MacEachainn went along, too. He and Flora were related and knew one another well. Although terrified by the very idea of what was being suggested to her, Flora allowed herself to be persuaded. The plan was for the Prince to disguise himself as Flora's maidservant, supposedly an Irish girl named 'Betty Burke'. Her stepfather would give her a travel pass for two women, who, because of their gender, would be less likely to arouse suspicion, and they would cross the Minch to Skye.

When the Prince wanted to secrete a pair of pistols under his dress, Flora demurred, asking how it would look if they were searched and a maidservant was found to be carrying weapons. Charles replied – and maybe we can allow him a twinkle in his bonnie brown eyes as he said it – that if anyone searched him so closely as to find pistols, the game would certainly be up.

Appalled by how bad the Prince was at playing the part of a woman, still taking manly strides in his petticoats, Neil said he was the worst 'pretender' he'd ever seen. He went with him and Flora to Skye, and, like Flora, said his farewells at Portree.

Except that for Neil it was only *au revoir*. Almost three months later, he was one of the Jacobite fugitives who accompanied the Prince back to the safety of France. He spent the rest of his life there, serving as a soldier in the regiment in the French Army commanded by Jacobite exile Lord Ogilvy. Neil had a son who became one of Napoleon's generals, a marshal of France and the Duke of Tarentum. The good ship *L'Heureux – The Happy* – put in at Loch nan Uamh near Arisaig and left on 20 September with several of the clan chiefs and gentlemen who had been involved in the Rising on-board. One of the passengers in this illustrious company was Neil MacEachainn.

Simple country boy? Aye, that'll be right.

23

ODE TO HIS WOUNDED FOOT: DONALD ROY MACDONALD

NO LONGER DO I HUNT, OR JUMP, OR SWIM, NOR CARE TO TOUCH THE SWELLING BREASTS OF GIRLS

Donald Roy MacDonald was a volunteer to the Jacobite Army, a captain in MacDonald of Clanranald's Regiment. He was in his late thirties at the time of the '45, six feet tall, strong and vigorous. The MacDonalds who had come out for the Prince did their utmost to persuade their fellow clansmen to follow suit, and Donald Roy was their messenger.

As the Jacobites retreated north after the Battle of Falkirk in January 1746, Donald Roy was sent with a letter to Sir Alexander MacDonald, signed by all the Highland chiefs, imploring him to join them with every man he could muster. Donald Roy reached Skye and handed over the letter on the very same day that Sir Alexander received another letter from Lord Loudoun, Duncan Forbes of Culloden and the Laird of MacLeod, asking him to form his clansmen into a militia and join in on the Government side.

Sir Alexander gave Donald Roy a letter to take back to his clan chief, MacDonald of Keppoch. He did not know what was in it until he delivered it, when Keppoch told him its contents:

Seeing I look upon your affairs as in a desperate way I
will not join you; but then I assure you I will as little rise
against you. If any misfortune shall happen to yourself I
desire you may leave your son, Ranald, to my care, etc.

Sir Alexander had tried to persuade Donald Roy not to go back to
the Jacobite Army, saying he did not like the idea of him being killed
by one of 'his own blood relations'. Several of his cousins were serving
under Lord Loudoun.

Donald Roy was not to be dissuaded. Heading for the ferry back to
the mainland, he met a very close blood relation indeed: his brother
Hugh MacDonald of Baleshare, captain in the local militia and Flora
MacDonald's stepfather into the bargain. The MacDonald brothers
spent three days together, eating, drinking and making merry at the
expense of King George. Donald Roy kept his white cockade in
his blue bonnet and many in the Skye Militia happily toasted the
Prince's Cause.

At Culloden, Donald Roy saw MacDonald of Keppoch fall wounded
to the ground, not once but twice. The second time, Keppoch looked
at Donald Roy and said, 'O God, have mercy upon me. Donald, do the
best for yourself, for I am gone.'

Donald Roy did as he was bid but was shot as he was leaving the
field, the bullet going through the sole of his left foot and out at the
top of it, taking his shoe with it. He walked five miles barefoot, his
wound bleeding all the way. He did not dare to stop until he got to
Bunchrew, two miles beyond Inverness. He got a horse there and rode
on for another eight miles, heading doggedly for Skye, although he
could not put his injured foot in the stirrup because it had swollen so
much. By sheer luck, he met up the next day with William Balfour,
surgeon to MacGregor's Regiment.

The young man 'dressed the foot by only putting some dry tow
upon the hole beneath and the hole above and rolling a bandage
above all'. That was all the medical attention Donald Roy's foot got

until he reached Skye one week later, where he went to stay with John MacLean, a surgeon who lived in Trotternish.

MacLean dressed the wound, which had now become infected, giving off 'such a stink that one could scarce enter the room where he was'. Two months later, Donald Roy was still lodging at the surgeon's house and about to become involved in the plot to keep Charles Edward Stuart out of harm's way after he came over to Skye with Flora MacDonald and Neil MacEachainn.

There were plans for the Prince to lie low on an island off the coast from Trotternish. Donald Roy's brother, Hugh, was involved in this, and he asked him to help by keeping a look-out and going across to the tiny island to deliver some supplies to Charles. The Prince was short of everything, especially shirts. He was also very keen to have the latest newspapers, which Lady Margaret MacDonald was already sending to him as often as she could.

Baleshare gave his brother an instruction to which Jacobite plotters were well used: burn this letter. Donald Roy was to make sure any incriminating missives, most especially any which came from the Prince, were to be read carefully and then immediately flung into the fire.

When Donald Roy gave a letter to Lady Margaret from Charles thanking her for sending him the newspapers, she was upset at the thought of destroying such a precious souvenir of the Prince. She did burn it later, though, when the unpleasant Captain Fergusson and his men came to her house looking for him.

Lady Margaret had six of her husband's best shirts washed and told the maid who did the laundry they were for Donald Roy, who had lost all his with his baggage at Culloden. There had to be an excuse for Donald Roy to go out to the little island, so he told the man he asked to row him over that he wanted 'to divert himself some time at fishing'. When the boatman told Donald Roy the fishing was fine where he was, Donald Roy had to admit what he was really up to, drawing his dirk and asking the man to swear by 'the Holy Iron' that he would never breathe a word to anyone. The oath was taken and kept.

Lady Margaret MacDonald then had a boat sent out to the little island on the pretext of gathering shells to make lime, Donald Roy going along to supervise and also taking some fishing lines with him, in keeping with the cover story. He also had the six shirts and twenty guineas for the Prince – but found he was on a fool's errand.

The Prince was not on the island, nor on a small flat rock near it, where Donald Roy suspected a couple of men could hide. Despite his bad foot, he scrambled onto the rock from the rowing boat and climbed to the top of it. It, too, was empty.

A few days later, a letter from Lady Margaret asked him to come to her home at Monkstadt. Donald Roy borrowed the horse belonging to his landlord the surgeon, and set out. He found Lady Margaret with Alexander MacDonald of Kingsburgh, and very agitated. Kingsburgh was Lady Margaret's factor, and his son Allan was later to become Flora MacDonald's husband.

The Prince had only just got to Skye and had landed no distance from her house. Lieutenant MacLeod of the Militia was currently in the dining room of the house with Flora MacDonald, and the Prince was still in the rowing boat disguised – not very convincingly – as a woman. Even worse, Lieutenant MacLeod had a troop of men under his command with orders to investigate every boat they saw.

Lady Margaret, Donald Roy and MacDonald of Kingsburgh discussed what to do but 'all choices were bad'. Then Donald Roy had a brainwave. The coast was being closely watched, so why not send the Prince overland to Portree, 14 miles away? Kingsburgh asked if Donald Roy would go down to the shore and communicate the plan to Charles. As Donald Roy 'had been in the scrape', the Prince was more likely to take advice from him. Donald Roy demurred, saying that 'as the Prince he was sure would make a monstrous appearance in women's cloaths', it would look suspicious if he was seen talking to him. He suggested that Flora should go instead.

While this agonized discussion was going on, Charles Edward Stuart was sitting on a rock gazing out to sea, wearing his flowery frock and 'patiently waiting his fate'. Kingsburgh took a bottle of wine and some bread down to the shore, and Donald Roy went off in search of the laird's son known as young Raasay, who was currently staying near Portree. The island from which young Raasay took his name, just across the water from the north-east coast of Skye, had already been harried by Government troops. They had done their work well, burning every house and hut on it. Since there was now no reason for the Redcoats to return there, it seemed, at least temporarily, to be likely to provide a safe refuge for the Prince. The MacLeods of Raasay had provided a small regiment to the Jacobite Army. Given their support for the Cause and the destruction done to their island home, they were only too willing to help Charles escape.

Charles and Neil MacEachainn walked overland to Portree on a night of wind and rain and were met there by Donald Roy, who had arrived on horseback. The Prince was soaked through, and at the inn which is now the Royal Hotel he changed into a clean shirt and dry clothes, and sat down to a dinner of butter, cheese, bread and roasted fish with Neil, Donald Roy and Flora, who had gone there by 'taking a different road'. The three men drank from a bottle of whisky they bought from the landlord.

Being in a public place was making Donald Roy nervous. Anyone might walk in. He thought Charles should move on as soon as possible. Charles wanted to stay the night, understandably reluctant to go back out into the torrential rain. He wanted to smoke a pipe, too.

When the landlord weighed some tobacco and asked for fourpence halfpenny for it, the Prince gave the man sixpence and told him to keep the change. Donald Roy insisted the Prince keep it because 'in his present situation he would find bawbees very useful to him'. Amused, Charles slid the coins into his purse.

He then set about trying to persuade Donald Roy to come with him on the next leg of his journey. Donald Roy begged him not to even think of it. The wound in his foot was still open, making it difficult for him to walk. If he undertook any sort of a journey, he would have to do it on horseback, and if the search parties saw two riders they would undoubtedly come up and question them.

The Prince countered by saying he always felt safe when he had a MacDonald with him. The Stuart charm strikes again. Donald Roy was, however, still on his guard. He would join him later. He stopped Charles from paying over the odds for their meal, again worried that too big a tip would make the landlord suspicious.

The Prince said goodbye to Flora MacDonald, paying back to her a half-crown he had borrowed, kissing her hand and telling her, 'For all that has happened I hope, Madam, we shall meet in St James' yet.' Then he took his leave of Neil MacEachainn. Neil, Donald Roy and Flora spent that night in Portree.

Donald Roy saw Charles to his rendezvous with the next safe pair of hands. Attached to his belt, the Prince had what was left in the whisky bottle, a bottle of brandy, the clean shirts and a cold, cooked chicken. Donald Roy spotted the landlord looking very closely at Charles as they went out of the inn and deliberately turned the wrong way. They went round in a big circle to get back to the quayside, where Charles stepped into the boat which was to take him to Raasay.

It was now the early morning of Tuesday, 1 July, and Donald Roy returned to the inn and slept as best he could in the short Highland night. The next morning, the landlord was curious as to who the fair-haired young man had been. Donald Roy told him he was a comrade-in-arms from the Jacobite Army, to which the landlord replied that he had wondered if he might be Prince Charles in disguise, 'for that he had something about him that looked very noble'.

Donald Roy went back to the west coast of Skye, happily spending the night with his friend Lieutenant MacLeod, the man who had been in the dining room with Flora MacDonald while the Prince was sitting on the beach. It was also to MacLeod that Donald Roy had officially surrendered his weapons when he returned to Skye after Culloden. He bought some rough old ones for the purpose, sending his good ones to his brother for safe keeping, which MacLeod probably knew very well. What Lieutenant MacLeod didn't know was that the Prince had waltzed off from under under his nose. He had his men still watching the Minch.

Over the next couple of days, Donald Roy returned the surgeon's horse to him, armed himself with a new pistol and a dirk, and wore himself out and hurt his foot again after walking too many Highland miles. The plan had been that he would go to Raasay to join the Prince, but Charles had moved on. He sent a mysterious stranger with a letter to Donald Roy:

> Sir, I have parted (I thank God) as intended. Make my
> compliments to all those to whom I have given trouble.
> I am, Sir, your humble servant, James Thomson.

Donald Roy kept this letter, signed with one of Charles's many aliases, until the day his niece, Flora, was arrested. Then, with regret, he destroyed it. He also persuaded Flora to part with the safe conduct her stepfather had written for her and 'one Bettie Burk [sic], an Irish girl, who as she tells me is a good spinster'.

Despite his continuing caution, when it came out that he had been seen in Portree in company with the man whom people were now beginning to realize had been the Prince, Donald Roy had to take to the heather. More precisely, he had to take to three different caves in which he spent the next eight weeks, until the fuss had died down.

Lady Margaret MacDonald made sure he had food. Late at night and early in the morning, when no one would see him, he took a bottle to a nearby spring to get water. The surgeon sent dressings for his wounded foot, but Donald Roy was lonely and he was skulking during July and August and the midges and the flies drove him crazy.

He found distraction in writing poetry – in Latin. One is a lament for the slaughter at Culloden, another an ode to his wounded foot. It's not comic. The pain was obviously still too great for that. In his verses, he lamented that his injury was stopping him from doing the things he loved to do, like hunting and swimming. He didn't even feel like 'touching the swelling breasts of girls'. He could only hope and pray that 'the benign Founder of the World' would heal his foot and his situation.

Both did get better. Once it was realized that Charles had left Scotland and things began to quieten down, Donald Roy came out of hiding. He had enough friends in high places, including Lady Margaret's husband, Sir Alexander MacDonald of Sleat, that he was able to quietly get on with his life.

In the fullness of time, his wounded foot healed. When he visited Edinburgh a year or so after Culloden, he walked there from Skye in 12 days.

24

NOT WITHOUT ORDERS:
FERGUSSON, LOCKHART & SCOTT

MONSTROUS TRANSACTIONS THAT WERE DELIBERATELY
PERPETRATED IN THE FACE OF THE SUN BY GENTLEMEN
AND (SHALL I SAY IT?) CHRISTIANS

It's an unpalatable truth that three Redcoat officers who earned themselves an enduring reputation for terrible cruelty after Culloden were all Scotsmen: Captain John Fergusson, Major James Lockhart and Captain Caroline Frederick Scott. In the summer and autumn of 1746, there were plenty of Englishmen running amuck through the Highlands raping, burning and destroying – Captain Cornwallis is one who earned his place in the hall of infamy – but it's these three Scotsmen who are most bitterly remembered.

Captain John Fergusson, master of the Royal Navy's *Furnace*, appears again and again in the stories of horrors committed along the western seaboard and throughout the Hebrides. One of the most dogged of the summer hunters of the Prince, he was afterwards fond of boasting that he had several times come within an hour of finding him.

A native of Oldmeldrum in Aberdeenshire, Fergusson came from a family with a long tradition of enmity towards the Stuarts. He seems also to have been motivated by the price on his quarry's head. After it was all over, a relative in Edinburgh asked him if he would have killed Charles if he had succeeded in capturing him. Fergusson's answer was unequivocal:

> No by God, I would have been so far from doing any such thing that I would have preserved him as the apple of mine eyes, for I would not take any man's word, no, not the Duke of Cumberland's for £30,000 Sterling, though I knew many to be such fools as to do it.

A cruel man by nature, he was also a boor. In pursuit of the Prince on South Uist, he went to Lady Clanranald's house. She was not at home but with the Prince and Flora MacDonald a few miles away on the other side of Loch Uiskevagh, the escape over the sea to Skye in the planning. Fergusson spent the night in Lady Clan's bed. In the eighteenth century, when it was shocking for a gentleman who was not a close relative to even enter a lady's bedroom, this was a deliberate insult.

Dissatisfied with her explanation when she returned home the following morning, that she had spent the night sitting up with a sick child, Fergusson arrested her and her husband. Despite Clanranald being ostensibly a friend of the Government, his wife spent many weary months under house arrest in London.

To add to his many unlovely qualities, Fergusson was a hectoring bully. Some people had the courage to stand up to him. Mrs MacDonald of Kingsburgh was one of them, telling him to his face the word was that he was a 'cruel, hard-hearted man'. Fergusson told her people should not believe everything they hear.

The Prince having once more given him the slip, Fergusson was paying Mrs MacDonald an unwelcome visit in the wake of the 'Betty Burke' episode. In the course of his interrogation, he asked her to show him where her most recent visitors had stayed. Hoping to shock her into an admission of guilt, he asked if she had put the Young Pretender and Flora MacDonald in the same bed. Mrs MacDonald of Kingsburgh remained as cool as a cucumber:

Sir, whom you mean by the Young Pretender I shall
not pretend to guess; but I can assure you it is not the
fashion in the Isle of Skye to lay the mistress and the
maid in the same bed together.

Ferguson observed drily that it was odd the maid seemed then to
have slept in a better bedroom than the mistress. Later that summer,
having failed to capture the Prince, he took some prisoners to
London on the *Furnace*. He kept them half-starved, with the little
food they did get brought to them 'in foul nasty buckets wherein the
sailors used to piss for a piece of ill-natured diversion'.

Before that, Father Alexander Cameron, Jesuit priest, Lochiel's
brother and Catholic chaplain to his regiment, fell into Fergusson's
clutches. Taken prisoner and held on the *Furnace* while the vessel was
still in the Hebrides, he had no bed to lie on other than the coils of
rope in the hold.

When he became ill, some of his friends on shore grew concerned
about his well-being. Getting no response from Fergusson, they went
over his head to the Duke of Albemarle. The Duke of Cumberland had
by now left Scotland, appointing Albemarle commander-in-chief in
his stead. He sent his own physician to examine Alexander Cameron.

The doctor's opinion was that Father Cameron should either be
brought ashore or given better treatment on-board. When Albemarle
sent a platoon of soldiers to pick him up, Fergusson was having none
of it. The man was his prisoner, and he was not obliged to hand him
over unless he had an order from the prime minister or the Lords of
the Admiralty.

A party of Alexander Cameron's friends then rowed out to the
Furnace with a bed, sheets and blankets. Fergusson refused to take these
on-board, threatening the small boat with sinking if its occupants
even tried to unload their cargo. Although Father Cameron was later
transferred to Inverness and away from Captain Fergusson, he did
endure a sea journey to London on a different ship. He died a few
months after he got there on one of the prison hulks moored on the

Thames to accommodate the hundreds of Scottish prisoners who had been shipped south from Inverness.

Felix O'Neil, one of Charles Edward Stuart's companions while he had been hopping about the Hebrides, was also unlucky enough to fall into Fergusson's hands. The captain treated him 'with all the barbarity of a pirate' and ordered him to be flogged when he refused to say where the Prince was. O'Neil was stripped and pinioned, on the point of being lashed, when Lieutenant MacCaghan of the Royal Scots Fusiliers – whose name sounds more Irish than Scottish – stepped forward, drew his sword and told Fergusson 'that he'd sacrifice himself and his detachment rather than to see an officer used after such an infamous manner'. He succeeded in preventing the flogging.

There were others who served under Fergusson who found his cruelty and the brutality he encouraged in others too much to stomach. Marines under his command and that of Captain Duff – another Scotsman who earned himself a notorious reputation – went ashore with the express aim of raping all the women and girls on the island of Canna. One of their number 'who had some grains of Christian principles about him' warned the islanders, thus thwarting this chilling plan.

Major James Lockhart was a senior officer in Cholmondley's Regiment. From their base at Fort Augustus, he and the gang of thugs under his command sallied forth to ravage the surrounding countryside. Lockhart's speciality was encouraging his men to gang-rape women and hang men, whether he had proof they had been in the Jacobite Army or not.

Many of these stories are confirmed by more than one source and many name names. There was Isabel MacDonald in Glenmoriston, raped while her husband, in hiding nearby, had to watch. If he had tried to stop it, Lockhart and his men would undoubtedly have killed him.

One infamous story has Lockhart personally shooting dead two old men and one young lad while they were doing nothing more than working in their fields. Another man, Grant of Daldriggan, was tied up and forced to watch as the dead men were strung up by their feet on a makeshift gallows. Not having jumped quickly enough when Lockhart ordered him to round up some cattle, Daldriggan was set to join them – until once more a man with a conscience stepped forward to stop the barbarity. This time it was a Captain Grant of Lord Loudoun's Regiment.

Like Captain Fergusson, James Lockhart clearly had a cruel streak. He enjoyed seeing people suffer, and he enjoyed watching their growing terror as they realized what he was going to do to them. Yet there's something about Lockhart which gives an even more sinister edge to his exploits: the sense of a man out of control. During these months of bloodletting, all limits were breached. He is reported to have murdered one boy of four by plunging his sword into him 'in at a belly and out at the back'. Something very powerful and very negative was driving James Lockhart.

These reprisals against Jacobite soldiers and the civilian population which had produced them were not only perpetrated by Englishmen and Lowland Scots. Highlanders were also involved. As the Camerons under Lochiel had played such a vital part in the Rebellion, Lochaber was singled out for special treatment. Among those who delivered it were Munro of Culcairn – taking his revenge for being defeated at Inverurie – and Captain Grant of Knockando and Strathspey.

According to John Cameron, Presbyterian minister at Fort William, and another of the chaplains to Lochiel's Regiment, Grant 'burnt and plundered as he marched' and 'stripped men, women and children without distinction of condition or sex'. An officer in Lord Loudoun's Regiment, he did so at the head of a company of 200 men. To know they were heading your way must have been absolutely terrifying.

Someone took revenge, though, shooting Munro of Culcairn dead. The Reverend Cameron knew who it was, knew too that the bullet had been intended for Captain Grant, who was walking beside Munro at the time. Grant had murdered the adult son of the old man who fired the shot which killed Munro.

The most infamous of these sadistic Redcoat officers was Captain Caroline Frederick Scott. He served in Guise's, the same regiment as the well-mannered and friendly Captain Sweetenham, but was a man of a very different stamp.

Scott first distinguished himself honourably, conducting a determined, focused and successful defence of Fort William when it was besieged by the Camerons early in 1746. His diary of the siege was published in the *Scots Magazine,* making him something of a hero among the friends of the Government. He was already a personal favourite of the Duke of Cumberland.

After Culloden, Scott led many raiding parties out of Fort William to harry the clan lands which lay around it. He paid particular attention to Appin, whose regiment of Stewarts in the Jacobite Army had been headed by Charles Stewart of Ardsheal.

Ardsheal's strong-minded wife, Isabel Haldane, had encouraged her husband to go out for the Prince. Like many men, he had hesitated, justifiably fearful of the consequences of failure. According to legend, Isabel untied her apron, took it off and handed it to him, saying that if he would not lead the men out, she would, and he could stay at home and look after the house and children. Ardsheal led the men out.

Many of them did not come home again, killed in the desperate charge of the right wing of the Jacobite Army and the subsequent heroic attempts to save the Appin banner. Held now at Edinburgh Castle, it is one of the few Jacobite colours to survive, along with that of Lord Ogilvy's Angus Regiment, kept safe now at the McManus Galleries and Museum in Dundee. In a ritual act of humiliation, the other Jacobite flags and banners were burned in Edinburgh by the public hangman.

Caroline Frederick Scott liked to humiliate his defeated enemies, too. Correctly suspecting that Charles Stewart of Ardsheal was skulking not too far from his home, Scott swooped down on Isabel Haldane and her young children. He took her house and her life apart, in the most literal sense.

Her meagre stores of butter and cheese were taken. On the direct orders of Cumberland himself, most of her livestock had already been driven off. This confiscation of assets and tools of trades happened to many Highland families after the '45. Ploughs were burned and cows taken to Fort William and elsewhere to be sold to cattle farmers from the south, who journeyed north to buy them at bargain prices, leaving people destitute and with no means of tilling the ground, working the land or feeding themselves.

Many houses were burned, too, leaving a family with no shelter. In August 1746, Caroline Frederick Scott further refined the cruelty of this heartless policy. He stripped Ardsheal House bare, to the extent of having every piece of wood in it removed. Doors were taken off their hinges, panelling removed from the walls, the slates taken off the roof. Under Scott's orders it was all done very slowly and carefully, the nails straightened out so they too could be taken back to Fort William and sold. He even took the children's school books.

The lady of the house was then asked for her keys. Surrounded by her frightened children, pregnant with another, a confused Isabel handed them over. In a parody of gentlemanly behaviour, Caroline Scott offered her his hand, led her to the door and told her to go. She had no business here any more. Ardsheal House was no longer her home.

Isabel Haldane penned a furious letter of protest to Major General John Campbell of Mamore, the father of Colonel Jack of the Argyle Militia. Although both father and son were robust in their treatment of the defeated Rebels, by the standards of their time they were also humane, and she was not the only person who appealed to them for help. Many skulking Jacobites let it be known they were prepared to surrender, but only 'to a Campbell', meaning either Lord Loudoun, Colonel Jack or his father.

Considering the bad press the Campbells have had throughout Scottish history, it's interesting that these defeated clansmen clearly believed they would get better treatment from a Scotsman and fellow Highlander than they would from an Englishman or a Scottish Lowlander.

By birth, that's what Caroline Frederick Scott was, although it might also be fair to call him an Anglo-Scot. His father, George Scott of Bristo in Edinburgh, was British Ambassador to the Hanoverian Court during the reign of Queen Anne, before the House of Hanover succeeded to the British throne.

When George Scott's wife, Marion Steuart of Goodtrees, gave birth to a son, his godmother was Princess Caroline. As the wife of George II, she was to become Queen Caroline and the mother of the Duke of Cumberland. Caroline Frederick Scott was named in her honour, thus acquiring a first name which was as unusual for a man in his own day as it would be in ours.

Through both his father and his mother – whose surviving letters show that she believed in raising children with kindness – Caroline Frederick Scott was very 'weel-connecktit' in Scotland, too. In this he was not unusual. Sometimes it can seem that everyone involved in the '45 was related to everyone else.

Like many people, Scott had relatives who were friends of the Government, others who kept their opinions to themselves and others again who gave him a bad case of Embarrassing Jacobite Relatives Syndrome. One of his cousins was Provost Archibald Stewart of Edinburgh, whom Alexander Carlyle and John Home and their friends suspected of collusion with the Prince and his army. The provost's wife was the sister of Lord Elcho, colonel of one of the cavalry regiments in the Jacobite Army. For Caroline Frederick Scott, there weren't even seven degrees of separation in it.

Isabel Haldane of Ardsheal also belonged to the Scotland-wide network of friends and closely related families. This crossed the Highland–Lowland divide. She herself was one of the Haldanes of Lanrick, near Doune, just north of Stirling. Besides which, the Highland gentry often had houses in Edinburgh, where Flora MacDonald went to boarding school, or at least paid regular visits there.

The chances that Isabel and Caroline Frederick Scott knew one another are therefore pretty high. Tellingly, in her letter to John Campbell of Mamore senior, she said she could hardly believe 'that any man especially bred in a civilized country and good company could be so free of compassion or anything at all of the gentleman to descend to such a low degree of meanness'.

There's a strong implication here that Isabel knew the 'good company' which her ruthlessly cool and cruel tormentor had kept. She and Captain Scott were around the same age, in their early thirties in the mid-1740s. Could he have been a rejected suitor? Or had they simply already met and taken a hearty dislike to one another before their encounters in the summer of 1746?

The eighteenth century was a robust age, especially when it came to crime and punishment. Clan justice could be as brutal as any. When Angus MacDonell of Glengarry was accidentally shot in the streets of Falkirk by a man cleaning his gun, the man was immediately shot dead in reprisal. Captain Fergusson persuaded some of those he captured to talk by means of an instrument of torture which had been invented by MacDonald of Barisdale. It was a sort of rack, and Barisdale had previously used it to punish thieves.

Nevertheless, the idea that the Jacobite Army as a whole acted humanely to those whom it defeated and did not wage war on women and children is not just a romantic notion. The evidence is there in story after story. They were ferociously brutal in battle but merciful afterwards. There are stories of cruelties committed by Jacobites, but you have to look hard to find them, which does not, of course, excuse those which did take place.

There is Mrs Grossett of Alloa, whose husband, Walter, was an exciseman who detested smugglers and Jacobites and did much to thwart the plans of both. The revenge the latter took on him makes for unpleasant reading, with echoes of what happened to Isabel Haldane and her family:

> The Rebells robbed and plundered his house at Alloa and his house in the country to such a degree that they did not leave his infant children even a shirt to shift them, and pursued his wife and daughter to an uncle's house, to whose estate they knew Mr. Grosett was to succeed,

plundered that house, stript his wife and daughter of the very clothes they had upon their backs and used them otherwise in a most cruel and barbarous manner.

Mrs Grossett died not long afterwards. Her husband suffered a second bereavement when his brother Alexander was killed at Culloden. His death, too, was claimed as a Jacobite atrocity. A contemporary print called 'Rebell Ingratitude' shows him being shot by a Jacobite soldier whose face is twisted with malice. Caught at the moment of death, falling backwards off his horse, Captain Grossett's neat white military wig has slipped off his head. Behind him, two other Redcoats rush forward to avenge their captain. The text under the picture tells the story:

> Or a **Representation** of the Treachery and Barbarity of Two **Rebell Officers**, at the **Battle of Culloden**, who had their Lives Generously given them by the **Earl of Ancram**, (who had a considerable Command that Day) and by **Captain Grosett** Engineer & Aid De Camp to the General.
>
> The One attempted to shoot His Lordship behind his back, with a **Pistol,** which he had kept concealed & which luckily only Flash'd in the Pan. The Other Shot **Captain Grosett Dead** with his own **Pistol,** which happened Accidentally to fall from his as he was on **Horseback,** under pretence of restoring the same to the Captain.
>
> These **Rebells** received the Just reward of their **Perfidy**, By being immediatly cut to pieces by the **King's Troops**. And it is Generally believed that this their Ingratitude and Treachery greatly heightened the Slaughter that was that Day made of their Party.
>
> Captain Grossett left behind him a Distressed Widow, with Six young Children.

Captain Alexander Grossett was indeed killed at Culloden, but there is no other detailed account of how he died. It's interesting that his death was being used as justification for '*the Slaughter that was that Day made of their Party*'. It did not take long for people in Edinburgh, London and elsewhere to begin to think that, in stamping out the Rebellion, too many Government officers had gone too far. Robust punishment had tipped over into sadistic cruelty.

Leading the storm of fire, rape and death which raged through the Highlands and Islands in the summer and autumn of 1746, none of the men responsible thought they were going too far. Yet Fergusson, Lockhart and Scott would all have called themselves gentlemen, and would not have dared behave in Edinburgh as they did while they were north of the Highland Line.

When one of his officers remonstrated with him, telling him he *was* going too far, Caroline Frederick Scott told him he knew very well what he was doing, which was 'not without orders'. Close as he was to the Duke of Cumberland, he knew better than anyone what was wanted: Scotland was to suffer. It never seems to have occurred to Cumberland, as it occurred to others, that such harsh and profoundly unfair reprisals might be counter-productive, as they have been – to this very day.

In their own minds, Fergusson, Lockhart and Scott, as much as many of their English fellow officers, seem to have felt themselves in the Highlands to be in a land of savages. The people they hounded were not people like them and, as such, did not deserve to treated with humanity. The class structure of the time forced them to rein in their more violent impulses when dealing with the Highland gentry. The common man, woman or child had no such protection.

Yet Caroline Frederick Scott spoke, or at least understood, Gaelic. Was it a form of self-hatred which propelled him? As red-coated Scotsmen did he, Fergusson, Lockhart and the others feel they had something to prove? In putting down this 'Scotch Rebellion' were they trying to show not only that they could be as rigorous as any Englishman but also how much they despised so many of their fellow Scots?

In the case of Major James Lockhart, there may have been more to it even than that.

25

The Shah of Persia, the Magic Penny & Embarrassing Relatives: The Lockharts of Carnwath

They offer'd to let me go if I would give my parole of honour, wch I utterly refused to do

The Lockharts of Lee and Carnwath were Jacobites to their fingertips. Sir George Lockhart was a member of the Scottish Parliament before the Union in 1707 and a Jacobite plotter in the run-up to the Rising of 1715. It was he who first made it public that many of his fellow Members of the old Scottish Parliament had accepted English bribes to vote in favour of the Union, publishing a list of their names. King James VIII's agent in Scotland, his extensive correspondence and his *Memoirs of the Affairs of Scotland* were later published as *The Lockhart Papers*.

Sir George died in 1731, but several of his children and grandchildren played their part in the '45, if not necessarily in ways of which he would have approved. He would undoubtedly have been proud of his son-in-law and two of his grandsons. Married to Lockhart's daughter Mary, the former was John Rattray, golfer, doctor and personal

241

physician to Charles Edward Stuart. The grandsons were George and James. George, known in 1745 as Young Carnwath, was one of Charles Edward Stuart's aides-de-camp. His younger brother, James, was also in the Jacobite Army. Both fought at Culloden and subsequently spent many years in exile in Europe.

James was only 18 at the time of the battle, which did not stop him from undertaking an epic journey afterwards, crossing Europe and hiring out his sword and his soldiering skills to the Shah of Persia. Nobody knows how he got there. He fetched up a year or so later fighting in the War of the Austrian Succession in the army of the Empress Maria Theresa. He rose to become a general and was ennobled by her as Count Lockhart-Wishart, taking his mother's name in his title as well as his father's, in the Austrian style.

The Empress also gave him a very special box to house a very special object, whose origin may indicate that James had felt some sort of pull towards the Middle East. An ancestor had fought in the Crusades, acquiring there what has been known throughout history as the Lee Penny. A silver coin with a red stone in its centre, it was credited with healing sickness in humans and animals, and remains in the possession of the Lockhart family today. Sir Walter Scott took inspiration from it to write his novel *The Talisman*.

The figure which stands on top of the memorial at Glenfinnan that commemorates the Raising of the Standard is James Lockhart's brother, George, the aide-de-camp to the Prince. It was sculpted by John Greenshields of Carluke. Told there was a painting of Charles Edward Stuart at Lee Castle, Greenshields went to have a look at it. Only the housekeeper was at home, and she showed him two paintings of two young men, which hung side by side, and left him to it.

When Greenshields discovered he had assumed Young Carnwath was the Prince and modelled his statue accordingly, he was philosophical. He thought George Lockhart junior looked a lot better than 'the Prince in tartan pantaloons'. So the '45, inextricably associated with the Highlands, is marked at its birthplace in one of the most beautiful glens in the Highlands by the figure of a

Lowlander. There's a yet more intriguing twist to the story of the Jacobite Lockharts of Carnwath.

Major James Lockhart, Government officer and brutal persecutor of Jacobite fugitives and Highlanders, fought with his regiment, Cholmondley's, at Falkirk. As his men panicked, he did his utmost to rally them but fell from his horse and hurt his hip and thigh, which, as he later wrote when required to answer for his conduct at Falkirk, 'swell'd prodigiously, & made me very Lame'. Forced into 'resting on Captn Websters shoulder', he was helped onto another horse, his own presumably having bolted, but found he could hardly sit on it because of the pain in his leg.

They had to move. Everyone had now realized the Jacobites had won the battle. Despite his injury, Major Lockhart was ordered to see to the collecting of tents from the Government camp. He issued orders in his turn for that to be done and was helped onto his third horse of the afternoon. It was not to be third time lucky. He 'had not rode a few Yards, when the Horse fell & tumbled Over me'. The pain of it made him lose consciousness.

When he came to, he found himself in nearby Callendar House, home of the Jacobite Lord and Lady Kilmarnock. They'd had him put to bed, and a doctor was bleeding him. It was very difficult to get Lockhart's boot off, and the pain was so great he was shouting out and crying with it.

Once the doctor had done what he could to make his patient comfortable – Lockhart told the maid the next day when she enquired that he was 'a little easier' – Lord and Lady Kilmarnock promised not to hand the major over as a prisoner of war. It's very possible that they all knew each other. One of the Kilmarnocks' sons, James, Lord Boyd, was a serving British officer, a 2nd lieutenant in the Royal Scots Fusiliers.

Yet the very next day they broke their promise. The major was handed over to Mr Murray, possibly John Murray of Broughton, the Prince's secretary, who:

after much insignificant Discourse, Offer'd to Let me
go, If I would give my Parole of Honour, not to Serve
Against Them for 12 Months, wch I utterly refus'd to do;
On wch they ordered a Guard into the Room wth me
& next day was offer'd my Liberty, on the above Terms,
wch I absolutely refus'd; On which, Though I was then
Extremely Ill, I was forc'd down Stairs, with Half my
Cloths on, in Presence Of Lord, Lady Kilmarnock &
Son, who told me, as I had refus'd my Parole, & show'd
so little Respect to them I deserv'd no Favour.

They put him in a chaise, which took him to Stirling where Jacobite
commander Lord John Drummond again asked him to give his parole
and Lockhart again refused to do so. He was then asked to write to
General Hawley to ask for the release of 'Kinloch Moidart or some
such Person', as he later haughtily put it, in exchange for himself. He
wouldn't do that, either.

Held at Stirling, he and other Government prisoners were later
moved out to Doune Castle by a company of Jacobites commanded
by John Roy Stuart. The colonel of the Edinburgh Regiment also
asked for their parole of honour but required of them only that they
would not try to escape on the way to their new prison. If they gave
their parole, they could march like officers.

This time Lockhart agreed to make the promise and was outraged
to find himself 'betwixt A Party of Men, wth Fix'd Bayonets, & all
Kinds of Pris^{rs}'. He called up to John Roy in protest and the two
men threw angry words at one another, John Roy threatening to have
Lockhart tied with ropes. Although the threat was not carried out,
the major was clearly outraged. The account he wrote bristles with
indignation that an officer and a gentleman such as himself should
have been so insulted.

And what does he have to do with the Lockharts of Carnwath?
Well, possibly rather a lot. While he was a prisoner of the Jacobites,
he was locked up with John Gray of Rogart, the cattle drover from

Sutherland who gave evidence at Lord Lovat's trial. Major Lockhart had a visitor, and, when he left, Gray asked who he was. Lockhart replied that it was Young Carnwath.

This was George Lockhart, aide-de-camp to Prince Charles. Frustratingly, John Gray said nothing about their conversation, even whether it had been cordial or aggressive. The family tree of the Lockharts shows that Old Carnwath, the Sir George Lockhart who had been King James's agent in Scotland, had a son called James. Born in 1707, he died in 1749 while serving as lieutenant colonel of 'Hacket's Regiment in the Dutch service'.

There's a misprint here. Hacket's Regiment was stationed for many years on the island of Menorca. The Mediterranean island had been captured by the British Navy in 1708 during the War of the Spanish Succession and, with interruptions, remained in British hands until 1802.

If Lockhart died in Holland, he may well have done so as lieutenant colonel of *Halkett's* Regiment. This was commanded by Sir Peter Halkett of Pitfirrane in Fife, the man who asked the Jacobite doctor John Rattray if he could help Lee's Regiment's inexperienced young surgeon after the Battle of Prestonpans.

Was Young Carnwath visiting his Uncle James at Stirling, offering to see what he could do for him? It seems highly likely. It's clear from his written defence of himself that James Lockhart felt humiliated and insulted by what had happened to him at Falkirk. It's also clear he thought his conduct as an officer and his honour as a gentleman were being called into question.

Was this because he felt he always had to defend himself from allegations that he was a secret Jacobite? Was that why he kept refusing to give his parole? In the angry final paragraph of his passionate defence of himself, he states that his colonel will speak up for him as to his character and his conduct. The final lines he wrote were these:

> As to my Principles, & Education, from my Youth
> They are Notorious, to all the World, & I beg my Coll;
> will inform Himself, as to Them, from His Majesty's
> Sollicitor, Lord Justice Clerk, or any Other Person He
> Pleases.

He may have been born and reared a Jacobite but had he decided very early on in life that he would not grow up one? Given what we know about his character, when his nephew came to visit him in Stirling, did he angrily tell him to get lost?

There may be a revealing glimpse of the boy who was to become the dreaded Major Lockhart in a letter Sir George Lockhart wrote to another of his sons:

> Jamie hath been ane undutiful child, and shows no inclinations to do well, but hes young and not to be dispaird of, and he must be cherishd or discouraged according to his good or bad behaviour.

Just as we sagely nod our heads at this clue as to why James Lockhart turned out the way he did, we read in *The Lockhart Papers* that a note 'in a feeble hand' was added to this letter: 'Jamie, since writing this letter, having alterd his way and behaved to my satisfaction, I have intirely forgot all offences in his younger years.'

All the same, did he perhaps continue to rebel against his family and their commitment to the Stuart Cause? Was he getting back at them when he acted so cruelly in the west Highlands? It's an intriguing possibility.

Lockhart suffered another mishap at Falkirk. A man called Dunbar, a deserter to the Jacobites at Prestonpans, stole 'a suit of laced clothes' from the major's baggage. When Dunbar was hanged at Inverness, he was dressed in Lockhart's fine clothes. He hung in them, twisting in the wind and the streets of Inverness, for two days.

The account which gives this story also confirms the brawl between

Scottish and English Redcoats in those same streets which took place after the hanging of young Malcolm Forbes of Pitcalnie.

If Major Lockhart was involved in that, I think we can probably guess on which side of the street he lined up.

26

THE ESCAPE OF JOHN ROY STUART

GREAT IS THE CAUSE OF MY SORROW,
AS I MOURN FOR THE WOUNDS OF MY LAND

After Culloden, John Roy Stuart marched with the survivors of the Edinburgh Regiment to Ruthven Barracks near Kingussie. There is no record of this having been an agreed rendezvous point in the event of a Jacobite defeat, but it seems it must have been. Two to three thousand men who had escaped the battlefield met up there.

Nowadays we see Culloden as a decisive final blow, the death knell to the '45, the Jacobites and any further hope of a restoration of the Stuarts. This wasn't necessarily how they saw it at the time. When James Johnstone reached Ruthven, he was 'delighted to see the gaiety of the Highlanders, who seemed to have returned from a ball rather than a defeat'.

Next day, the mood underwent a drastic change. A letter from the Prince reached those assembled at Ruthven. It was read out to them, very probably by John Roy, who seems to have taken charge. By this time Lord George Murray had already sent a bitter letter to the Prince resigning his commission. The last order to the men who had followed Charles Edward Stuart to hell and back was succinct, if nothing else: 'Let every man seek his own safety the best way he can.'

It was John Roy Stuart who disbanded the Jacobite Army, telling everyone it was time to go. It was a painful farewell, men in tears at the realization that it was all over. They were fearful too of the reprisals they rightly anticipated were going to be meted out to them, their families and the Highlands.

Now a notorious Jacobite, John Roy would have been entitled to be scared, too. Yet he was one of those who still had the stomach to continue the fight, one of those who hadn't yet lost hope.

Two weeks later, on 2 May 1746, two French ships sailed into Loch nan Uamh, running the gauntlet of a flotilla of British warships. The Frenchmen unloaded gunpowder and six casks of gold coins and took some fugitives away with them. The louis-d'or they left behind had an estimated value of £38,000: a huge sum of money in those days. It didn't take long for it to cause dissension, the remnants of the Jacobite leadership arguing bitterly over how the money should be used. At the time, it gave encouragement to those who were left. Some of the money was used to help those who were now destitute.

John Roy Stuart, Lord Lovat, Cameron of Lochiel, Gordon of Glenbucket and Clanranald met with some others a couple of days later at Murlaggan near the head of Loch Arkaig. The meeting broke up without any decision having been taken on what to do next. The bulk of the French money was stashed away, possibly buried, possibly hidden away in a cave. The now legendary Jacobite gold has never been found, but it's still out there somewhere.

Redcoat military patrols were now spreading out across the Highlands and Islands. Unsurprisingly, the movements of the mercurial Mr Stuart once again become a little hazy. Some historians claim he was dispatched by the Prince to France with the news of the defeat and then returned to Scotland, which sounds both highly unlikely and highly risky.

The evidence of his own poetry and the traditions of Badenoch and Strathspey are that he spent much of the next four months there, moving from one hiding place to another, including a cave where he held his foot under a waterfall in the hope of relieving the pain of a sprained ankle. The pain of the defeat he poured out into poetry. Translated from the Gaelic, his '*Latha Chuil-Lodair*' or 'Culloden Day' begins: 'Great is the cause of my sorrow, / As I mourn for the wounds of my land' and continues:

> Woe is me for the host of the tartan
> Scattered and spread everywhere,
> At the hands of England's base rascals
> Who met us unfairly in war;
> Though they conquered us in the battle,
> 'Twas due to no courage or merit of theirs,
> But the wind and the rain blowing westwards
> Coming on us up from the Lowlands.

After lamenting the white bodies of the dead lying unburied on the hillsides and that those 'who survived the disaster are carried to exile o'erseas by the winds', the poem throws some bitter words at Lord George Murray. John Roy was one of many who believed he had betrayed the Cause.

John Roy's poems and songs are full of Biblical references, comparing the Jacobites to the Children of Israel being delivered from slavery in Egypt. In John Roy's 'Prayer', he bemoans the injury to his foot:

> By a streamlet, worn and tired,
> The poor Christian John Roy sits.
> A warrior still lacking rest,
> His ankle sprained, and wretched the time.

He continues by invoking the charms and incantations which had been chanted in the Highlands for centuries as an aid to healing:

> I'll make the charm Peter made for Paul
> When his foot was sprained leaping a bank,
> Seven prayers in name of Priest and of Pope
> As plaster to put round about.

One charm more for Mary of grace
Who can a believer soon heal:
I believe, without doubt or delay,
That we shall discomfort our foes.

Perhaps his most well-known poem is a parody of the 23rd psalm:

The Lord's my targe, I will be stout,
With dirk and trusty blade,
Though Campbells come in flocks about
I will not be afraid.

Either the waterfall or the incantations must have done the trick as far as his ankle was concerned. An old story has it that Marjory Stewart of Abernethy, who died at the age of 100 in 1830, remembered that as a young girl in her teens she had danced with John Roy Stuart at a wedding in Balnagown.

In September 1746, back on the mainland after his adventures in the Hebrides, the Prince was asking if anyone knew where John Roy was. Charles was at this point with Cluny Macpherson, skulking in a bothy on Ben Alder which was 'superlatively bad and smockie'. This was before they decamped to the hiding place on the same mountain known as Cluny's Cage. A kind of tree-house woven into a rockface, an account thought to have been written by Cluny himself describes it as 'a very romantic comical habitation'. Intriguingly, this account at one point refers to 'John Roy Stewart (whom the Prince used to call THE BODY)'. Sadly, the writer does not explain how or why the nickname had been earned.

Back at the smoky bothy, John Roy Stuart had been found but not told who he was going to meet there. Alerted to his approach and wanting to surprise him, Charles wrapped himself in his plaid and lay down. As John Roy entered the hut, the Prince showed his face. Astonished and overwhelmed with relief that he was alive and well, John Roy cried out, 'O Lord! My master!' and promptly fainted. He ended up in the puddle of water in the doorway, causing great hilarity all round.

A week later, having crossed over to the west coast, Charles Edward Stuart stepped on to *L'Heureux*, the French privateer which had anchored in Loch nan Uamh. Those who were with him as he left Scotland, never to return, included Cameron of Lochiel, his brother Dr Archie Cameron, Neil MacEachainn and John Roy Stuart.

Once back in France, the former colonel of the Edinburgh Regiment soon exited stage left. Yet again the accounts differ. One story has him dying in 1747, leaving his wife and young daughter to the charity of the Stuart court in exile. Another says he died in 1752, offering as his place of death only as somewhere in Europe. The man whose light shone so brightly during the '45 steps back into the shadows and vanishes.

A roadside cairn placed there by the 1745 Association marks his birthplace at Knock of Kincardine. His poetry and songs live on.

27

FORTUNE'S TRICKS IN FORTY-SIX: DONALD MACDONELL OF TIRNADRIS

LUDICROUS WITH HIS FETTERS . . .

Fortune played the cruellest of tricks on Donald MacDonell of Tirnadris, the man who kicked off the '45 by taking Captain Sweetenham prisoner and ambushing the Royal Scots at High Bridge. In the growing darkness and torrential rain which accompanied the Battle of Falkirk in January 1746, he mistook a group of Government officers for Jacobites and walked right up to them.

Thinking on his feet, Donald MacDonell tried to pass himself off as a Campbell, the white cockade he wore being so dirty from heavy rain and gunsmoke that 'there was no discovering the colour of it'. General Huske of Barrell's Regiment was having none of it. He pointed at MacDonell's sword, which was 'covered over with blood and hair', and immediately shouted out 'to shoot the dog instantly'. Seven or eight muskets were raised, all aimed at Tirnadris's chest.

They would have killed him there and then if Lord Robert Kerr had not intervened, 'beating down the muskets'. Tirnadris admitted defeat and said he would hand over his weapons to General Huske.

The Government commander angrily said he would 'not do the Major that honour'. Once more Lord Robert Kerr intervened:

> Upon which Lord Robert Ker politely stept forwards to receive the Major's arms. When the Major was pulling off his pistol from his belt he happened to do it with such an air that Husk swore the dog was going to shoot him. To which the Major replied, 'I am more of a gentleman, Sir, than to do any such thing, I am only pulling off my pistol to deliver it up.' When the Major at any time spoke to a friend about delivering up his good claymore and his fine pistol, he used to sigh and to mention Lord Robert Ker with great affection for his generous and singular civilities.

Lord Robert was killed at Culloden, another of those men who was mourned by friend and foe alike.

Tirnadris was at first imprisoned in Edinburgh Castle where one of the sentries was an Irishman called Trapeau, a lieutenant in Bligh's Regiment. Trapeau went to some pains to ingratiate himself with the prisoners, particularly Donald MacDonell and Mrs Jean Cameron. This was the famous Jenny Cameron of the '45, who had led the Camerons of Glendessary to the Raising of the Standard at Glenfinnan.

When the sentry's regiment was ordered to sail to Aberdeen in February to join the Duke of Cumberland, 'the said Trapeau took care to have recommendatory letters to Keppoch and Lochiel from Major MacDonell and Mrs Jean Cameron, for fear of the worst'. At this stage it was not clear to anyone who was going to win this war. Trapeau changed his tune after Culloden, being in favour of severe measures while at the same time denying that Cumberland was capable of inflicting the cruelties of which he stood accused. The duke apparently had 'a soul much above these things'.

Tirnadris spent six months and more in Edinburgh Castle. Another of his fellow captives was MacDonald of Kingsburgh, accused of helping the Prince escape when the net was closing around him in the Hebrides. The prisoners were all glad to have company but found their confinement intolerable, 'waiting the freak and humour of an officer to be let out when he thinks fit to walk for an hour or so within the narrow bounds of the Half-moon', this being the battery from which those of the castle's guns which pointed at Edinburgh were fired.

The trials of Jacobite officers were held in London, Carlisle and York between August and November 1746. They were charged with high treason 'in compassing and imagining the king's death, adhering to his majesty's enemies, and levying (with other false traitors) a cruel and destructive war in these kingdoms, &c.'

Because of Cumberland's fears that Scottish juries would be too lenient, no cases were held north of the border. Brothers Alexander and Charles Kinloch, on trial in London, argued that as they were born in Scotland they ought to be tried under the laws of Scotland. Their plea was unsuccessful and they were both sentenced to death, although later reprieved. They had friends in high places, including, bizarrely, the Sardinian Ambassador.

Donald MacDonell of Tirnadris was not so lucky. As the man who had lit the spark at High Bridge which ignited the fire, he was probably always going to hang. On 24 August 1746, he wrote from Carlisle Castle to Robert Forbes in Edinburgh, 'making offer of my compliments to yourself and the Leith ladies'.

It's very possible that Tirnadris met Forbes while the latter was also imprisoned in Edinburgh Castle, in his case merely on suspicion of being on his way to join the Prince. The 'Leith ladies' may have visited them there, especially if Trapeau had allowed them access while he had been trying to ingratiate himself. Donald MacDonell might also have met the women while the Jacobites occupied Edinburgh in September and October of the previous year, although not Robert Forbes, who was already a prisoner by then.

Donald MacDonell's letter to Forbes is polite and cheerful, yet what he is relating is awful, describing how there are 100 'gentlemen who came from Scotland' all crowded in together. Not everyone is manacled, but he himself is. Typically, he makes a joke of it, asking Robert Forbes to make those compliments 'especially to Miss Mally Clerk, and tell her that notwithstanding of my irons I could dance a Highland reel with her'. Other people said he was 'ludicrous with his fetters'.

Robert Forbes wrote back, returning the compliments and telling Tirnadris that people in Edinburgh were collecting money to send to them in Carlisle in the hope it would buy them some comforts. Forbes also wanted to pass on his regards to one of Tirnadris's fellow prisoners, Robert Lyon. Both young men were ministers of the Episcopalian Church. In a P. S., Robert Forbes let Tirnadris know that 'The lady prisoners in the Castle are well.' The picture which emerges is of a group of friends all desperately worried about one another.

Three weeks later, Donald MacDonell wrote a joint letter to Robert Forbes and another friend, John Moir, described as a merchant in Edinburgh. He wanted to let them know he had been tried the day before and found guilty of treason. He had not yet been sentenced, but he was hoping for the best and preparing for the worst.

MacDonell's concern was for his 'dear wife'. She wanted to visit him in prison, but he did not think this would be allowed. In any case, he wanted her to go home. He knew he had little hope of a reprieve, and it's clear he was desperate to get her as far away as possible from the impending horror of his execution. He makes the request several times during the course of the short letter to his two friends in Edinburgh: 'I never will forgive either of you if you do not manage this point.' A few lines on, he emphasizes the point yet again: 'And for God's cause, see my wife fairly on her way home.'

He wrote again ten days later to tell Robert Forbes he'd had a bit of a fever but was now once more in good health. If it was his fate to go to the scaffold, 'I dare say that I'll goe as a Christian and a man of honour ought to do.' Once more he asked for his regards to be given to everyone, 'Miss Mally in particular'.

He wrote a farewell letter to his friend John Moir the day before he died. He had written to his wife and his brother, and he asked John Moir to help his wife sort out her finances. She wasn't going to have much money, but Tirnadris had sent 'fourteen pounds sterling and half a dozen shirts':

> I conclude with my blessing to yourself and to all the honourable honest ladies of my acquaintance in Edinburgh, and to all other friends in general, and in particular those in the Castle. And I am, with love and affection, My dear Sir, yours affectionately till death, and wishes we meet in Heaven. Donald MacDonell.
>
> Carlisle Castle, October 17ᵗʰ, 1746.
>
> P. S. Remember me in particular to my dear Mr. Robert Forbes.

His dying speech, which condemned prisoners gave from the scaffold and had been printed to be handed out to the crowd, was solemn and dignified. He had taken part in the Rising out of principle and conviction, believing it to be his duty to take up arms for 'Charles, Prince of Wales' in support of having 'our ancient and only rightful royal family restored'.

He also believed that 'nothing but the king's restoration could make our country flourish, all ranks and degrees of men happy, and free both Church and State from the many evil consequences of Revolution principles'. 'Revolution principles' were held by Whigs and friends of the Government, whose political philosophy stood on the rock of what they called the Glorious Revolution of 1688, when the Stuarts had been deposed and William of Orange had come to the throne.

Tirnadris contrasted the 'publick, cruel, barbarous and (in the eyes of the world) an ignominious and shameful death' with the magnanimous conduct of Charles Edward Stuart and the 'charity and humanity' he himself had shown to 'my enemies, the Elector's troops, when prisoners and in my power'. He died 'an unworthy member of the Roman Catholick Church, in the communion of which I have lived'. He was at pains to point out he had never had any wish to impose this on others:

> But I hereby declare upon the word of a dying man that it was with no view to establish or force that religion upon this nation that made me join my Prince's standard, but purely owing to that duty and allegiance which was due to our only rightful, lawful and natural sovereign, had even he or his family been heathen, Mahometan, or Quaker.

He hoped his 'dear son' would show the same loyalty as his father had to 'his King's, his Prince's and his country's service', and finished:

> I conclude with my blessing to my dearest wife and all my relations and friends, and humbly beg of my God to restore the King, to grant success to the Prince's arms, to forgive my enemies and receive my soul. Come, Lord Jesus, come quickly! Into thy hands I resign my spirit!

He was hanged at Carlisle on Saturday, 18 October 1746.

28

FAITHFUL UNTO DEATH:
ROBERT LYON OF PERTH

LET US PRAY WE MAY HAVE A JOYFUL AND HAPPY
MEETING IN ANOTHER WORLD

Lord Ogilvy's Regiment had two chaplains, one Church of Scotland and the other Episcopalian. The latter was Robert Lyon of Perth, who joined the Jacobite Army along with many of his parishioners as it swept south in the late summer of 1745. He did not carry arms and took no part in any battle, believing that 'to be inconsistent with my sacred character'.

Despite that, he was arrested in Perth after the defeat at Culloden and taken to Carlisle for trial. Imprisoned with many other Jacobite prisoners, he continued his ministry, leading services, and giving them communion, solace and comfort. He also wrote to their relatives to let them know what had happened to their loved ones.

One of his fellow prisoners was Laurence Mercer of Lethenty. A gentleman volunteer, he had served as a cavalry officer in the troop in the Perthshire Squadron commanded by the nephew of Isabel Haldane of Ardsheal. Tried and condemned to death, he died in Carlisle Castle before the sentence could be carried out. Robert Lyon wrote to Laurence's mother, Lady Mercer, to let her know. His letter is addressed to her at Carlisle, so she cannot have been allowed inside the castle to be with her son as he lay dying. Robert Lyon offered her the comfort of their shared religious beliefs and some very practical suggestions as to what might be done with Laurence Mercer's clothes:

> Your worthy Son Mr Mercer was remov'd from the Miseries of this World about one o'clock this Morning, during which time I was recommending his Soul to God; I hope the Consideration of his Happiness in the other World, will allay in You all immoderate Grief, & make You thoroughly resigned to God in all his wise Disposals.

Telling Lady Mercer that Laurence had died wearing a shirt belonging to a Mr Clark, who understandably did not want it back, Robert Lyon suggested she might send Mr Clark a new nightshirt. The young clergyman had a further suggestion to make:

> I beg leave to suggest to you that Mr Randal has been of great Use to your Son during the time of Distress which shou'd not be forgot, & as your Son had a new big Coat, which I know Mr Randal stands in need of, I presume it wou'd be a very acceptable Compliment to him.

Robert Lyon finished his letter by hoping God would support Lady Mercer in her grief and asking for her prayers for himself, as he believed he, too, would soon be leaving behind the miseries of the world. Three days later, he did.

He had already written his last letter to 'my dear mother and sisters' in Perth, telling them that by the time they received it he would be dead. He was his mother's only son, and his father had died while Robert was still a schoolboy. In his dying speech, he made an illuminating comment about his Protestantism:

> I declare upon this aweful occasion, and on the word
> of a dying man, that I ever abhor'd and detested and do
> now solemnly disclaim the many errors and corruptions
> of the Church of Rome; as I do with equal zeal the
> distinguishing principles of Presbyterians and other
> dissenting sectaries amongst us who are void of every
> support in our country but ignorance and usurping
> force, and whom I have always considered the shame
> and reproach of the happy Reformation, and both alike
> uncatholick and dangerous to the soul of a Christian.

For him, his own Episcopalian church was the real Church of Scotland. He believed, too, in the divine right of kings, in the sense that it was up to God to decide who ruled, not man.

Robert Lyon was outraged that he had been tried and condemned to death when he had committed 'no overt act of treason' and deeply regretted that he had gone against his religious principles and his commitment to the Stuart Cause by submitting a petition for clemency to the 'Elector of Hanover'. This he had done because of 'fear, human frailty, the persuasion of lawyers and the promise and assurance of life'. He retracted it completely before he died.

In his last letter to his family, he entreated his womenfolk to put their faith in God and expressed his regret that he was not leaving them in a better position financially. He was sorry he had spent so much of his sister Cicie's money but hoped they would all understand because it had gone not on riotous living but 'on the late glorious cause of serving my King and country'.

He asked the Lyon women to take care of Stewart Rose, the girl whom he had hoped to marry and whose first name leaves no doubt of her family's commitment to the Jacobite Cause. Robert hoped his family would treat her like a daughter and a sister. He also asked them to pass on his last good wishes to various friends and every member of his congregation.

Living up to his vocation, he asked, too, that his mother and sisters would forgive – as he did – George Miller, the Perth town clerk. Miller had earned himself a terrible reputation for vindictiveness, his evidence hanging many of his fellow citizens who had been involved in the Rising.

Robert Lyon finished his 'too long' letter to his family by hoping God would pour down His blessings on them, and gave them his own:

> Farewel, my dear mother! Farewel, my loving sisters! Farewel, every one of you for ever! And let us fervently pray for one another that we may have a joyful and happy meeting in another world, and there continue in holy fellowship and communion with our God and one another, partakers of everlasting bliss and glory to the endless ages of eternity.
>
> The grace of our Lord Jesus Christ and the love of God and the communion of the Holy Ghost be with you all evermore, is the prayer and blessing of, my dear mother, your obedient and affectionate son, and my loving sisters, your affectionate and loving brother.

He wrote that from Carlisle Castle on 23 October 1746 and, after having comforted the dying Laurence Mercer and his bereaved mother, 'stepped into eternity' at Penrith five days later:

> He suffer'd at Penrith upon Tuesday, October 28th, the festival of St. Simon and St. Jude, 1746, and perform'd the whole devotions upon the scaffold, with the same calmness and composure of mind and the same decency of behaviour, as if he had been only a witness of the fatal scene. He delivered every word of his speech to the numerous crowd of spectators.

His sister Cecelia Lyon personally gave that report to Bishop Robert Forbes, and the existence of a macabre piece of mourning jewellery seems to confirm that she personally witnessed her brother's execution. A ring was made in commemoration of Robert Lyon's life and death, its centrepiece a drop of his blood. Someone must have stepped forward to the scaffold and gathered that, perhaps soaking it up in a linen handkerchief. If it was Cicie, then at least Robert Lyon, who had given comfort to so many, was comforted himself in his last moments of life. Perhaps Cicie, the loving and much-loved sister, stood in that numerous crowd of spectators and locked eyes with him until the light dimmed for the last time in his.

29

THE LAST-MINUTE REPRIEVE: FRANCIS FARQUHARSON OF MONALTRIE & FRANCIS BUCHANAN OF ARNPRIOR

AND I'LL BE IN SCOTLAND AFORE YE

Francis Farquharson of Monaltrie on Deeside was said to be the most handsome man in the Jacobite Army. He was tall and fair and, in the parlance of the time, 'wore his own hair' – that is, he did not cover short hair or a balding head with a wig. At the age of 40, he still had a fine head of it, his golden locks falling to his shoulders. These earned him his nickname of 'Baron Ban', *ban* being Gaelic for fair.

He was the nephew of Farquharson of Invercauld, the clan chief, who had fought in the '15 but was too old to take an active part in the '45. With his blessing, Monaltrie led out the clan. Serving with him as the regiment's other colonel was his cousin James Farquharson of Balmoral. Another cousin was Captain Henry Farquharson of Whitehouse. The family relationships do not end there. Yet another of Francis Farquharson's cousins – he was a witness at her wedding in Aberdeen in 1740 – was Lady Anne Mackintosh, the Jacobite 'Colonel' Anne.

Monaltrie and Balmoral's Regiment first joined the Jacobite Army at the shambolic siege of Stirling in January 1746, although they also saw action at the Battle of Falkirk and the skirmish at Inverurie. At Culloden, they fought with the Mackintoshes under Dunmaglass and were in the thick of the fight. Many were killed. Monaltrie himself survived but was taken prisoner on the field.

He later wrote his own account of the battle, a copy of which can be read today in the National Archives of Scotland. It confirms other accounts, detailing the mistakes made in the day and weeks before the battle. Writing of the abortive night march to Nairn, Monaltrie commented on how many of the men had gone off before it in search of food:

> The thing was this; numbers of men went off to all sides, especially towards Inverness and then the officers who were sent on horseback to bring them back came up with them, they could by no persuasion be induced to return again, giving for answer they were starving, and said to the officers they might shoot them if they pleased but they could not go back until they got meat.

Francis Farquharson of Monaltrie made the hellish journey to London on-board one of the overcrowded ships on which Jacobite prisoners suffered so much and was held at the New Gaol at Southwark with several other Jacobite officers, including Andrew Wood, the young Glasgow shoemaker.

Curiously, Charles Gordon of Terpersie, one of the members of Monaltrie's Regiment held at Carlisle, wrote to his wife the night before his execution to tell her how kind Francis Farquharson had been to him. 'I think my butchered body will be taken care of and buried as a Christian, by order of Francis Farquharson, who has acted a father to me.' Although Monaltrie was never held at Carlisle, he must have found a way of sending some money there to pay for that Christian burial. Gordon was the man who had been skulking close to his home near

Alford and whose identity was fatally confirmed when Government soldiers marched him to his own home whereupon his young children ran out calling 'Daddy, Daddy'.

Like most of the prisoners at Southwark, Francis Farquharson was tried, condemned and sentenced to hang. The night before the date set for his execution, a reprieve came for him, a petition for clemency having been submitted and granted. The condition of his release was that he should not return to Scotland but remain in exile in England. He endured this separation from his homeland for almost 20 years.

He had the consolation of the love of a good woman. Elizabeth Eyre of Hassop in Derbyshire, member of a devoutly Catholic and Jacobite family, visited the prisoners in Southwark Gaol, bringing them what comfort she could. She and Francis Farquharson fell in love and married during his period of exile.

He lived for a long time in Berkhamsted, where he applied himself to the study of agriculture. When he was, at last, allowed to return home to Deeside, he put much of what he had learned into practice. He is credited with having initiated the changes which transformed Aberdeenshire from a wild upland place full of bogs and stones into the fruitful farming county it is today. He also developed Ballater as a spa, a place to go to take the waters. In so doing, he might also be credited as being one of the fathers of Scottish tourism.

The story of another Francis, Buchanan of Arnprior, is quite different. Arnprior did not serve in the Jacobite Army and never publicly declared himself for the Prince. Or did he? There's more than one mystery in his case, one of which involves the unexplained death of a man found in Arnprior's house at Leny near Callander with a pistol in his hand.

Shortly before Culloden, when Government forces were once more in charge of southern Scotland, Francis Buchanan was arrested at Leny and taken to Stirling Castle. The case against him seemed thin. There was no hard evidence to say he had been a Rebel, his arrest made on the basis of suspicion only. Thinking it highly unlikely he would be found guilty, the commanding officer of Stirling Castle allowed him the run of the place. The officers who escorted him to Carlisle were equally relaxed:

> These officers knowing well the case of Mr. Buchanan, and having witness'd the usage he had met with in Stirling Castle, treated him in a quite different manner from the other prisoners. In the forenoon, as if he had been only a fellow-traveller, they would have desir'd him to ride forwards to bespeak dinner at a proper place, and to have it ready for them against the time they should come up. In the afternoon they also desir'd him to ride on to take up night quarters and to order supper for them, and all this without any command attending him; so that he had several opportunities every day of making is escape had he dream'd that he ran any risque of his life.

This all changed when they arrived at Carlisle. To the astonishment of Francis Buchanan and the escorting officers, he was immediately thrown into a dungeon and clapped in irons. Shocked by this brutal treatment, Arnprior asked to see Captain James Thomson, one of the soldiers who had brought him to Carlisle. Equally shocked, Thomson came immediately to him and undertook to do what he could for his erstwhile travelling companion.

When Thomson approached the officer in command of Carlisle Castle, he was told the prisoners were now the responsibility of the English Solicitor General, who had come to Carlisle to oversee their trials. The Solicitor General drew a list of names out of his pocket and asked Thomson if the Mr Buchanan of whom he spoke was Francis Buchanan of Arnprior. When Thomson said yes, the Solicitor General said a curious thing: 'Pray, Sir, give yourself no more trouble about that gentleman. I shall take care of him. I have particular orders about him, for HE MUST SUFFER!'

Captain Thomson went back to Arnprior and told him what had happened 'in the softest manner he could'. The story of his interview with the Solicitor General was told to friends of Arnprior's in Edinburgh after his execution by Lieutenant Archibald Campbell, the other officer who had been in charge of escorting the prisoners to Carlisle.

The evidence brought against Francis Buchanan at his trial was flimsy, and, although the jury found him guilty, no one thought he would hang. A reprieve would surely come. Only it didn't, leaving everyone with the distinct impression that Arnprior's fate had been sealed even before he had been arrested.

Although he left no printed dying speech, Francis Buchanan did declare himself before he died:

> as he was persuaded in his conscience King James the 8th had the sole undoubted right to sit on the throne of these realms, so the only action that stared him most in the face was that he had acted the prudent and over-cautious part in not joining the Prince immediately upon his arrival, and drawing his sword in so glorious a cause . . .

Curiously, there is a letter in the National Archives of Scotland which would seem to provide the hard evidence of Arnprior's involvement with the Jacobites. Although the writer refers to 'poor Arnpior', he also writes that: 'they swore him at Glasgow two days between Christmas and the New Year walking with the Rebels in arms highland cloaths and white Cockade.' However, this letter does not seem to have been used as evidence at his trial.

At the time, his case was something of a cause célèbre. Bishop Robert Forbes did his damnedest to get to the bottom of it. He was helped in this by Robert Lyon, who spoke with Arnprior about his case shortly before they both died. Francis Buchanan himself thought people believed him to be guilty of murdering the man found dead in his house and that this, as much as anything, was what was going to hang him. With death staring him in the face, Arnprior was prepared to say what he believed had happened to Stewart of Glenbucky:

> Now I take this opportunity to declare publickly to you and my fellow prisoners that Glenbuckie and I liv'd many years in close friendship together, and altho' he was found dead in my house, yet, upon the word of a dying man, I declare I myself had no hand in his death, nor do I know any other person that had. And I am persuaded that I can likewise answer for every one of my servants, since all of them were acquainted with and had a particular love to that gentleman. So that I declare it to be my opinion that he was the occasion of his own death.

Was Arnprior reluctant to add to the pain Glenbucky's death caused to his family by saying it was suicide? Did this damage his own case? Or did the powers that be have it in for him anyway? Take a bow, Dougal Graham. The rhyming reporter mentions Arnprior in his *History of the Rebellion*.

According to Dougal Graham, while the Prince was marching south and Johnnie Cope was turning round at Inverness, a council of war was held at Leny:

> *While Charles yet, he lay at Down,*
> *And the dragoons at Stirling town:*
> *A council call'd at his desire,*
> *Held in the house of Arnprior,*
> *With chiefs and heads of ev'ry clan,*
> *Their expedition south to plan.*

If Dougal Graham was right, that Arnprior had hosted a meeting of Jacobite leaders at his home, this would certainly have been enough to hang him. And hang he did at Carlisle on 18 October 1746, along with Donald MacDonnell of Tirnadris; Thomas Coppack, the chaplain of the Manchester Regiment; Donald MacDonald of Kinlochmoidart, colonel and aide-de-camp to the Prince; and John MacNaughton. A watchmaker in Edinburgh before the outbreak of hostilities, MacNaughton was accused of having been the man who killed Colonel Gardiner at Prestonpans, which he denied. He was also the messenger instructed by Murray of Broughton, the Prince's secretary, how to steal the mail from the postboy. Although Murray himself betrayed the Cause, turning king's evidence, John MacNaughton refused to do the same.

On the sledge which dragged the prisoners to their execution, he was offered his life and a lifetime's pension if he would give evidence against his former comrades. As Bishop Robert Forbes later recorded in *The Lyon in Mourning*: 'He answered that they had done him much honour in ranking him with gentlemen, and he hoped to let the world see he would suffer like a gentleman.'

One of the Jacobite prisoners hanged at Carlisle is traditionally said to have written the poignant love song 'Loch Lomond'. The singer bids farewell to his friend, who will be returning to Scotland by the high road of life, while he will have to travel on the low road of death, returning home only as a ghost.

It's not known who wrote 'Loch Lomond'. If only on the basis of where he lived, Francis Buchanan of Arnprior would seem to be a likely candidate.

30

THE CAPTAIN'S HALFPENNY:
ANDREW WOOD OF GLASGOW

ALL THAT YOUR FOREFATHERS EVER FOUGHT FOR IS GONE

Shortly before nine o'clock on the morning of Friday, 28 November 1746, a young man in Southwark Gaol, on the south bank of the Thames, was told to prepare himself. In three hours' time, he was to be hanged on nearby Kennington Common. He was Captain Andrew Wood, and he was the man who wasn't there – if only according to Provost Cochrane of Glasgow. There were no Jacobites in his city.

Andrew Wood asked about one of his fellow prisoners, John Hamilton from Huntly, who had been left with Colonel Townley of the Manchester Regiment in the doomed attempt to hold Carlisle Castle after the Jacobite Army's retreat from England. Was he to hang, despite his years? 'Yes,' came the answer, to which Andrew replied, 'I am sorry for that poor old gentleman.'

Wood, Hamilton, Sir John Wedderburn, Captain Alexander Leith, James Lindsay and Jem Bradshaw of the Manchester Regiment were to be executed that day. Before they left the prison, they were offered refreshment. Andrew Wood called for white wine and toasted King James and Prince Charles Edward Stuart, defiantly giving them what he believed to be their proper titles.

The condemned men were to be drawn to Kennington Common on straw-covered sledges pulled by strong shire horses. As they were submitting to having their hands tied, a reprieve came for James Lindsay. He and Andrew Wood knew each other well from the campaign and from their sojourn in Southwark Gaol. They also had a profession in common: they were both shoemakers.

Such last-minute reprieves were not uncommon. Francis Farquharson of Monaltrie had received one just the night before. Jamie Lindsay broke down in tears, unable to do more than embrace his friend before he was led away.

There is a curious little souvenir of the six months or so which Andrew Wood spent in Southwark Gaol. It is a George II halfpenny, with the following inscription on the reverse: 'Given to me by Captain Andrew Wood of the Rebel Army whilst confined at Southward, 1745. Wm. Stapley.'

The year must, of course, have been 1746, but the mistake only adds authenticity to the piece. Anyone faking a Jacobite relic would have made sure to get the date right. The logical assumption is that William Stapley was a prison warder. In those days, prisoners had to pay for their own food and drink, but since Stapley kept the halfpenny it obviously wasn't given in payment. We know, too, that Andrew was short of cash, 'not so plentifully supplied' as some of his fellow prisoners were. The halfpenny must have been a token gift, perhaps for some kindness rendered in a prison whose chief gaoler was known for his greed, brutality and lack of humanity. Stapley must have felt more compassion for the Scotsmen so far from home. Andrew Wood, too, must have made an impression on Stapley, enough for him to have the coin engraved and keep it as a memento of the young Glaswegian.

To the representatives of the Government of King George, whose authority he and every other Jacobite did not recognize, Andrew Wood adopted a policy of non-cooperation. The notes of the official who interrogated him illustrate this. Other than acknowledging his name, time and again it is noted that 'he refuses to answer further'. When asked where he was born, he replied only, 'Scotland, I think.'

Others tried to help him escape his fate. The Glasgow men whom he had saved at Falkirk, seeing them through the Jacobite lines, composed a petition for clemency. As they put it:

> had it not been for his humanity and safe conduct of us
> we should have been carried Prisoners by the Rebells
> further North and should have been stript and robbed
> of all we had if not deprived of our Lives.

Nine men signed the petition: James Steven, John Bannatyne, James McKean, John Buchanan, Alexander Sutherland, Robert Logan, William Thomson, Thomas McKinlay and Robert Philipshill. There were two separate affidavits in support of clemency from William Aitken, a student of divinity, and Joseph McCray, a fencing-master. They, too, believed they owed their lives to Andrew Wood.

Provost Andrew Cochrane, the man who fell over backwards to affirm his city's loyalty to the Government and the House of Hanover, also signed the petition. He was careful not to minute this. There is no reference to Andrew Wood's case in any of the archives of Glasgow from this period. At the same time, Cochrane did make the petition official, affixing to it the seal of the Corporation of Glasgow.

Defiant though he was, Andrew Wood must have hoped against hope that, like Monaltrie, he, too, might receive a last-minute reprieve. As James Lindsay's case shows, hope could last to the steps of the scaffold.

Andrew Wood was distressed the day before his execution but not because of fear. A Presbyterian minister visiting Southwark Gaol had refused to give him communion. He was a Rebel. What's more, he refused to acknowledge that what he had done was wrong.

Bishop Gordon was a Scottish Episcopalian who visited Southwark later that day. With tears in his eyes, Andrew Wood told him the story. According to the other clergyman, Wood was no better than a murderer. He had Christian blood on his hands, and he was guilty of 'rebelling against the wisest, most just, most pious & best of Kings in favour of a Popish Pretender, & with a great deal more of Such like unbecoming Rant'. Unless he repented and asked God's Pardon for what he had done, the minister would not give him communion or have anything more to do with him. At this point Andrew Wood saw red, too angry to care that his words were being overheard by at least a dozen bystanders, including 'those in the Room & those looking in at the Windows'.

First, he was no Rebel. He had taken up arms in support of the lawful king and if he got the chance he would do the same again. Second, Charles Edward Stuart's religion was neither here nor there. Everyone owed him and his father James their allegiance. Third, look at what Scotland had lost:

> I bid him remember too the Massacre of Glencoe, & Destruction of the Scots in Darien; the base & Scandalous Union, the Articles of which had constantly been violated as often as ever it Served the Wicked Purposes of the Usurpers & their infamous Tools; & particularly on the present Occasion with regard to us the poor Prisoners, who are brought up here out of our own Country, the ancient Kingdom, to be tried, condemn'd and murthered by Strangers & Foreigners, who most inhumanly thirst after our Blood.

Andrew's final point to the Presbyterian minister, whose full and silent attention he now had, cited the 'Murders & Massacre in cool Blood after the Battle of Culloden, So barbarous and unchristian, that I verily believe the like had never before been heard of in any civilized, much less Christian Country'.

Recovering at last from the verbal onslaught, the minister told the young man to mind his tongue. He could be endangering his fellow prisoners. Andrew Wood retorted that he had to speak the truth, at which point the clergyman rose to his feet and left without a further word.

Feeling deeply sorry for the young captain, whom he described as being 'in the utmost Distress, quite bewildered', Bishop Gordon sat down and talked it all through with him. A lengthy theological discussion followed, in which the good Bishop convinced Andrew Wood that a Presbyterian minister had no right to give or withhold communion anyway. The only true Church of Scotland was the Episcopalian one.

With Andrew's agreement, he baptized him a member of it and gave him the solace of communion which he so craved. Afterwards, he was 'easy and cheerfull, like a person indeed thoroughly Satisfied in his Mind: And this Ease and Cheerfulness, I have good reason to believe continued with him to the last Moment of his life'.

No reprieve came for him. On the scaffold at Kennington Common, not far from where the Oval cricket ground now stands, he was calm and forgave his enemies. He affirmed his support for the Stuarts and appealed to his fellow Scots to realize that, by uniting with England, 'all ever your forefathers fought for is gone'.

He asked God to bless King James and Prince Charles and committed his spirit to the Lord. He was 23 years old.

31

Warm Ale on a Cold Morning: The Escape of Lord Pitsligo

I had ate, and drunk, and laughed enough

And then there are the ones who got away. Alexander Forbes, 4th Lord Pitsligo, was one of them. After Culloden, he made it back to Elgin, hiding there for a while before heading east to his home at Pitsligo Castle near Fraserburgh. The plan was to take ship for France. It didn't work out that way.

Alexander Forbes was, after all, one of the most important Jacobite leaders, a man who'd had an enormous influence on his neighbours, not by bullying and coercion but through the strength of his mind and the force of his arguments. A huge military operation swung into place to prevent his escape. This man was dangerous.

This man was also no longer young nor in the best of health, making it all the more remarkable that he eluded his pursuers for so many years. It's a tribute to his own lust for life and the loyalty of his tenants, who sheltered him and shared what they had with him. He shrugged off the discomforts of being a fugitive, saying: 'I had ate, and drunk, and laughed enough.'

Disguised as a beggar and going under the alias of 'Sanny Brown', the noble lord stravaiged the Buchan coast and countryside for several years, occasionally managing a flying visit to see his second wife, Elizabeth Allan, whom he had married after Rebecca's death in 1731. Often he hid in a cave a mile or two west of Rosehearty and on other occasions concealed himself under the arches of the old bridge at Craigmaud, several miles inland. The latter he found extremely uncomfortable, the arches being low and the space beneath them very cramped.

His narrow escapes while he was skulking are the stuff of legend. On one occasion, he was taken badly by an asthma attack on the road at the very moment that a troop of Government soldiers were marching past. Unable to move, he played his beggar's role so well the men gave him some coins and sympathized with him about his illness. Another time, sleeping at one of his tenant's houses, he was surprised by cavalrymen searching for him. In his disguise, he conducted them around the house himself, carrying a lantern to help them see better. Satisfied their quarry was not there, the soldiers departed, giving their guide a shilling for his pains.

While he was in hiding, his friend the Countess of Erroll kept in touch with him via messages carried by Jamie Fleeman. We know him as the Laird of Udny's fool, but he was a loyal and discreet messenger.

At last, after four years of this exhausting way of life, Alexander Forbes was able to seek the shelter of his son's house at Auchiries, inland from Fraserburgh to the north of the Mormond Hill, Buchan's famous landmark. The search for him was periodically renewed. A full ten years after Culloden, when he was seventy-eight, the household was disturbed by an early morning raid in search of the infamous Lord Pitsligo.

Hurriedly bundled into a small recess behind the wood panelling of one of the bedchambers, the dust, confinement and anxiety provoked an asthma attack. The young lady occupying the room, Miss Gordon of Towie, pretended she was having a coughing fit to mask the noise coming from behind the wall. Despite the soldiers getting close enough to assure themselves she wasn't a man in a woman's nightdress, her ruse worked.

Safely tucked up in his own bed, the exhausted Lord Pitsligo asked his servant James to see to the Redcoats, who were still outside the house. It was March, and a cold morning, and James was to make sure that 'the poor fellows', who, after all, had only been doing their duty, got some breakfast and warm ale.

Gradually the search eased off. It seems many of those ostensibly looking for him had little real desire to catch him. He was a man respected as much by his enemies as his friends.

In his final years, he turned once more to his beloved books and produced another series of moral and philosophical essays. His message was a positive one. He wrote of the joys of friendship and the beauty of the world: its trees, flowers, rivers and seas.

Surrounded by his family and friends, he died shortly before Christmas, 1762. He was 84 years old and a free man still. He is buried in Old Pitsligo church on the hill above Rosehearty.

32

Sore Feet & Tender Kisses: The Escape of James Johnstone

I pity his situation. Will you take an oar?

James Johnstone was 26 years old in 1745. Well off and well connected, his father had despaired of his only son, who seemed interested only in the pursuit of pleasure and the pursuit of the opposite sex. Mr Johnstone senior, an Edinburgh merchant, dispatched James to stay with two uncles in Russia for a while, in the hope the experience would broaden his horizons.

Back in Scotland in September 1745, when James found a cause he could believe in, his father was appalled. Jacobite in sympathy though Mr Johnstone senior was, he was violently opposed to James joining the Prince's army. James went all the same.

His family connections secured him an introduction to the Duke of Perth and Lord George Murray, and he acted for a while as aide-de-camp to the latter. He was to become a passionate supporter of Lord George and was accordingly sometimes highly critical of the Prince.

On the battlefield, fighting on the left wing next to Donald MacDonald of Scotus, Johnstone was momentarily stunned when he saw him fall. Then he deployed the blunderbuss Sergeant Dickson had used to such effect in Manchester:

I remained for a time motionless, and lost in astonishment; then in a rage, I discharged my blunderbuss and pistols at the enemy and immediately endeavoured to save myself like the rest. But having charged on foot and in boots I was so overcome by the marshy ground, the water on which reached to the middle of the leg, that instead of running, I could scarcely walk.

He had left his servant, a man called Robertson, on a little rise about 600 yards behind where the battle was being fought. This was near to where the Prince stood, and Johnstone had told Robertson to stay there with their horses so he would be sure of finding him afterwards. When Johnstone looked for Robertson, he was gone.

Spotting what he thought was a riderless horse, he ran up to it. Unfortunately, its rider, though lying on the ground, was still holding onto its bridle. A ridiculous argument over possession of the horse then ensued. Even when they were showered with mud from grapeshot from the Government cannons, it continued until Johnstone called on a friend by the name of Finlay Cameron who was also making his escape from the field.

Finlay 'flew to me like lightning, immediately presented his pistol to the head of this man and threatened to blow out his brains if he hesitated a moment to let go the bridle'. The man let go of the bridle and ran off. Since the 'cowardly poltroon ... had the appearance of a servant', Johnstone obviously felt he was more entitled to his horse than he was. At times, young Captain Johnstone could be the most awful snob.

The day after the battle, he reached Ruthven Barracks. When the order came that each man should seek his own safety, the survivors were devastated:

> Our separation at Ruthven was truly affecting. We bade one another an eternal adieu. No one could tell whether the scaffold would not be his fate. The Highlanders gave

vent to their grief in wild howlings and lamentations; the tears flowed down their cheeks when they thought that their country was now at the discretion of the duke of Cumberland and on the point of being plundered, whilst they and their children would be reduced to slavery and plunged, without resource, into a state of remediless distress.

James Johnstone was highly critical of the Prince for abandoning the fight when he did. Considering the situation years later, he still believed, as he always had done, that many of the Scottish officers in the Government army could have been persuaded by national pride to come over to the Jacobites. He could not understand why the Prince 'preferred to wander up and down the mountains alone' when he might have been 'at the head of a body of brave and determined men, of whose fidelity and attachment he was secure, and all of whom would have shed the last drop of their blood in his defence'.

Had distance lent a romantic glow to James Johnstone's memories? It's hard to know. In his memoirs, he wrote of his confidence that the regrouped Jacobite Army could have marched back to Inverness and fought the Duke of Cumberland again within the space of a fortnight – and won.

Failing that, Johnstone suggested something that has often been speculated on since: that they could have melted away into the hills and emerged from them to wage a guerrilla campaign against the Government forces, what he described as 'mountain-warfare'. His summing-up of what happened instead has huge resonance. His 'last war' in the following passage was the Seven Years War of 1756–63:

> in a revolt, 'when we draw the sword we ought to throw away the scabbard'. There is no medium; we must conquer or die. This would have spared much of the blood which was afterwards shed on the scaffold in England, and would have prevented the almost total

extermination of the race of Highlanders which has since taken place, either from the policy of the English government, the emigration of their families to the colonies, or from the numerous Highland regiments which have been raised, and which have been often cut to pieces during the last war.

Johnstone was to spend the next few months wandering up and down the mountains himself, seeing them as the most secure hiding place he could find. He had been at school with one of the Grants of Rothiemurchus and, although his old school friend was in the Government army, both he and his father had assured James that he would always find a welcome under their roof.

At a time when mountains and untamed nature were not admired as they are today, James Johnstone loved them. Waxing lyrical about the waterfalls and the glens, he described the Grants' home at Rothiemurchus as being in 'one of the most beautiful valleys imaginable' and 'on the banks of a very beautiful river, the Spey'.

He found other fugitives at Rothiemurchus, including Sir William Gordon of Park and Gordon of Avochie. They had resolved to head home to Banffshire, and Johnstone decided to go with them. His brother-in-law lived in Banff, 'where he had the inspection of merchant-ships, in virtue of an office lately obtained by him from the government', and he thought he would help him to escape. The group didn't go far on the first day of their journey, spending the night at a friend's house 'near a mountain called Cairngorm':

> These gentlemen yielded to the entreaties of their friend to stay a day at his house, and I was not displeased at it. Forgetting our disasters for a moment, I rose at an early hour and flew immediately to the mountains among the herdsmen, where I found some pretty and beautiful topazes, two of which, sufficiently large to serve for seals, I afterwards presented to the Duke of York, at Paris.

This Duke of York was the Jacobite holder of that title: Henry, Bonnie Prince Charlie's brother, a cardinal in the Roman Catholic Church. When he came back in with a bag of cairngorms, Johnstone's friends burst out laughing and suggested he ought to be concentrating on saving himself from being hanged rather than on 'collecting pebbles'.

It's obvious, however, that he found his stravaig through the hills searching for cairngorms soothing and distracting. His head must have been full of the terrible sights and sounds of Culloden. Only too well aware of the danger they were all in, he was also haunted by thoughts of the scaffold on which he was likely to end his days if he were captured. These thoughts were to torment his imagination in the weary weeks and months of flight which followed.

They reached William Gordon's home at Castle of Park, halfway between Huntly and Banff, four days after they left Rothiemurchus. On the way, they spent one night with a Reverend Stuart. A Church of Scotland minister, he was a covert Jacobite. The minister's servant swapped clothes with James Johnstone, so that instead of a 'laced Highland dress' he now wore 'an old labourer's dress, quite ragged and exhaling a pestilential odour'. He assumed the man must have worn the clothes only when he mucked out the minister's stables, because they reeked of manure. Despite his appalled distaste, Johnstone was happy to admit that 'these rags were to contribute to save my life'.

Banff was swarming with English soldiers, a good 400 of them, but the clothes with the pestilential odour kept them away. It was a crushing disappointment when Johnstone's brother-in-law refused to help him. Every ship leaving Banff was being searched for escaping Jacobites, and he would not risk smuggling a fugitive on-board.

Johnstone decided there was nothing for it but to head overland towards Edinburgh. It took him weeks to get there. Every port and every river was being watched, and getting across the Tay was to be a major problem. Persuaded it might help if he bided his time until the fuss had died down a bit, he spent more than a fortnight with two other fugitives in the humble home of a man called Samuel in Glenprosen, near Cortachy.

Samuel, his wife and their married daughter, who lived nearby and kept a lookout for any approaching Redcoat patrols, risked their lives for James Johnstone, and he was profoundly grateful to them. He did get bored with their diet, although he had to admit it was healthy:

> Samuel was a very honest man but extremely poor. We remained seventeen days in his house, eating at the same table with himself and his family, who had no other food than oatmeal and no other drink than the water of the stream which ran through the glen. We breakfasted every morning on a piece of oatmeal bread, which we were enabled to swallow by draughts of water; for dinner we boiled oatmeal with water, till it acquired a consistency, and we ate it with horn-spoons; in the evening, we poured boiling water on this meal in a dish for our supper. I must own that the time during which I was confined to this diet appeared to pass very slowly, though none of us seemed to suffer in our health from it; on the contrary we were all exceedingly well.

Johnstone had the money to be able to send Samuel to buy some food or drink to vary this monotonous regime, but everyone was scared this might arouse suspicion. There were too many Government soldiers patrolling the area. A similar problem arose when the 'very honest man' at last guided Johnstone to Broughty Ferry, from where he hoped to cross the Tay. When James offered him the horse on which he had ridden away from Culloden as a present, Samuel refused. If people saw him in possession of such a fine horse that would arouse suspicion, too.

So James threw the saddle and tack down a well and sent the horse off into a field. Someone was bound to find him, take him for a stray and give him a home. It took the faithful cuddy some time to get the message that, for him, the war was over: 'We had great difficulty in getting quit of this animal, for he followed us for some time like a dog.'

A combination of Samuel's local knowledge and Johnstone's social network produced the fugitive's next helper. Leaving him in a field where he was concealed by a mass of broom bushes, Samuel returned with Mr Graham of Duntroon. He asked James Johnstone what he would like for breakfast. His answer is not hard to guess: anything as long as it's not oatmeal and water:

> He left me and soon after sent me his gardener, in whose fidelity he could confide, with new-laid eggs, butter, cheese, a bottle of white wine and another of beer. I never ate with so much voracity, and devoured seven or eight eggs in a moment, with a great quantity of bread, butter and cheese.

Johnstone gave Samuel a generous tip – he still had six or seven guineas on him – said his farewells and lay down for a sleep among the broom. Mr Graham woke him at midday to take his order for dinner and with the good news that he could get him across the Tay that evening. 'He mentioned a piece of beef, and I begged he would send me nothing else.' Graham brought it back himself, plus a good bottle of claret, which the two of them shared.

When James arrived at the pub in Broughty Ferry to which he had been covertly led, the boatmen who were to row him across the Tay reneged on the deal, fearful of what might happen to them if anyone ever found out they had helped a Jacobite fugitive to escape. The landlady's daughters, 'who were as beautiful as Venus' and clearly as charmed by James Johnstone as he was by them, were a lot bolder:

> The beautiful and charming Mally Burn, the eldest of the two, disgusted at length, and indignant at their obstinacy, said to her sister, 'O, Jenny! they are despicable cowards and poltroons, I would not for the world that

> this unfortunate gentleman was taken in our house. I
> pity his situation. Will you take an oar?'

James 'clasped them in my arms and covered them in turns with a thousand tender kisses'. For the sake of Mally and Jenny, hopefully the stay at Samuel's had allowed his smelly clothes to become a little fresher.

It took two hours to row across the river, and they reached the other side at midnight. Affectionate farewells were exchanged under the stars. More tender kisses, one assumes. The girls would take no money from him, but he slipped ten shillings into Mally's pocket without her realizing he had done it.

Heading through Fife towards St Andrews, where he had another relative, he stopped by a burn to bathe his feet, which were blistered and bleeding. After the romantic drama and the kindness of the girls the previous night, it's here that he reached his lowest point, suddenly swamped by images of himself being hung, drawn and quartered.

He wished he had died with his comrades at Culloden. He saw his current situation as hopeless. How on earth was he to reach safety? As he sat on the banks of the burn, he mulled it all over and seriously considered taking his own life.

A spark of hope and a prayer to God that one way or another his troubles might soon be over stayed his hand. His shoes and stockings were encrusted with dried blood. He soaked them in the burn for half an hour, put them on again and continued to St Andrew's to his cousin, Mrs Spence.

She sent him to one of her tenants, with a note that the man should give James a horse and conduct him to Wemyss, where he could get a boat to cross to Edinburgh. However, Mrs Spence's tenant was not willing to cooperate:

> I delivered the letter to the farmer and the answer I
> received from this brute petrified me. 'Mrs. Spence,' said
> he, 'may take her farm from me and give it to whom she

pleases, but she cannot make me profane the Lord's day by giving my horse to one who means to travel upon the Sabbath.'

James got his revenge on this man in his memoirs, going into full rant mode about the hypocrisy of this 'holy rabble' who 'never scrupled to deceive their neighbours on the Lord's day, as well as other days'. At the time, the man's refusal to give him the horse was a disaster. Johnstone's feet were in a terrible state, every step bringing fresh agony.

He remembered that a former maid to his mother had married a gardener who worked for Mr Beaton of Balfour, whose home was ten miles away. His feet were so sore by the time he got there that he had to hold onto the doorpost to stop himself from falling over. Even if it was to save himself from being hanged, he could not have walked another step.

The gardener was horrified when he realized his visitor was a Jacobite fugitive, but his wife immediately said, 'Good God, I know him; quick – shut the door!' Like many people in Scotland at the time, her husband fortunately drew a distinction between disliking someone's politics and not wanting to see a fellow Scotsman hanged. He bathed James's feet in whisky before applying salve to them, his wife cooked him steak for his supper and James Johnstone slept the clock round.

His troubles were by no means over. The only fisherman who might even consider taking him across to Edinburgh when he went to Leith to sell his fish the following morning was 'a very zealous Calvinist and a violent enemy of the house of Stuart' by the name of Salmon. He would do James no harm, he said, and was not capable of informing against him, but he would not help. Money could not persuade him either.

As well as being a fisherman, Salmon kept an alehouse. James suggested they all have a beer together. After an hour of matching him 'glass for glass', during which he did not mention the lift to Leith, Salmon suddenly changed his mind, exclaiming to the gardener:

'What a pity, that this poor young man should have been debauched and perverted by this worthless rebel crew! He is a fine lad!'

And so it went on. In Leith, his old governess sheltered him. He saw his father but could not risk seeing his mother, who was very ill and not fit enough to leave the family home, which everyone feared was too risky for James to visit. Being persuaded out of running that risk was something he was to regret for the rest of his life. He never saw his mother again, as she died soon afterwards.

He travelled overland to London and, at last, after several narrow escapes, made it to the Continent. He was to spend his life in exile in France, soldiering in Europe and in Canada, becoming known as the Chevalier de Johnstone.

In old age, he published *A Memoir of the 'Forty-Five*. It's sharply observed, intelligently and well written, and his descriptions leap off the page. Few who write about the '45 can resist quoting him.

He never came home to Scotland.

33

A Chiel Amang Ye Takin' Notes: Bishop Robert Forbes

I love truth

It's not much to look at: ten small notebooks bound in dark brown leather. Over the two and a half centuries since a man with a quill pen first wrote in them, some of the covers have come off. They are secured now to the handwritten pages they protect by linen tape tied in a bow. You can hold one of them in your hand for a moment or two without realizing what you have. This is *The Lyon in Mourning*, and there are riches beyond measure in here.

When its compiler, Robert Forbes, designed, drew and wrote the title page in 1747, he was committing an act of treason for which he could have been sentenced to death. Over the next 30 years, he kept his notebooks carefully hidden when he was not copying letters, poems, dying speeches and eyewitness accounts of events and personalities of the '45 into them.

Born in Old Rayne in Aberdeenshire, Robert Forbes was 37 in 1745, an Episcopalian for whom commitment to the House of Stuart was bound up inextricably with his religious faith. With a group of friends, he was arrested at Stirling on his way to join the Prince. He was held captive in the castle there and subsequently at Edinburgh

Castle from the beginning of September 1745 until the end of May 1746.

So he never met Charles Edward Stuart, and he never knew what it was like to be in Edinburgh while a Stuart prince held court at Holyroodhouse. He must have been so frustrated by that.

He seems to have met Donald MacDonell of Tirnadris after the latter was taken prisoner at the Battle of Falkirk on 17 January. Although they cannot have spent more than a few weeks together, the friendship forged under such circumstances ran deep. Robert Forbes and the men with whom he'd been captured were transferred to Edinburgh Castle in February 1746, on the orders of the Duke of Cumberland, who was then at Stirling. Taken out of the castle at nine o'clock in the morning, Forbes and his fellow prisoners stood in the street till the middle of the afternoon 'as so many spectacles to be gazed at'.

When the Duke of Albemarle came riding up and 'with a volley of oaths' demanded to know why the prisoners weren't tied, Captain Hamilton, who was in charge of them, said it was because they were gentlemen. 'Gentlemen,' snarled Albemarle, 'damn them for rebels. Get ropes and rope them immediately.'

Hamilton demurred. The gentlemen had been arrested on suspicion only. He didn't think they had actually committed any rebellious acts. Albemarle roared his head off and insisted on the ropes. 'Tied two and two by the arms, the gentlemen laughing at the farce,' Captain Hamilton apologized as it was done. Once they were away from Stirling, he told them to throw away the ropes. Might this have been the same Captain Hamilton who rescued Ranald MacDonald of Belfinlay on the battlefield at Culloden?

Writing in the third person about this incident, Bishop Forbes added a discreet footnote to the story: 'This account about the prisoners I wrote from my own eyesight and experience.' The modesty is typical of the man, as is his acknowledgement of the reluctance of Captain Hamilton to rope his prisoners. *The Lyon* contains searing accounts of cruelties perpetrated by Government troops and commanders, but where credit is due to them for restraint and kindness, Bishop Forbes is always scrupulous to give it. 'I love truth,' he wrote, 'let who will be either justified or condemned by it. I would not wish to advance a falsehood upon any subject, not even on Cumberland himself, for any consideration whatsoever.'

In May 1746, he was released from Edinburgh Castle without charge and went to stay in Leith with a wealthy parishioner, Dame Magdalene Scott, Lady Bruce of Kinross, well known for her Jacobite sympathies. He married twice, his first wife dying after only a year. His second wife was Rachel Houston and they seem to have been devoted to one another. She shared her husband's politics and was as committed as him to the compilation of *The Lyon in Mourning*.

Charles Edward Stuart was aware of both of them. Rachel often sent the Prince little presents, and he said of her husband that he was an honest man and that he held him in high esteem. Robert Forbes' collection does not include only words. There are Jacobite relics, too.

They include a scrap of the flowery material of Betty Burke's dress and a tiny piece of wood from one of the oars of the boat which carried Charles, Flora MacDonald and Neil MacEachainn to Skye. There's a large strip of tartan material, its reds, greens and yellows still jewel bright after 250 years. As ever, the Bishop was careful to record in writing where this piece of tartan came from: a waistcoat which MacDonald of Kingsburgh gave the Prince after he changed out of his female clothes. Unfortunately, since the waistcoat was 'too fine for a Servant', Charles had to discard it.

Compiling *The Lyon in Mourning* was Robert Forbes' life's work. He went on gathering information until a month before his death in 1778. By this time, Jacobitism was a spent force, no longer viewed as a danger to the status quo. The Episcopalian church was to officially separate itself from the Cause two years later. Despite a gradual easing of attitudes towards the vanquished Jacobites, the Bishop could never be persuaded to allow his collection to be published.

He may have been right to continue to view it as containing too many 'truths of so much delicacy and danger' or perhaps it had simply become too precious to him. His wife Rachel survived him by 30 years. Short of money, she sold the notebooks in 1806, but it was to be another 25 years before some of the information in them was released to the public between the covers of writer and publisher Robert Chambers' *History of the Rebellion of 1745–6*.

The Lyon in Mourning in its entirety was subsequently published by the Scottish History Society. It gave a great boost to writers investigating the '45 in the late nineteenth and early twentieth centuries and continues to be an amazing resource for anyone fascinated by the events of 1745–6.

Some people don't like it. Academic historians accuse Bishop Forbes of having a bias towards the Jacobites. Revisionist historians who try to persuade us that the cruelties encouraged by the Duke of Cumberland and perpetrated by some of the officers and men in his army are exaggerated accuse the Bishop of peddling Jacobite propaganda.

Of course Robert Forbes had a bias towards the Jacobites. He was impelled to start compiling *The Lyon in Mourning* because of a sense of burning injustice over how defeated Jacobites were being treated: they were being hanged and hounded and persecuted. Those are hard facts, not propaganda.

The Bishop, as he said, loved the truth. Read *The Lyon in Mourning* and you keep coming across letters from him to the people who were sending him information. He always wants the truth, he always wants to check if there are other sources to corroborate a story, as he is scrupulous about recording the names of those Government soldiers who acted to stop cruelty.

All history is selective. What we leave out is as important as what we leave in. Robert Forbes did his absolute best, working with a quill pen by candlelight, to put everything in.

Epilogue: On Culloden Moor

Behave yourself. People died here

Scotland's broken heart lies here. Even the name hurts. The vicious battle fought on this windswept moor four miles east of Inverness meant the death of the Jacobite dream, the end of the line for the House of Stuart and the abandonment of any hope of Scotland, the ancient Kingdom, regaining her centuries-old status as an independent European country. This is where the clocks stopped.

The massacre of wounded Jacobites by the victorious Government forces initiated that devastating summer of bloodletting and reprisals. Throughout the Highlands and Islands, men and boys were shot, women and girls were raped, houses, farm buildings and chapels were burned. The treatment meted out to Jacobite prisoners who survived Culloden and its aftermath is a chilling example of man's inhumanity to man.

Many of the thousands carried south in the holds of filthy, overcrowded and disease-ridden ships did not survive the journey, their bodies flung overboard into the chilly waters of the North Sea. Those who did survive endured incarceration on prison hulks moored on the Thames or were cooped up in Tilbury Fort, where excursions were run so people could gawp at them. Hundreds of men, women and children were transported to the West Indies to work as forced labour on the sugar plantations.

Thirty-six men were hanged in the streets of Inverness. Eighty-four more suffered the medieval barbarity of being hung, drawn and quartered in Carlisle, York and London. Their heads were placed on spikes as a terrible warning to anyone who might ever again contemplate delivering such a shock to the British state as the Jacobites did.

After Culloden, there was a determined effort to diminish and marginalize the culture which was seen to have nurtured the 'unnatural rebellion'. Highlanders were no longer allowed to carry weapons. The wearing of kilts and tartan was banned. One of the men sent to enforce this prohibition was Captain Sweetenham. Whether he thought it was suitable work for an engineer is debatable.

Culloden symbolizes the end of the clan system and is bound up irrevocably with the Highland Clearances, which were to see the emigration of hundreds of thousands of Scots to the farthest ends of the Earth.

For so many sad reasons, it's easy to understand why so many of those who visit the battlefield today do so in a spirit of solemn pilgrimage and can be overheard admonishing their children to 'Behave yourself. People died here.'

Each year, at the annual commemoration of this last full-scale battle fought on British soil, flowers are laid to remember the sons, fathers, brothers and friends who fought and died here. Nobody ever lays flowers for the Redcoats.

The men whose choices led them to this place to fight under the Standard of Prince Charles Edward Stuart did so for a variety of reasons. Some had no choice.

Many on the Government side were in the army through economic necessity. Many on the Jacobite side were here because their clan chiefs, lairds and landlords had demanded it. That rigorous obedience was mirrored in those among their leaders whose mystical, near-religious loyalty to Scotland's royal house evokes so much admiration in those who take the romantic view of the Jacobite Cause.

For the men who felt this unswerving loyalty to the Stuarts, the '45 was the final act in the War of the British Succession, the culmination of all the other failed attempts to regain the British crown and throne for the ruling house to whom they believed it rightfully belonged. As they saw it, this right was God-given, not to be questioned or usurped by man.

For them and many others, what they were also fighting for was their country's nationhood. They were to be bitterly disappointed when it became clear that Scotland alone was not enough for Charles Edward Stuart. Nevertheless, at the start of the great adventure, he gave all those disaffected to the status quo a focus for their discontent and a leader they could follow. In the days before democracy and universal suffrage, it was one of the few ways ordinary people might hope to change things.

On the field and off it, there were Scots who sincerely believed Scotland's best hopes for peace and prosperity were dependent on remaining in the Union. Others, with regret for the loss of nationhood, were unwilling to plunge their country into bloodshed and turmoil for the sake of which royal house sat on the throne in a conflict between a German king and a Polish-Italian prince.

Yet that European dimension meant the stage on which the drama of the '45 was acted out was as big as it could be. If the attempt to regain the throne for the Stuarts had succeeded — and there were certain pivotal moments when it might have done — the subsequent history of Britain, Europe and the world would have been very different.

Once the Jacobites had been so comprehensively defeated, the French no longer had the opportunity to meddle in Britain's affairs and cause trouble for their old rival, England. With Scotland on-board, reluctantly or not, there was now the freedom to concentrate on the building of the British Empire. The Highland warriors who might have destroyed a united Britain ended up putting their swords, fighting spirit and loyalty at its disposal.

Culloden is often presented as a mythic Last Battle, the final conflict between the old Scotland and the new. Even as they line up on that windswept moor four miles east of Inverness, ready to run into the history books, a hundred sentimental songs and Scotland's collective memory, the Jacobites are the romantic but doomed warriors of a way of life already fading into the mists of time and legend. Their loyalty and courage is lauded, their suffering condemned, but essentially they are consigned to the footnotes of history.

According to this scenario, modern Scotland – the Enlightenment, the Industrial Revolution, Scots seizing their opportunities as so many did in Britain and the British Empire – could only be born out of the death throes of old Scotland.

Culloden does symbolize the death of an ancient way of life, but it was changing anyway. It had to, and the people living it understood that better than anybody. The Jacobite ranks were filled with men who were looking not to the past but the future.

There were Highlanders and Lowlanders who had lived through the famines which ravaged Scotland in the early 1740s. They were passionate about the planting of trees and other long-overdue improvements to agriculture and the land which would enable the country to feed itself and make such periodic catastrophes as famine a thing of the past.

Many of the committed Jacobites and Episcopalians of Scotland's east coast were involved in trade with Scandinavia, Europe and the Baltic which had been going on for hundreds of years. There was a trade in ideas, too. Catholic Scots were not permitted to attend their own universities and although they were also banned by law from going abroad to seek a Catholic education, many of them did, studying in Rome, Paris and Leyden.

Presbyterians and Episcopalians studied on the Continent, too, as a matter of course acquiring the necessary language skills. Among the merchants, doctors, lawyers, students, clergymen and poets who stood at Culloden were many fluent in several languages over and above their native Gaelic, Scots and English.

When they came home to Scotland, they kept their fluency up

by reading Voltaire in the original and corresponding with men and women throughout Europe on religion, philosophy, engineering, science and every other subject under the sun.

Scottish Jacobites were in the mainstream of contemporary European thought. In their attitudes to women, personal liberty and religious freedom they were light years ahead of their adversaries. These were modern men. They were also individuals who had thought long and hard about what they were doing and who understood only too well the consequences of failure.

That they were prepared to risk those consequences shows they could see a different path stretching forward into the future, one they thought was worth fighting for. At a time when Scotland stood at a crossroads of history, they were prepared to stand up and be counted. They have inspired Scotsmen and women to do the same ever since.

Two hundred and fifty years ago, the *Gentleman's Magazine* reported the Battle of Culloden under the headline 'Rebels Totally Defeated'.

In Scotland? How wrong can you be?

Select Bibliography

Manuscript Sources

Public Record Office, London *State Papers Domestic George II, Treasury Solicitors Papers (TS11), The 1745 Rebellion Papers (TS20), Court of King's Bench Papers (Baga de Secretis), Patent Rolls*

National Archives of Scotland NAS mss including *GD12 Records of the Episcopal Church of Scotland, GD158 Hume of Polwarth Earls of Marchmont Papers (Lady Jane Nimmo's letters), GD220 Papers of the Graham Family, Dukes of Montrose (Montrose Muniments), GD498 Records Relating to Colonel James Gardiner*

King's College Special Collections, Aberdeen University Library *The MacBean Collection*

National Library of Scotland NLS mss including *The Lyon in Mourning (manuscript originals)* and *The Blaikie Collection*

Royal Archives, Windsor *RA/CP/MAIN/10/173* and *RA/CP/MAIN/10/176*, quotations from which are reproduced by the permission of Her Majesty Queen Elizabeth II

Published Papers

The Albemarle Papers New Spalding Club, Aberdeen, 1902

Blaikie, W.B., *Origins of the 'Forty-Five* Scottish Academic Press, Edinburgh, 1975

The Cochrane Correspondence Regarding The Affairs Of Glasgow 1745–46 Maitland Club, Glasgow, 1836

Cottin, Paul, *Un Protégé de Bachaumont: Correspondance Inédite de Marquis d'Eguilles* Revue Rétrospective, Paris, 1887

Duff, H.R., *Culloden Papers* T. Cadell & W. Davies, London, 1815

Forbes, Bishop Robert, *The Lyon in Mourning* Scottish History Society, Edinburgh, 1895

Howell, T.J. (Compiler), *A Complete Collection of State Trials and Proceedings for High Treason and Other Crimes and Misdemeanours* Longman, London, 1816

Lockhart, George, *The Lockhart Papers* Wm. Anderson, London, 1817

MacGregor, George, *The Collected Writings of Dougal Graham, 'Skellat' Bellman of Glasgow* Thomas D. Morison, Glasgow, 1883

Nicholas, Donald (ed.), *Intercepted Post* Bodley Head, London, 1956

Report of the Proceedings and Opinion of the Board of General Officers on their Examination into the Conduct, Behaviour, and Proceedings of Lieutenant-General Sir John Cope . . . London, 1746

Seton, Sir Bruce Gordon & Arnot, Jean Gordon (eds), *The Prisoners of the '45* Scottish History Society, Edinburgh, 1929

Warrand, D. (ed.), *More Culloden Papers (Vol. III 1725–1745)* Robert Carruthers & Sons, Inverness, 1927

Woodhouselee Manuscript Edinburgh, 1907

Other Sources (Books, Journal Articles & Websites)

Ainsworth, William Harrison, *The Manchester Rebels* Printwise Publications, Bury & Manchester, 1992

Campbell, John Lorne, *Highland Songs of the Forty-Five* Scottish Academic Press, Edinburgh, 1984

Colley, Linda, *Britons: Forging the Nation 1707–1837* Yale University Press, New Haven & London, 2005

Doddridge, Rev. P., *Some Remarkable Passages in the Life of the Honourable Col. James Gardiner* London, 1791

Doran, Dr, *London in the Jacobite Times* Richard Bentley & Son, London, 1877

Duffy, Christopher, *The '45: Bonnie Prince Charlie and the Untold Story of the Jacobite Rising* Cassell, London, 2003

Eardley-Simpson, L.E., *Derby and the Forty-Five* Philip Allan, London, 1933

Forbes, Alexander (Lord Pitsligo), *Essays Moral and Philosophical on Several Subjects* J. Osborn & T. Longman, London, 1734

Forsyth, William, *In The Shadow of Cairngorm: Chronicles of the United Parishes of Abernethy and Kincardine* Northern Counties Publishing Company, Inverness, 1900

The Gentleman's Magazine for 1745 & 1746

Fergusson, Sir James, *Argyll in the Forty-Five* Faber, London, 1951

Gibson, John S., *Ships of the '45* Hutchinson, London, 1967

Gibson, John S., *The Gentle Lochiel: The Cameron Chief and Bonnie Prince Charlie* NMS Publishing, Edinburgh, 1998

Gordon-Taylor, G. (1945), 'The Medical and Surgical Aspects of the 'Forty-Five', *The British Journal of Surgery*, Vol. 33, Issue 129, pp. 4–16

Hancox, Joy, *The Queen's Chameleon: The Life of John Byrom* Jonathan Cape, London, 1994

Harrington, Peter, *Culloden 1746: The Highland Clans' Last Charge* Osprey Publishing, London, 1991

Home, John, *The History of the Rebellion in Scotland in 1745* Peter Brown, Edinburgh & Ogle, Duncan & Co., London, 1822

Johnstone, James, Chevalier de, *A Memoir of the 'Forty-Five* Folio Society, London, 1958

Lawson, John Parker, *History of the Scottish Episcopal Church* Edinburgh, 1843

Livingstone of Bachuil, Alistair, Aikman, C.W.H. and Stuart Hart, Betty (eds), *No Quarter Given: The Muster Roll of Prince Charles Edward Stuart's Army 1745–46* Neil Wilson Publishing, Glasgow, 2001

MacGregor, Neil (2006), 'John Roy Stuart, Jacobite Bard of Strathspey', *Transactions of the Gaelic Society of Inverness,* Vol. LXIII, pp. 1–24

McKim, Anne, *Defoe in Scotland: A S.P.Y. Among Us* Scottish Cultural Press, Dalkeith, 2006

Maclean, Fitzroy, *Bonnie Prince Charlie* Canongate, Edinburgh, 1988

McLynn, F.J., *The Jacobite Army in England 1745: The Final Campaign* John Donald, Edinburgh, 1983

MacNaughton, P. (1965), 'Medical Heroes of the '45', *Transactions of the Gaelic Society of Inverness,* Vol. XLII

Menary, George, *The Life and Letters of Duncan Forbes of Culloden, Lord President of the Court of Session, 1685–1747* Alexander Maclehose & Co., London, 1936

Monod, Paul Kléber, *Jacobitism and the English People, 1688–1788* Cambridge University Press, Cambridge, 1989

National Trust for Scotland, *Cùil Lodair/Culloden* Edinburgh, 2007

Prebble, John, *Culloden* Penguin, London, 1961

Reid, Stuart, *Cumberland's Army: The British Army at Culloden* Partizan Press, Leigh-on-Sea, 2006

Scots Magazine for 1745 & 1746

Tayler, A. & Tayler, H., *Jacobites of Aberdeenshire & Banffshire in the Forty-Five* Oliver & Boyd, Aberdeen, 1928

Tayler, A. & Tayler, H., *1745 and After* T. Nelson and Sons, London, 1938

Tomasson, Katherine & Buist, Francis, *Battles of the '45* B.T. Batsford Ltd, London, 1962

Watts, John, *Scalan: The Forbidden College, 1716–1799* Tuckwell Press, East Linton, 1999

Watts, John, *Hugh MacDonald, Highland, Jacobite & Bishop* John Donald, Edinburgh, 2002

Whittet, Martin M. (1967), 'Medical Resources of the Forty-Five', *Transactions of the Gaelic Society of Inverness,* Vol. XXIV, pp. 1–41

http://www.battleofprestonpans1745.org

http://www.abdn.ac.uk/historic/actsofunion/ (online exhibition by the University of Aberdeen)

INDEX

DAMN' REBEL BITCHES

The Women of the '45

MAGGIE CRAIG

DAMN' REBEL BITCHES
THE WOMEN OF THE '45
MAGGIE CRAIG

ISBN 9781840182989
Available now
£9.99 (paperback)

Damn' Rebel Bitches takes a totally fresh approach to the history of
the Jacobite Rising by telling fascinating stories of the many women
caught up in the turbulent events of 1745–46. Many historians have
ignored female participation in the '45: this book aims to redress the
balance. Drawn from many original documents and letters, the stories
that emerge of the women – and their men – are often touching,
occasionally light-hearted and always engrossing.

'This is a superb book, a fascinating historical work that
is deeply researched and completely riveting'
– Roddy Phillips,
Aberdeen Press and Journal

'takes a refreshingly new look at the history of the
Jacobite Rising of 1745–46 by recording the stories of
the many women caught up in the events . . . a racily
written, well-researched and heart-warming account'
– Elizabeth Sutherland,
Scots Magazine

'a worthy tribute to all those unsung heroines'
– *The Herald*

'bold and argumentative . . . resounds with authority'
– *Scotland on Sunday*